REFLECTIONS IN AFRICA

ALSO BY HAROLD F. MILLER

Encounters in Africa

The Murang'a Murals (editor)

Reflections in Africa

Harold F. Miller

MANQA
books

NAIROBI

ISBN: 978-9966-7360-2-4

A catalogue record for this book is available from the British Library.

Published by Manqa Books
www.manqa.net

Cover art: adapted detail—with images representing past, present, and future—of a multi-panel carved mural by Expedito Mwebe Kibbula located in the foyer of the All Africa Conference of Churches headquarters, Nairobi, Kenya
(Photos by E.M./Manqa)

Editing and book design by Edward Miller and Keith Miller

First Edition
10 9 8 7 6

For Annetta, Keith, and Edward

Contents

Introduction

MY WIFE, ANNETTA, was born in 1940 to missionary parents who lived and worked in a remote northwest corner of Tanganyika, then a League of Nations trust territory under the custody of Great Britain. When Annetta was five years old, her father died of malaria. He lies buried in the lakeside village of Mugango. At the age of fourteen, she moved to the United States with her mother and siblings to attend high school and, subsequently, college. We met in college, were married in 1963, and served as high school teachers for several years. Then Annetta declared: "I want to go home." Her declaration catalyzed scattered strands of my introduction to Africa.

One of those strands can be traced to my mother's knee. There she read to her children from the book *Uncle Tom's Cabin*. During those readings—my first conscious encounter with the African-American experience—a sense of tragedy and pain swept over me in waves. A second strand emerged at the conclusion of a three-year stint of reconstruction work—a pacifist alternative to service in the US Army—in postwar Germany. Following a hitchhiking jaunt from the north German town of Espelkamp in the general direction of London, I landed at Harwich after an overnight ferry ride from France. During disembarkation, a tall fellow passenger, an African-American gentleman, asked, "Are you headed for London?" After my affirmative answer, he asked, "Can I show you around? I know the city." In religious and cultural terms, his identity was Muslim; he was a descendant of African slave ancestors who had come to America as Muslims. During the train ride to London, he recounted how his family had struggled with that heritage in a racist, religiously chauvinist America.

During my college years—another strand—I had much interaction with African students; they comprised a cluster of hugely optimistic young people who had received primary and secondary education in missionary-sponsored schools and were now enjoying newly achieved national independence from colonial rule. Africa, long a mysterious *other* in my awareness, was on the move. Both Annetta and I felt a strong urge to witness and participate in that historic shift of fortunes.

As an initial step toward the fulfillment of that impulse, we applied to the Mennonite Central Committee's (MCC's) Teachers Abroad Program for secondary school teaching assignments in East Africa, hoping for placements somewhere within the vicinity of Annetta's childhood home. In the event, we found ourselves assigned in 1965 to Dar es Salaam, Tanzania (Tanganyika had become Tanzania in 1964 when the Omani sultanate of Zanzibar was overthrown by African revolutionaries who then merged with mainland Tanganyika) by the Eastern Mennonite Board of Missions, a sister agency to MCC. Annetta took on the position of music teacher in one of the city's primary schools, while I was seconded to the Christian Council of Tanzania as Secretary for Relief and Service.

Our arrival in Tanzania's capital city triggered sensations of love at first sight. The coastal city was easy on the eyes: the palm-lined harbor front was spectacular, as were the attendant German colonial buildings. It was suffused with languid air and the cordial and measured pace of human interaction. Business was dominated by members of the Asian community, but representatives of the British and Greek communities were also active in conspicuous ways. For newly arrived folks like ourselves, everything about the place was exotic and interesting.

At national and regional levels, the atmosphere was electric with expectation, thanks in significant measure to the tone set and sustained by Julius Kambarage Nyerere, the charismatic first president of independent Tanzania. At the national level, Nyerere was promoting the ideology of *Ujamaa*, a Swahili term approximating the notion of "familyhood," referred to in more formal political science parlance as "African socialism." According to Nyerere, Ujamaa was not contiguous with Marxism; rather, it was a modern expression of Africa's age-old communitarian culture. It was a point severely contested by Marxist academics clustered, at the time, around and within the University of Dar es Salaam, located several miles inland on "the hill." As Nyerere's ideology was subsequently translated into and implemented as national policy, many Tanzanians experienced Ujamaa as a harsh form of governance. Near the end of his life, Nyerere admitted that the national economic policies of Ujamaa had not succeeded. But he could and did take great satisfaction in the countrywide cohesion achieved by his enthusiastic promotion of Swahili as a national language.

At the regional African level, Nyerere's leadership was widely recognized and selectively admired. Early on in his political career, he had embraced the stated vision of the Pan-Africanist movement—"Africa for Africans"—for a continent free of colonial rule. At the time of our arrival, the government of Tanzania was serving as host to the Liberation Committee of the Organization of African Unity (OAU), a continental configuration of African independent countries, with Nyerere serving as its dynamic chairman. Tanzania was recognized by the OAU as a "frontline state," situated on the border area with countries in the southern portion of the continent still under diverse forms of colonial rule.

Rhodesia (now Zimbabwe) was ruled at the time by a small European minority. According to the understanding of the Portuguese government, Mozambique, Angola, and Guinea Bissau were considered since the 1500s to have existed as "departments" (not colonies) integral to Portugal. South West Africa (now Namibia) was being (mal)administered by South Africa as a United Nations trust territory, while South Africa itself had been dominated and governed since the mid-1600s by a succession of European settler configurations and, beginning in 1948, by the avowedly racist National Party (apartheid) government, widely condemned by the global community of nations as illegitimate. Territories to the south of Tanzania were variously under siege by one or several armed rebel groups, virtually all of which were represented in Dar es Salaam, seeking recognition and legitimacy as "governments in waiting" under the scrutiny of the OAU's Liberation Committee.

Our context and immediate point of reference at that dramatic moment and place was "church," expressed in a complex multilayered configuration of relationships. Mennonite missionary activity in Tanzania had been focused since the mid-1930s on an area to the north and south of Musoma town, on the eastern littoral of Lake Victoria. Annetta's parents were among the pioneer Mennonite missionaries, her father serving as an ordained bishop of the Mennonite Church in Tanzania. Like other missionary communities in the region, Mennonite missionaries had been strongly influenced by the East African Revival, which greatly affected missionary–African relationships, including the shift during the 1960s from missionary to African church leadership.

Institutional and governance polity within the Mennonite mission and church community in Tanzania compared favorably with general missionary praxis of the day, though from a North American perspective Mennonites had been aligned more closely with evangelical nuances than with ecumenical or mainline Protestant denominations such as Lutherans, Anglicans, and Presbyterians. However, in the ebullient independence atmosphere affecting both nations and churches, the Tanzania Mennonite Church had become a constituent member of the Christian Council of Tanzania. My assignment to Tanzania, and specifically within the Christian Council, was understood by Mennonites in the USA and in Tanzania as a fraternal gesture, the term "ecumenical" not common in missionary parlance at the time. Such was the immediate context of our presence in Dar es Salaam, but soon "church" took on additional dimensions.

We now found ourselves working alongside colleagues from a range of Tanzania's Protestant churches, all affiliate members of the national ecumenical entity, the Christian Council of Tanzania. Like the Tanzania Mennonite Church, these member churches were also preoccupied, variously, with the shift from missionary to African church leadership, dynamics that informed significant portions of the council's agenda. Aspects of that church-leadership transition were readily understood against the backdrop of the political winds of change sweeping across the continent, shifting the political pendulum from colonial to independent rule.

National Christian councils in Africa had taken form during the 1960s and were widely understood to be heirs of the earlier missionary-established councils or "fellowships" that had been formed to facilitate the coordination of multidenominational missionary efforts dedicated to the provision of medical, educational, and Bible translation and distribution services. With the coming of political independence, some of those services had been absorbed by the respective national governments of the day or assigned to specialty institutions managed by boards with members appointed by constituent churches. As in other national Christian councils, the Christian Council of Tanzania's agenda had shifted after the achievement of national independence from the aforementioned missionary agenda to urgent issues of the day. Among the most pressing of those was the matter of refugees, an agenda item firmly lodged within the department to which I was assigned in the council.

By the mid-1960s, refugees in Africa were everywhere on the move. Tanzania was hosting thousands of refugees from Mozambique, Burundi, Rwanda, and Kenya, among other countries. In the year before our arrival, ecumenical response to the prevailing refugee situation in Tanzania had taken form in the Tanganyika Christian Refugee Service, established on the basis of a tripartite agreement between the Government of Tanzania, the United Nations High Commission for Refugees, and the Lutheran World Federation. From the perspective of Christian council member churches, the newly established refugee service was understood as an ecumenical initiative, and as such was expected to report regularly to the churches of Tanzania. It did so during the annual assemblies of the Christian council, always within the framework of the department in which I was serving as the administrative secretary.

The Christian Council of Tanzania's refugee agenda and its dotted-line relationship with the Tanganyika Christian Refugee Service involved links with a range of ecumenical agencies, including the World Council of Churches, the National Council of Churches of the United States, and a variety of European Protestant ecumenical organizations. By this time, the Christian ecumenical world had firmly declared solidarity with the cause of liberation from all vestiges of Africa's colonial past. It was a posture supported by vigorous theological reflection and by flourishing multinational ecumenical relationships. Typically, leaders of liberation movements and the newly installed leaders of African churches had shared common education experiences in mission- and church-sponsored schools. In conscious and unconscious ways, leaders of the African ecumenical movement had taken on the liberation cause articulated originally in the late 1800s by personalities in the African diaspora—notably those from Caribbean countries, widely acknowledged in political and academic circles as founders of the Pan-Africanist movement.

One of the frequent visitors to the Christian Council of Tanzania was the representative of Church World Service, an agency based in New York and working under the aegis of the National Council of Churches of the USA. Among much else, he provided updates on developments in southern Sudan, where a rebel movement known as the Anyanya was agitating for a still undefined degree of autonomy from the government in Khartoum, the capital city. Sudan had gained its independence from Britain in 1956, but southern Sudanese felt that independence had disproportionately favored the northern "Arab" and Muslim populace at the expense of their black African and primarily Christian counterparts. Following years of rebel activity in southern Sudan, mediation initiatives undertaken by staff members of the All Africa Conference of Churches and the World Council of Churches resulted in the 1972 Addis Abba Peace Agreement between leaders of the Anyanya rebel movement and the government of Sudan. As a result, a ten-year period of relative peace and reconstruction prevailed in Sudan. It was against that complex backdrop that a second assignment in Africa transferred us to Khartoum, Sudan, where I took on the position of logistics officer within the newly constituted Relief and Rehabilitation Commission of the fledgling Sudan Council of Churches.

If Dar es Salaam had provided an introduction to the complexities of southern Africa's liberation dynamics, Khartoum was an introduction to one of Africa's "fault lines" where, since AD 650, northern, primarily desert cultures met cultures honed by tropical forests and open savannahs. The contrasts between these two venues are not easily exaggerated. In Dar es Salaam we had been introduced to the results of more than a century of Christian missionary activity, on the one hand, and, tantalizingly, to elements of Africa's incredibly rich indigenous religious and cultural heritage, on the other. In Khartoum our reading and our interaction with a range of people soon provided introduction to the historic residue of empires, monarchies, and "holy war" campaigns—both Muslim and Christian—that had shaped the environment in which we now found ourselves. Everything about the place, past and present, was intriguing. But this initial exposure to Sudan was relatively short-lived, serving, in the event, as an introduction to a ten-year encounter with Sudan in the context of a subsequent assignment with the All Africa Conference of Churches, a continental African Protestant ecumenical organization.

Within the span of several months in 1963, two African organizations with continent-wide mandates were established. One was the abovementioned All Africa Conference of Churches, bringing together mainline Protestant Christian churches that had been birthed by Western missionaries during the previous century. The second was the Organization of African Unity, a continental assemblage of heads of independent African states. Both organizations were heir, in varying degrees, to the visions articulated by an earlier generation of Pan-Africanists; both drew leadership from common or greatly overlapping institutions of Western-style education; both were seized by the challenges and promises of the immediate postcolonial period; and both were greatly exercised by the still unfinished quest for political independence, especially in countries situated in the southern portion of the continent.

From 1989 to 1999, I was seconded by MCC to the All Africa Conference of Churches to the position of consultant with the International Affairs Desk. During that period, the Anglican archbishop Desmond Tutu from South Africa served as the chair of the organization. His participation in the essential deliberations of the body provided a window onto the complex dynamics of southern Africa, but he also expressed through his infectious personality the spirit of *ubuntu*. According to Wikipedia, ubuntu (a term original to South African Nguni languages such as Xhosa and Zulu, with cognates in African languages further north) is defined as "the belief in a universal bond of sharing that connects all humanity." Today the term is claimed alike by African theologians, philosophers, politicians, and religious and civil society groups as the realization of aspirations, struggles, and achievements in the quest for renewed and enhanced self-identity throughout independent Africa.

If ubuntu encapsulated broadly the values and the cosmology of the Bantu peoples throughout central and southern Africa, the vast diversities of northern Africa had yet to be captured by commonly recognized nomenclature. Within the past several hundred to several thousand years, Nilotes, Cushites, Semites, Berbers, and Eastern and Western Bantu, as well as Arabs, Indians, and Europeans, had rendered East and North Africa a melting pot of diverse human communities. As of this writing, an "Arab Spring" is underway, the eventual form and content of which has yet to be discerned. Clearly the African continent and the African peoples are still in formation.

My sojourn in Africa over a period of more than five decades has been infused with sustained amazement. Though born in the United States in a separatist religious (Amish-Mennonite) minority, the larger backdrop was nevertheless provided by the achievements and claims of Western European culture. I experienced African culture as vastly "other"; from the beginning of that exposure there was a sense of being absorbed into another, larger cosmos. There was an unspoken but clearly communicated societal ethic that seemed to be saying: "You are welcome here; you are one of us if you join and enlarge our common well-being." I was being included into the "other."

The reflections in this book constitute, more than anything else, conversations with myself. With one or two exceptions, these are not peer-reviewed inquiries, nor did they emerge from the cut and thrust of academia. They are not offered as conclusions or "findings," but rather as engagement with multilayered realities during a remarkable transition period among remarkable people on a remarkable continent.

We realize our historic becoming by being there with others.

—JOHN MBITI

1
Africa—Past, Present, and Future: Religious, Temporal, and Political Crosscurrents

It seems that we all belong, ultimately, to Africa.

—ROLAND OLIVER

Introduction

In ancient times, Africa (north of the Sahara Desert) was referred to by the Latin dictum *Ex Afrika semper aliquid novum* ("Out of Africa there is always something new"). "Exotic, primal Africa," anticipating the anthropologist's paradise or perhaps the booming twentieth-century tourist trade!

For centuries, the Africa of antiquity was estranged from European awareness. Eventually, the logic of Africa's geography made its claim. When Ali Mazrui, the Kenyan social scientist, refers to Africa as "the center of the world," he is corroborated in his hyperbole by the renowned British historian, Roland Oliver: "Almost certainly, the Garden of Eden . . . lay in the highland interior of East Africa, where the equatorial forest belt is broken by mountains and high savanna parklands running south from Ethiopia to the Cape."

According to Robert W. July, "History begins with geography." The most important feature about Africa is not its size, though it ranks as the second largest of the continents. Africa's significance as a continent lies in its location, its northernmost and southernmost points equidistant from the equator at 37° 21' North and 34° 51' South, respectively; fully four-fifths of Africa lies between the Tropics of Cancer and Capricorn. It is this equatorial position that determines the pattern of the continental rainfall, which in turn has had a profound influence on African ecology and human history. Indeed, Oliver and Mazrui reflect a consensus among archaeologists and paleontologists to the effect that the forebears of humankind had their beginnings in the East African highlands.

For centuries, Africa functioned merely as a troublesome peninsular obstruction around which European sailors cautiously picked their way en route to the known and unknown treasures of the Far East. Beginning in the 1500s, Europe's explorers and adventurers gave some attention to Africa's treasures, but mostly in the form of random looting and petty trading, leading eventually to the massive "triangle slave trade" in support of the plantation economies of North and South America.

Africa (south of the Sahara Desert) served both as a source of slaves and as an element of the global, slave-driven plantation system. Even after this system of servitude yielded to the moral outrage of abolitionists and the logic of Europe's industrial economies, Africa was still in many ways the big loser. With the abolition of slavery, relationships with Europe changed, but not decisively; Africa continued its function as a reservoir of raw materials.

Africans persistently and rightly perceive themselves to have been exploited and abused. When European explorers, adventurers, and missionaries began crisscrossing the continent in earnest, they encountered a continent on which time had come to a halt, thanks to centuries of looting and exploitation. How else could they account for the dramatic contrasts between the socioeconomic conditions in Europe and Africa? Africa's integration with Europe was premised on European terms, serving European ends. The metaphor of European or "Christian" time was one of the elements at work in this encounter.

Wrinkles in Time: An Analytic Framework

Every people that has tried to separate itself from its time has disappeared and is no longer remembered among the living.

—JEREMY RIFKIN

"Christian time admits of no interruptions. Its advance is rectilinear; it strides from the age of Judaism to our own, passing by way of the primitive church, the Middle Ages, the Renaissance and modernity. Conversion [to Christianity] means integration into this current," says Father Eboussi Boulaga. It followed that, until recently, the encounter between the African and the Western world was characterized by explanations or apologies for apparent differences between modern and traditional realities, usually critiquing the tradition and doing obeisance to modernity.

One of the most famous, and also one of the most controversial, of such attempts is the temporal schemata proposed by Kenyan theologian John Mbiti. Particularly contentious was his assertion that Africans inherently have a weak sense of "future." According to him, the greater portion of African awareness is lodged in the *zamani*, i.e., in the past. For in Africa, time flows from the present and accumulates in the zamani, ever augmenting the vast store of wisdom generated by the human encounter with life.

The *sasa*, the present, in which we all live, can be subdivided into "potential time" and "actual time," with the former representing solar or lunar time, setting the pace for all of life. Actual time, on the other hand, refers to the "time we have on our hands," or "willed time"—that manifestation of time beholden to human volition; actual time functions only when so willed by human agency. "Time is ours; it will wait till we decide what to do with it," is a frequent comment. In the African concept of time, there is the sense of a seamless whole, bounding willed human action and the function of time. However, within the recognized whole, time was and is respectively dominated, according to Mbiti, by the zamani and the sasa.

Mbiti's time schemata will serve as the framework within which I reflect on a variety of dynamics infusing the African continent, partly because of its provocative nature and partly because the cross-cultural function and behavior of time has attracted increasing attention. While African academics have disagreed with aspects of Mbiti's temporal thesis—especially with regard to his assertions on the future—it will be noted in the final section of this chapter that the issue of time in Africa is a project attracting continuing investigation. Augustine Musopole observed that Mbiti's temporal paradigm has been variously critiqued but not easily ignored. Mbiti must at the very least be given credit for having identified a critical component of the African cosmology.

The African Zamani: A Font of Religious Sensibility

At the onset of the missionary era, Africa was appropriately designated the "dark continent," thanks to the ravages of European plunder and the scourge of the slave trade throughout the continent. Western linkages with the ancient churches of Africa were either nonexistent or extremely tenuous. What is today acknowledged generically as African Religion was not yet articulated by African scholarship and hardly recognized as an underlying religious or cosmological reality by the missionary community.

Indeed, much of the missionary initiative was premised on an assumption that African religion and culture was at best a reality to be ignored and at worst relegated to the demonic. An appreciation of Africa's religious heritage developed only slowly. And with regard to relationships between the ancient churches of Africa and the churches birthed by the modern missionary movement, the conversation continues. The following brief survey of the continent's cultural and religious traditions touches on a remarkable religious heritage.

Christian Africa

Historians have established that Africa's first Christian church was founded during the decade of the 60s (AD) in Alexandria, Egypt, known today as the Egyptian Orthodox Church. Its counterpart in Ethiopia, the Ethiopian Tewahedo Orthodox Church, was established circa AD 331 when two Christian Syrian lads made their way into the king's court at Axum, thanks to the initiatives of a Christian trader from the Middle East. Later, in what is today northern Sudan, the Christian Kingdom of Nubia flourished between approximately AD 500 and 1500 before succumbing to Muslim expansion. It can be noted, parenthetically, that in their attempts to reach India, Portuguese explorers had as one of their objectives an encounter with Prester John, the legendary Christian priest-king whose location had been variously reported to be in Africa or even as far afield as the Middle East or India. Eventually, the Portuguese had their quest sated when they met the Christian monarch of Ethiopia.

Jewish Africa

"Jewish Africa" flourished in the land of Kush, usually associated with the Ethiopian highlands and extending westward to modern Sudan's northern region. The largest portion of the Ethiopian Jewish community—known as the Falasha—migrated in the late 1980s and early 1990s to Israel, thanks to complex negotiated trade-offs between Ethiopia's former rulers and the state of Israel, reflecting the former's need for arms and the latter's standing welcome for all Jews in the diaspora.

Another significant Jewish community, known as the Lemba, is located in southern Africa, straddling the borders of South Africa and Zimbabwe. According to their myths of origin, the ancestors of the Lemba emigrated from Palestine in 586 BC and during subsequent millennia made their way across Africa. Today the Lemba have assimilated with their religious and social environs, some of them embracing Islam and some Christianity, though elements of the Jewish religion and culture are recognized and celebrated. DNA tests among the Lemba revealed clear genealogical congruence with the priestly line of Aaron (associated with the modern Jewish family name Cohen), the brother of the biblical Moses.

Muslim Africa

"Muslim Africa" traces its beginnings to the lifetime of Prophet Mohammed (circa AD 615), when a group of his followers came as refugees from Mecca in Arabia to Axum in Ethiopia, where they found protection under the Christian king Negus. In AD 652 Arab Muslims from Egypt made an attempt to expand into Nubia, today's northern Sudan. There they encountered armed Nubian Christians. Following extensive negotiations, the Nubian Christians and the Arab Muslims agreed to a *baqt* (pact) that provided guidance over the next six hundred years for the commercial, social, and religious interaction of the two communities.

In subsequent centuries Arabic-speaking Muslim traders penetrated deep into West Africa, where large Islamic communities took shape and are extant to this day. Similarly, on the East African coast Arab Muslim traders made their appearance as early as the ninth century, establishing far-reaching commercial networks and significant urban settlements. Towns and cities such as Lamu, Malindi, Mombasa, Zanzibar, and Dar es Salaam provide modern evidence of those early initiatives. Muslim traders intermarried with local communities throughout the continent and shared their Islamic faith. By the mid-1800s, Christian European missionaries had also made their presence felt across the continent. By the year 2000, the peoples of Africa were divided more or less evenly between Muslim and Christian adherents.

Thus, from antiquity Africa has been host to three of the great religious communities of the world—Judaism, Christianity, and Islam.

African Religious Antiquity

RELIGIOUS COMMUNITY	DATE
African Religion	0 to present
Judaism	0 to present
Egyptian Christianity	60s AD to present
Ethiopian Christianity	331 AD to present
Nubian Christianity	500 to 1500 AD
Islam	615 AD to present

African Traditional Religion

Under the rubric African Religions, African Traditional Religion, African Religion, or African World Religion, indigenous African scholars have been exploring the manner in which the continent's religious and cultural heritage has intersected over the past nearly two millennia with the three readily recognized Abrahamic faith traditions.

While recognizing notable exceptions (e.g., John V. Taylor), modern African writers have critiqued Western anthropologists and missiologists for inventing a continent characterized by images, concepts, and rituals that coincided with the Western need to explain and convert. As might have been anticipated, African scholarship (including Christian theological scholarship) has made heroic efforts, meanwhile, to counter Western stereotypes of the African religious world. Hence the growing body of exceptionally articulate representations by African scholars of both generic and particular characteristics of the African cosmology.

In the context of African Religion—currently the most common designation for the phenomenon—the singular consideration at hand is the *project of life*. The purpose of the project—the cycle of life—is the "completion of the human being." Thus are the several manifestations or stages of life committed to "increasing life," to the end that human beings might aspire to and achieve "successful deaths" and thence join the disembodied world of the ancestors, sometimes referred to as the "living dead." Both the unborn and the ancestors seem to inhabit a kind of "holding ground" of the life force, while the life cycle of human beings functions to renew and enlarge the whole of the life pattern.

Among the agents central to this project are the Supreme (creator/sustainer) Being, the human community, and the earth. Both the earth and the woman function as mediators, the former as the entry point to the world of the ancestors and the latter as the entry point to the physical life of humans. Facilitating this process are the rites of passage, beginning with human birth, ritualizing each of the successive age-group ceremonies until the final, successful rituals related to death have been accomplished.

Being human constitutes a "becoming." It is integral to a dynamic project, striving for an "increase in life," for maturity, for fullness, and for completion. Birth, life, and death provide the framework and the experience of God's holiness and sovereignty. In the Ghanaian Ewe tradition, as in many other African traditions, it is abundantly clear that human beings (*agbete*) are dependent on the Supreme Being (Mawu), the creator, who has taken the initiative to call them to life. Not only do humans owe their being to Mawu, they fulfill themselves only in becoming, remaining, being there with the Supreme Being. Furthermore, human beings can only realize their historic *becoming* by *being there with others*. Becoming a complete human being can never be the deed or initiative of a single individual. Malusi Mpumlwana says, "A person is a person because others are."

African cultures function in the undefined framework of an all-encompassing history, characterized by continuous expansion and unfolding. It is understood that ancestors continue to determine the present and the future, as their living space constantly penetrates that of their descendants living on earth. African cosmological space "represents not so much the *place* as the permanent *milieu* in which the undefined time of history is played out—a space by no means anonymous and individualistic, but personal and [communitarian], the origin and witness of the creative hope that animates the awareness of history, enveloping the below and beyond, the now and the always" (Robert Schreiter). Meanwhile, the Supreme Being is at the heart of the destiny of human beings, sustaining the project of *being*, which ancestors and soothsayers in turn interpret to the living.

Such, in broad generic strokes, are the dimensions of African Religion, put together by an imaginative Africanist theologian. He is joined by others who seek to demonstrate a long-standing engagement between African Religion and the "religions of the book"—Judaism, Christianity, and Islam—in addition to the great religions of Egypt and Greece. The available literature ranges from a strong Afro-centrist orientation to much documented evidence of profound continuity among African Religion, classical civilization, and European Christianity.

The following figure provides a summary of these components and the relationships among them.

Foundations of Western Christian Religion and Culture

European Latin Religious Tradition	European Christianity
Arabic/Jewish Scholarship	Bridging Middle East/Europe
Classic Greek Philosophy and Science	Ancient Greece
Classic Egyptian Culture	Ancient Egypt
African Primal World View	Primal Africa

Colonial Africa

In an effort to formalize what had long been random occupation and looting of the continent by Europeans, a conference of the major European powers was held in Berlin in 1884–85, a deliberation during which Africa was parceled out among European powers in ways more or less commensurate with European political and economic power configurations of the day. For Europeans, Africa was a void to be explored, organized, and "civilized." David Livingstone, the great missionary explorer, articulated Europe's contribution to Africa in the "three Cs" of this mission: Christianity, (legitimate) commerce, and civilization. It was a mission providing the foundations for colonial Africa and, eventually, for politically independent Africa.

Thanks to the colonial experience, Africa is to this day divided among Francophone, Anglophone, and Lusophone spheres of interest and influence. There were, of course, other colonial powers, namely, Germany, Italy, and Spain, though their influence in Africa was mitigated or ended by treaties after major world wars, among other dynamics. In addition to making their specific cultural and political imprints on the several bodies politic, the presence of the colonial powers had the effect of bringing the African continent into mainstream global intercourse, though not on African terms. Indeed, it was precisely this absence of participation by the peoples of Africa in the formation and structure of colonial rule that gave rise to the popular agitation, which led in turn to the political independence movement of the 1960s and beyond.

Dilemmas of Sasa: Africa between 1960 and 1990

Political and Economic

Following Mbiti's temporal categories, this section of the paper is preoccupied with the sasa, the African present, with its promise of *willed time*—volitional action—vis-à-vis its own social, religious, political, and economic destiny. If the Berlin conference of 1884–85 marked the formalizing of European colonial hegemony over Africa, 1960 represents the euphoric moment, the opening act, for the independence scene played out over the following three decades to 1990, a period which, for purposes of this paper, functions as the African sasa. The first black African country to become politically independent was Ghana in 1957, with the largest number of sub-Saharan countries achieving independence during the 1960s, followed by the Lusophone countries in the mid-1970s, Zimbabwe in 1980, Namibia in 1990, and finally, South Africa on April 27, 1994.

Africa's Transition from Medieval to Modern Times

Slavery	1400s to 1800s
Colonialism	1884–85 to 1957–1990s
Christian Mission	1800s to 1960s
Islamic Expansion	1960s to present
Political Independence	1957 to present

If 1960 defined the moment of African independence from the colonial order, the collapse of the Berlin Wall in 1990 marked the collapse of a world order firmly in place since World War II, but an order that demonstrated with its demise, for all to see, the fragile nature of Africa's position in the world. For the whole of its modern sasa, Africa had been defined—indeed, to a remarkable extent, defined itself—by the politics of the "East–West" ideological divide, essentially rendering Africa a pawn of the superpowers. War, peace, and understandings of normalcy in Africa were determined more by the strategic and ideological needs of the superpowers than by the deliberations of African leaders in their respective African countries.

Many Africans would argue that despite the coming of political independence and the collapse of the East–West ideological divide, the adverse economic relationships between Africa and the Western industrialized world were not changed in consequence; they only took on a new, more comprehensive exploitative character, comprising the combined initiatives of the World Bank, the International Monetary Fund, and the World Trade Organization. To this end, they cite the perceived negative effects of the World Bank's structural-adjustment programs and the effects of the Uruguay Round of the General Agreement on Tariffs and Trade talks on trade between Africa and the rest of the world. Indeed, Africa was the only major economic community in the world expected to experience a "net negative benefit" as a consequence of the General Agreement on Tariffs and Trade.

Beyond its immediate effects on trade, the agreement's influence was felt on issues such as intellectual property rights, including the patenting of plants and animals. Given the nature of the world's economic structures, Africa can be forgiven for any inclinations toward a siege mentality. On the other hand, African leaders are harshly accused of not thinking in economic terms: "[T]he cure for Africa's crises lies in freedom for business. A continent with enough [economic] lessons to draw from the rest of the world can only blame its problems on its own stupidity" (Okech Kendo). With the formation in the 1990s of regional trading instruments (e.g., Economic Community of West African States, Southern African Development Community, Common Market for Eastern and Southern

Africa) and the reconfiguration of the Organization of African Unity to African Union, fresh attention was in fact being given to Africa's potential as a continental economic trading block.

In political terms, it is difficult to exaggerate the multiple domino effects in Africa of the breakdown of the East–West divide. In the context of a rapidly changing international order, African governments with strong dependencies on the former eastern bloc of nations became destabilized or sued for accommodation with the new superpower, the United States. In this context, the pace of negotiations for majority rule in South Africa, political independence for Namibia, the departure of Cubans from Angola, contact between the FRELIMO government and the rebel RENAMO movement in Mozambique, and issues in other problematic states quickened dramatically.

Liberia and Somalia collapsed. Ethiopia's Marxist government yielded quickly to a thirty-year rebel movement, giving birth to the new state of Eritrea and effecting shifts in Sudan's civil war. With the loss of Ethiopia as a base, the Sudan People's Liberation Movement/Army in southern Sudan split into several factions, while the search for new benefactors and relationships got underway, leading eventually to Nairobi, Kenya, as its window to the world and as a base for regional peace negotiations in the context of the regionally constituted Intergovernmental Authority on Development (IGAD).

With considerable encouragement from the United States and international agencies such as the World Bank, international aid conditionalities shifted quickly and rather forcefully toward support of democratization. Across the continent, multipartyism came into vogue, altering the political landscape. In Anglophone countries, changes followed constitutional provisions, while Francophone countries opted for the mechanism of "national conferences"—representative nationwide talk shops—in which the excesses of the past were reviewed and revealed, moving slowly toward varying degrees of reconstruction or stalemate. In the absence of credible political leaders who could guide the way toward restructured bodies politic, church leaders suddenly found themselves coerced, in some instances, by popular demand to lead these delicate deliberations. After a period of relatively high-profile efforts toward democratization, there was later the sense that opposition leaders had failed to produce clear alternatives while world attention shifted quickly to the next crisis.

Ethiopia's drought in 1984–85, the collapse of Somalia in the early 1990s, Burundi's internal violence in late 1993, and the collapse of and genocide in Rwanda in 1994 transfixed the world community, thanks to global television networks (Flora McDonald, Canada's foreign minister, in a personal communication stated: "CNN directs our foreign policy"). Africa's sequence of disasters stimulated the formation of specialized (permanent) emergency agencies such as Médecins Sans Frontières on the one hand, while on the other there emerged the militarization of humanitarian assistance. Despite the more or less permanent nature of these emergency instruments, there is still a sense that disaster response is reinvented with each recurrence.

Debate on the efficacy of armed humanitarian assistance proffered by the United States in Somalia proceeded, while the French military entered and left Rwanda on its own terms, unilaterally declaring the mission "successful." Even within the ecumenical community, there was vigorous debate regarding the coordination of initiatives being taken by the respective members of the community. Like the secular disaster response, the ecumenical community did not succeed in prepositioning its disaster-response mechanisms.

Within both secular and faith communities, accumulating evidence suggests that massive international response to African disasters has the longer-term effect of marginalizing Africa ever further from the decision-making centers of the world. Large-scale disaster response in Africa is typically coordinated from Europe (even the sequence of flights into the small airport at Goma, Zaire, following the Rwandan refugee exodus, was coordinated from Geneva, Switzerland). Africa's submission to (armed) humanitarian assistance from distant donor countries must surely represent the ultimate humiliation. Following is a summary of the political and economic dynamics at work in Africa's three-decade sasa.

Political and Economic Scenarios: Africa in the 1990s

- "Second Liberation" (Political Reordering)
- "Democratization" (Aid Conditionality, Multipartyism, Ethnicity)
- Collapse of Economies
- Collapse of States (e.g., Somalia, Rwanda)
- Flourishing Informal Economic Sector
- Para-Church/NGO Development/Service Organizations
- "Free Markets" (Aid Conditionalities)
- European Common Market
- World Trade Organization (GATT)
- Militarization of Humanitarian Assistance
- Humanitarian Assistance as Marginalization

Religious and Cultural Africa

Roland Oliver, the grand British Africanist, provided a sweeping, highly nuanced overview of the missionary enterprise in Africa, a movement variously preceding, accompanying, protesting, or endorsing the colonial and settler regimes in Africa. He identified a clear distinction between the African Christianity of the first centuries after Jesus and the African Christianity that came to the continent during the modern missionary movement beginning in the mid-1800s. Even today, there is at best only vague awareness and an uneasy cohabitation between the churches of ancient Africa and the churches birthed by the modern, Western missionary movement.

If the advent of colonial rule in some ways stimulated, protected, or encouraged Western missionaries in Africa (or the obverse, as some critics aver, with colonial rule having been stimulated, protected, and encouraged by missionary activity), it must also be recognized that colonialism had its effects on the Muslim presence in Africa. Islam had been entrenched in both East and West Africa for nearly a thousand years by the time modern Western missionaries arrived (mid-1800s). Islam had been propagated more or less informally by Muslim traders who had crisscrossed the continent from North Africa down to present-day Botswana, providing a loose network of trade routes and trading posts servicing "normal" commercial activity and underwriting large sectors of the notorious slave trade. Famous Christian missionaries such as David Livingstone were facilitated in their explorations precisely by these Muslim traders.

To this day, those trade routes are easily identified in eastern Africa by the presence of Muslim adherents, by the far-flung use of the Swahili language (which draws heavily on Arabic), and by the presence of mango and coconut palm trees. According to the demands of popular Islamic expectation, it was assumed that successful traders would demonstrate their piety by building mosques, by demonstrating a positive public spirit, and by taking on business apprentices from the local population. Additionally, it was common for successful entrepreneurs to marry women from the local community. In this manner was business integrated with the host community and the message of Islam inculcated and spread.

In communities that developed around these kinds of dynamics, Islamic praxis could be described as laissez-faire, resulting in a syncretistic admixture of formal Islamic precepts and aspects of local indigenous culture. While this form of Islam bestowed a sense of respectability and identity upon its adherents, it was not immediately seen as coterminous with *modernity*, whose gatekeepers were the rising European colonial powers. In considerable contrast, modern Christian missions shared the Christian Gospel clothed in the languages and cultures of Europe. Moreover, by offering both formal education and technical training, Christian missions provided access to the continent's fledgling modern (European, Western) sector.

Between 1900 and 1914, the Christian population in Africa increased from approximately 4 million to 7 million adherents, while Islam may have increased its constituency from an estimated 60 million to 70 million people. By 1930 the number of Christians had increased to approximately 16 million, and by the 1950s the modern sector of the colonial economies was monopolized by those Africans who had had access to education provided by Christian missions. During the 1970s, the numbers of Christians and Muslims were more or less equal, a configuration expected to continue well into the new millennium.

During the African sasa, Muslim–Christian relationships have changed dramatically. Islam has become at once more modern and more orthodox. Taking its cue from the modern Christian missionary movement, Islam has taken both Koranic and secular education more seriously, strengthening Islam on the one hand, and entering the political arena of the modern world on the other. The remarkable alliance between the Vatican and Iran for purposes of addressing the issues of the September 1994 UN population conference in Cairo, Egypt, and the diplomatic use of Carlos the Jackal by the Islamic fundamentalist government of the Sudan as a bargaining chip to facilitate an escape from its pariah status in the world provide examples of a strong, self-conscious Islam making its way into Africa's major international forums of the day. Amid a rapidly changing political and religious international order, Islam is at once modernizing and restating claims regarding its preferred religious and social order. Africa provides an important arena for the changing order, both for Sudan's revivalist Islamic fervor and Iran's determined Islamic diplomacy.

Meanwhile, much is made in the Western Christian press of the numerical growth of Christians and churches in Africa. Already it is accepted that Africa has become the numerical locus of world Christianity in the new millennium. Many denominations, including Catholics, mainline Protestants, evangelicals, and newly arrived Pentecostals, are experiencing growth. Furthermore, virtually all church-growth methodologies seem to function successfully, though there is evidence that the higher growth rates are recorded among the newly arrived evangelical and Pentecostal groups. Why this phenomenon of growth within African churches? Basically because Jesus Christ as portrayed in the Bible is a convincing representative of the God of Africa. Additionally, the folk culture reflected in the Bible is in many ways similar to African folk cultures, hence the oft-heard comment by Africans: "The Bible must be true, because we see ourselves in it."

From the viewpoint of prospective church members, church is recognized as one of the few remaining institutions that has not succumbed fully to the wishes or whims of strongman African governments. But there are other reasons as well. During the early period of the modern missionary movement, Christians in Africa were known as "readers," qualifying for employment in the colonial administrative sector. During the 1960s and 1970s, churches became deeply involved with (some would say seduced by) so-called development activity and the concomitant growth of parachurch organizations, together with their secular counterparts now generally known as nongovernmental organizations (NGOs). Economic and political stagnation or hardening during subsequent years has by default permitted NGOs to dramatically enlarge their scope of activities, to the extent that NGOs are now viewed as major and, in some areas, dominant economic and social change agents. While churches insist on their unique religious identity, some of the activities they promote fall within NGO categories, with the consequence that churches are identified for select purposes as NGOs, both by African governments and the international donor community.

The activist character of church in Africa has been manifest in several ways. For decades, mainline churches were preoccupied with the eradication of apartheid in South Africa. Still in activist mode during the early 1990s after the cataclysmic changes in the global ideological climate, senior church leaders were coopted (more by default than by some grand design) into leadership postures that facilitated the transition from one-party states into multiparty democracy. Some church leaders chafed under what was considered an imposition by circumstance, while others saw the exercise as one of the high moments of prophetic witness by the African church.

Then came Rwanda, presenting the Christian church in Africa with an extreme dilemma. Beginning in the 1940s, Rwanda functioned for several decades as the font of the famous East African Revival Movement (or, more correctly, the Rwandan Revival Movement), which, among other issues, addressed and dramatically changed (some might say improved) the nature of missionary–African relationships. But as the world knows, and as CNN repeatedly emphasized, approximately one million people were killed in 1994 during several frenzied months of hand-to-hand slaughter. In this overwhelmingly Christian (90 percent plus) country, accusations of culpability in the genocide also touched church leaders, with details regarding their involvement pursued and prosecuted a decade later. Rwanda constituted an extreme example of the dilemmas facing churches in Liberia, Angola, Mozambique, Sudan, and Ethiopia, among other countries. In the language of the African ecumenical community, Rwanda's tragedy could be understood as a "sign of the times."

African church leaders claimed to have been reading the signs of the times. With the demise of the Berlin Wall and the ensuing global restructuring, the Protestant ecumenical community in Africa deliberated on the theology of reconstruction, with the implication that the Christian church would need to engage itself with the religious and cultural values, and in the process catalyze the reconstruction of both church and the body politic in Africa, ensuring its cultural rootedness and thus aspects of its authenticity. For Protestant churches the task was particularly challenging, thanks to their legacy of negative postures vis-à-vis African culture.

Catholics, on the other hand, had long engaged in a theological conversation with African culture, revisited in the 1994 African Synod held in Rome (though the venue was a source of great disappointment for many African Catholics). Culture, according to select Roman Catholic theology, functions as a means of grace; it is the task of the Christian Gospel to refine culture, thus rendering it a more efficacious means of grace, a process described as enculturation. Examples and descriptions of this process by African theologians (see Penoukou and Magesa) have become increasingly articulate.

But in the face of the Rwandan tragedy, are the initiatives by the Christian Church in Africa in any way relevant to the overwhelming challenges of the day, or are they always too little, too late . . . and too esoteric? Is Rwanda a one-time, unrepeatable phenomenon, or does it provide an alarming close-up view of Christianity's paper-thin presence and a general moral bankruptcy in Africa? Or has Christianity served merely as one of many variables in a dynamic that catapulted Rwanda into a political and social meltdown? Whatever the case, the Rwandan story has occasioned serious soul-searching on the part of African churches, generally serving as a new reference point in the history of the continent, key dynamics of which are summarized below.

Modern Religious Dynamics

- "End of Missionary Movement" (Penoukou, 1991)
- Christian/Muslim Encounter—"50 percent Christian/50 percent Muslim" (David B. Barrett, 1982)
- Fundamentalist Fringes: Christian, Muslim, New Religious Movements (Paul Gifford, 1992)
- Protestant "Reconstruction" (J. N. K. Mugambi, 1991)
- Catholic "Inculturation"—"Ongoing Dialogue between Gospel and Culture" (Aylward Shorter, 1991, and Laurenti Magesa, 2005)
- Ecumenical "Transition"—from Doctrinal Patriarchy to Multiple Loci of Insight/Discernment (Conrad Raiser, 1991)
- Rwandan Collapse

Kutwa: Imagining and Shaping an African Future

How is the future being done in Africa? In a remarkable treatise, a cross-section of African thinkers and planners in 1987 reported on their deliberations with regard to the future of the continent. As a point of departure, they distinguished between conventional wisdom and an African vision, the former referring to the body of knowledge received primarily from exogenous sources, linear in character; the latter spherical in character, open to new possibilities in multiple directions, conforming to a dynamic interpretation of Mbiti's volitional sasa. With the assistance of this analytic tool, they examined the possibilities for "surprise-rich" futures.

They chose, arbitrarily, to do their "futuring" between 1957 (Ghana's independence date) and 2057, a one-hundred-year span, following a generally accepted designation of the times: the *time of euphoria*, beginning in 1957 (or in the context of this paper, 1960) and extending until 1980; the *time of troubles*, beginning in 1980 and continuing to the end of the century; and the *time of renewal*, projected from the year 2000 to the year 2057. Participants accepted that the negative images of Africa could be attributed to both external and African forces. For them, history constituted the sum of initiatives by people. According to a personal communication from a participant, attendees deliberated on the basis of an expanded, malleable understanding of Mbiti's volitional sasa, capable of drawing on the wisdom of the elders from the past, capable of assessing and taking initiative in the perpetual sasa, and in so doing, shaping a preferred kutwa (future). These understandings and dynamics are summarized in the following matrix:

CONVENTIONAL WISDOM		AFRICAN WISDOM
	Conceptual:	
• unilinear		• dialectic
• crisis oriented		• beyond crisis
	Methodological:	
• surprise free		• surprise rich
• concentrated		• multiple and dispersed
• monopolistic		• pluralizing
	Operational:	
• donor fed and controlled		• locally owned and initiated
• directive and preemptive		• supportive and nurturing
• capital intensive		• people intensive
	Financial:	
• massive transfer		• seed money
• project specific		• matching funds

Source: Achebe, Hyden, Magadza, and Okeyo, 1990, p. 23

In their concluding chapter, written from the perspective of the year 2057, they wrote (both optimistically and realistically) of the new impetus for the whole continent realized by independence in Namibia; of the shift to majority rule in South Africa (this was written in 1987, seven years before majority rule was realized in South Africa); of the new pride and sense of nationalism replacing the low self-esteem of the twentieth century; of a renewal of the extended family tradition as part of a cultural revival; of the widespread use of regional lingua franca such as Swahili, Hausa, and Lingala; of development with a human face, i.e., development commensurate with African values; of the establishment of social welfare systems on a cooperative, egalitarian basis, and so on. According to their projected schedule, Africa's fortunes would experience an upturn, the indicators of which would be evident early in the new millennium.

Conclusion

If there has been a persistent recurrent dynamic pervading the deliberations of twentieth-century Africa, it has been the search for a legitimate place in the sun; for recognition of its contribution to the growth of history, to the increase of life, informed by the most seminal cultural and religious values. With notable exceptions such as Luthuli, Tutu, Mandela, Soyinka, Annan, and Maathai (the list of African Nobel Prize laureates is now extensive)—to say nothing of the host of African athletes—the contribution of the continent to the life of the world has been relatively invisible, undervalued, and ignored. Media images of Rwanda, Sudan, Liberia, Ethiopia, Somalia, Ivory Coast, and Liberia, among others, served merely to strengthen stereotypically negative images of the continent.

People of the African continent who consider themselves or are considered by others to be heirs to the missionary tradition, and now to a remarkable global fellowship of Christian believers, have a special task at hand with regard to the future of Africa. Church-growth statisticians glory in the rapid expansion of church in Africa. But the trauma of statistically Christian Rwanda serves as a reminder that the penetration of church into Africa's social and ethical realms may in fact be relatively shallow. Do Africa's distress indicators serve as reminders of the many layers of unfinished business or merely as flawed understandings that to this day plague relationships between the West and Africa?

Lamin Sanneh provided some clues to understanding Africa's complexities when he noted: "When missionaries sought to transmit the message through the mother tongue of Africans, they committed themselves to operating in a medium in which Africans have the first and last advantage." In some measure, the Christian "good news" was deployed by African believers as a form of resistance against missionary impositions, reasserting aspects of their own culture and reclaiming their own identity, much of which they saw mirrored in the Bible.

Sanneh emphasized the African power of receiving and the effects of the Christian Gospel message on many aspects of African life that in general were not beholden to Western perceptions. According to him, the act of receiving the Christian Gospel functioned both as an enrichment of the message and a renewal and enrichment of the receiving culture, activating insights on the good news that had eluded the Western messenger! According to Sanneh, these dynamics reflect the inherent genius of the Christian Gospel and, according to Catholic theologians, the genius of cross-cultural encounter.

With the collapse of the Cold War, it became clear that the political and cross-cultural agenda of the world was far from complete. Certainly, in the ongoing encounter between Africa and the West, much remained to be done, especially in the context of the missionary, development, and relief fraternities. Missionaries may have been too ready to count the ever-increasing numbers of coreligionists; development workers were preoccupied with multiplying ever more effective projects; and relief workers were supplying endless quantities of humanitarian assistance. Against all odds, and perhaps despite the plethora of international interventions, Africa has survived. As this survey indicates, Africa has long been engaged with an interdependent though highly inequitable world. In future, that engagement will only become more intense, but hopefully it will be mitigated and guided by the African (ubuntu) adage: "I am because we are: we are because I am."

—November 1994 (updated notes 2005)

This paper was first presented in oral, abbreviated form to a peace seminar in Limuru, Kenya, in September 1994.

Sources

Achebe, Hyden, Magadza, Okeyo. 1990. *Beyond Hunger in Africa—Conventional Wisdom and an African Vision.* London, UK: James Currey.

Adedeji, Adebayo. 1993. *Africa within the World: Beyond Dispossession and Dependence.* London, UK: Zed Books.

Africa Recovery. December 1993–March 1994. "Africa Seeks Redress for GATT Losses."

Atkins, Keletso E. 1993. *The Moon Is Dead! Give Us Our Money! The Cultural Origins of an African Work Ethic, Natal, South Africa, 1843–1900.* London, UK: James Currey.

Barrett, David B. 1982. *World Christian Encyclopedia: A Comparative Survey of Churches and Religions in the Modern World AD 1900–2000.* Nairobi, Oxford, New York: Oxford University Press.

Baur, John. 1994. *2000 Years of Christianity in Africa: An African History.* Nairobi, Kenya: Paulines Publications.

Bernal, Martin. 1987. *Black Athena: The Afroasiatic Roots of Classical Civilization (4 Volumes).* New Brunswick, New Jersey: Rutgers University Press.

Boulaga, F. Eboussi. 1984. *Christianity without Fetishes: An African Critique and Recapture of Christianity.* Maryknoll, New York: Orbis Books.

Byaruhanga-Akiki, A. B. T. 2004. "The African World Religion and Other Religions." In Mary N. Getui and J. N. K. Mugambi (eds.), *Religions in Eastern Africa under Globalization.* Nairobi, Kenya: Acton Publishers.

Diop, Cheikh Anta. 1991. *Civilization or Barbarism: An Authentic Anthropology.* New York: Lawrence Hill Books.

Gifford, Paul. 1992. *New Dimensions in African Christianity.* Nairobi, Kenya: All Africa Conference of Churches.

Haafkens, J. 1991. *Islam and Christianity in Africa.* Nairobi, Kenya: Project for Christian–Muslim Relations in Africa.

Hancock, Graham. 1993. *The Sign and the Seal: A Quest for the Lost Ark of the Covenant.* London, UK: Mandarin Paperbacks.

July, Robert W. 1992. *A History of the African People.* Nairobi, Kenya: East African Educational Publishers Ltd.

Kendo, Okech. September 13, 1994. "Africa in Turmoil." *The Standard.* Nairobi, Kenya.

Le Roux, Magdel. 2003. *The Lemba: A Lost Tribe of Israel in Southern Africa.* University of South Africa.

Lederach, John Paul. 2005. *The Moral Imagination: The Art and Soul of Building Peace.* New York: Oxford University Press.

Magesa, Laurenti. 2004. *Anatomy of Inculturation: Transforming the Church in Africa.* Nairobi, Kenya: Paulines Publications Africa.

Mbiti, John S. 1969. *African Religions and Philosophy.* London, UK: Heinemann.

Mpumlwana, Malusi quoted by Walshe, Peter. 1993. *Africa Faces Democracy.* Washington, DC: Africa Faith and Justice Network.

Mudimbe, V. Y. 1988. *The Invention of Africa: Gnosis, Philosophy and the Order of Knowledge.* London, UK: James Currey Press.

Mugambi, J. N. K. 1991. "The Future of the Church and the Church of the Future in Africa" in *The Church of Africa: Towards a Theology of Reconstruction.* Nairobi, Kenya: All Africa Conference of Churches.

Musopole, Augustine C. 1994. *Being Human in Africa: Toward an African Christian Anthropology.* New York: Peter Lang Publishing, Inc.

Obenga, Theophile. 2004. *African Philosophy—The Pharaonic Period: 2780–330 BC.* Popenguine, Senegal: Per Ankh.

Oliver, Roland. 1991. *The African Experience: Major Themes in African History from Earliest Times to the Present.* New York: HarperCollins Publishers.

Penoukou, Efoe Julien. 1991. "Christology in the Village" in Robert J. Schreiter (ed.) *Faces of Jesus in Africa.* Maryknoll, New York: Orbis Books.

Raiser, Conrad. 1991. *Ecumenism in Transition: A Paradigm Shift in the Ecumenical Movement.* Geneva, Switzerland: World Council of Churches Publications.

Rifkin, Jeremy. 1987. *Time Wars: The Primary Conflict in Human History.* New York: Simon and Shuster, Inc.

Sanneh, Lamin. 1993. *Encountering the West: Christianity and the Global Cultural Process—The African Dimension.* London, UK: HarperCollins Publishers.

Schonecke, Wolfgang. September 15, 1994. "What Does The Rwanda Tragedy Say to AMECEA Churches." Nairobi, Kenya: AMECEA Documentation Service/171994 No. 424.

Shorter, Aylward. 1991. *The African Synod: A Personal Response to the Outline Document.* Nairobi, Kenya: St. Paul Publications.

Standes, Justus. 1961 (reprint from 1896). *The Portuguese Period in East Africa.* Nairobi, Kenya: Kenya Literature Bureau.

Taylor, John V. 1963. *The Primal Vision.* SCM Press Ltd.

Vantini, Giovanni. 2009. *Rediscovering Christian Nubia.* Verona, Italy: Edizioni Nigrizia—College delle Missioni Africane.

2
The African Liberation Quest: Ecumenical Engagement

The whole body bends down to remove a thorn from the toe.

—AFRICAN PROVERB

Introduction

European colonial domination over Africa for more than seven decades functioned as a continental "thorn in the toe." From 1900 to 2011, the peoples of the African continent, including the African diaspora—"the whole body"—bent to remove the "thorn," resulting in the birth of fifty-four politically independent African nation-states. Accompanying and engaging with that remarkable process was an African Christian ecumenical community, ministering to wounds inflicted by the past and engaged with the dynamics that eventually rendered the African continent free of colonial rule. This overview traces aspects of that liberation narrative, augmented by "rabbit-hole" excursions into roles played by an eclectic supporting cast.

Within the African and the North Atlantic academe, generally, the colonial saga and the subsequent liberation narrative has been widely researched, documented, and debated by competent academics. However, this recounting of the African liberation narrative is narrowly based on select personal observations and impressions gained during twenty-five years of secondment as a fraternal staff member to four African ecumenical organizations. The perceptions thus acquired, set out in the following paragraphs, lay no claim to review by peers or academics as proper historiography would require. Rather, they have been shaped by select readings and by encounters with personalities, organizations, and processes variously engaged with the African liberation story. A significant portion of the narrative traced here transpired between the mid-1960s and 2011, a time during which my feet were on African soil, thus rendering these reflections proximate and immediate.

Berlin, Germany 1884–85

It is virtually impossible to reflect on modern Africa without reference to Berlin in 1884 and 1885. After centuries of diverse forays into the African continent by explorers, swashbucklers, merchants, and slave traders from Europe and the Middle and Far East, the advent of "Berlin" represented something akin to a formal, but self-serving, imperial gesture. Random exploration, competing trade, and informal claims on African territory were beginning to shift inexorably toward the need for more formal arrangements. From November 1884 to April 1885, representatives of fourteen North Atlantic nations (excluding Switzerland and the United States) met in Berlin, Germany, to deliberate on their common and conflicting interests in Africa.

By 1900, the whole of the African continent, except for Liberia and Ethiopia, had effectively been claimed and was being administered variously by European powers, thanks in part to the "imperial order" (thieves dividing the loot among themselves!) provided by the deliberations undertaken in the Berlin exercise. Following that process, Africa was effectively dominated by Anglophone, Francophone, and Lusophone spheres of influence; Spain and Italy claimed relatively small enclaves, while Germany's claims to substantial African territories survived only until World War I. But significant differences among the colonial governance regimes prevailed. For example, the Belgian Congo was managed for all practical purposes as the personal property of King Leopold of Belgium, while the territories of Mozambique, Angola, and Guinea Bissau were deemed to be "departments"—not colonies—integral to the country of Portugal. Among other consequences, World War I had had the effect of shifting some African territories from one colonial power to another or, in the case of Tanganyika and South West Africa, shifting colonial jurisdiction to trusteeship status under the supervision of the League of Nations and later under the United Nations. Until their respective achievements of independence in 1961 and 1974, Tanganyika (Tanzania after 1964) was administered by Britain and South West Africa (Namibia) was administered (and its mineral wealth shamelessly exploited) by South Africa as United Nations trust territories.

Religious Identities

With regard to Africa's religious identities, in 1900 there were an estimated 8.7 million Christians on the African continent. These were found within the Egyptian Orthodox Church, founded circa AD 61; the Tewahedo Orthodox Church of Ethiopia, founded circa AD 330; among descendants of Dutch and British Christians in South Africa; and among descendants of freed slaves from North America in Liberia and Sierra Leone. By this time Arab Muslims had long since crisscrossed Africa as merchants, slave traders, and promoters of the Islamic religion. Meanwhile, people such as David Livingstone had been in Africa as explorers, missionaries, and representatives of European culture and commerce.

Edinburgh 1910

In 1910 an International Missionary Conference (among the precursor events leading, eventually, to the formation of the World Council of Churches) was held in Edinburgh, Scotland, celebrating more than a century of global Christian mission activity and projecting its future direction. No African attended the Edinburgh convocation in an official capacity, though it has been determined that, in addition to several expatriate missionaries from Africa, one African was in attendance. During the conference deliberations, it was opined that the Christian Gospel could not be expected to flourish in Africa, thanks to the constraints presented by "tribal religions," referred to generically at the time as "animism."

One hundred years later (2000), half of Africa's 800 million people had become Christians, utterly defying the Edinburgh prognosis! The other half, according to ecclesial statistician David Barrett, were identified as adherents of Islam. However, subsequent research has demonstrated that "African Religion" in its myriad religious and cultural manifestations prevails at conscious and subconscious levels of society in much of sub-Saharan Africa. Aspects of both political and ecclesial dynamics underlying these astonishing statistics will be referred to in the rest of this chapter.

Resistance to Colonialism

The origins of resistance to European colonial domination of the African continent are multiple. Central America's Caribbean region was one such beginning point. Among the prominent Afro-Caribbean personalities were people such as George Padmore, Franz Fanon, Marcus Garvey, C. L. R. James, and Edward Blyden. Padmore was an activist closely associated eventually with Kwame Nkrumah of Ghana, the first president of the first sub-Saharan African country to achieve independence (in 1957). Fanon was engaged as a writer, ideologue, and activist devoted to the independence of Algeria, with only tangential activist links to sub-Saharan independence movements, though he enjoyed widespread influence among African nationalists because of his strident, insightful writings. Garvey devoted his life to a "back-to-Africa" movement among people of African descent in the Caribbean region, North America, and the United Kingdom. James was a highly educated academic and historian whose writings featured prominently within this activist cluster, subsequently referred to as the Pan-Africanists. Blyden became prominent in Liberia and the West African region as an educator, writer, and enthusiastic advocate of what he deemed to be Africa's promising future.

African-Americans

A second source of inspiration for African independence was comprised of African-Americans, prominent among whom was W. E. B. du Bois, a highly educated intellectual. He is remembered for his prescient and widely quoted statement: "The problem of the 20th century is the problem of the color line." Du Bois's forays into North American academia were fraught, as were his relationships with the likes of Marcus Garvey. As a gesture of protest and solidarity, he migrated to Ghana late in life and died there in 1963, improbably on the day of the Washington March when Martin Luther King, Jr., presented his "I Have a Dream" speech. Kwame Nkrumah was greatly influenced by Du Bois and other African-American academics he had encountered during studies at Lincoln University in Pennsylvania.

South Africa

South Africa was a third source of the African liberation quest. In 1952 the Rev. Albert Luthuli was chosen to serve as President of the African National Congress (ANC), the political womb within which a long line of South African independence activists, including Nelson Mandela, was born and nourished. As of this writing, the ANC is the ruling political party of modern majority-ruled South Africa. Luthuli was a pacifist and in some measure influenced the early ANC toward a pacifist posture—a posture sustained for some decades. Luthuli's pacifism was influenced and nurtured by the presence and nonviolent resistance praxis of Mahatma Gandhi of India, who had arrived in South Africa in 1893 and stayed for two decades advocating for the rights of the large Indian community. Gandhi in turn drew some measure of his pacifist understandings from the Russian writer Leo Tolstoy. And Tolstoy was touched in his pacifist inclinations by a Reformed (Herr-ite) Mennonite minister and physician by the name of Daniel Musser who published a tract during the American Civil War (1864) entitled *Nonresistance Asserted.* A Quaker peace advocate took this tract to Russia, where Tolstoy eventually received and commented favorably on it in his 1894 treatise *The Kingdom of God Is Within You.* Albert Luthuli was awarded the Nobel Peace Prize in 1960. Under the ANC, Nelson Mandela became the first African president of South Africa in 1994.

Like Nelson Mandela, South Africa's Anglican archbishop (emeritus) Desmond Tutu enjoys global recognition. In Africa, the Anglican Church is present in at least two ecclesial postures, recognized respectively as High-Church Anglo-Catholic and Low-Church evangelical. Tutu was nurtured in the former tradition and influenced in his priestly formation by British missionaries such as Trevor Huddleston. Tutu's career comprised a dizzy sequence of ecclesial and church-related positions: as administrator of an ecumenical theological training fund; as general secretary of the South Africa Council of Churches; as bishop and archbishop within the South African Anglican Church hierarchy; and as chair of the All Africa Conference of Churches from 1987 to 1997, among many other official and honorary positions.

At some point during his maturing career, senior leaders of the All Africa Conference of Churches approached Tutu with the proposition that he serve as an ecumenically designated "point person" to catalyze the anti-apartheid movement in South Africa and to persist in that position until majority rule, or independence, was realized. It was made clear, additionally, that his role was to be carried out explicitly within Africa's continental liberation ethos. After demurring initially, Tutu embraced that role with gusto. On February 11, 1990, when Nelson Mandela emerged from twenty-seven years of incarceration, courtesy of the South African apartheid regime, Tutu was there to receive and embrace him. Subsequently Tutu was appointed by President Mandela as chairman of South Africa's famous Truth and Reconciliation Commission, heartrending details of which are reflected in the book *No Future Without Forgiveness*. Mandela and Frederik de Klerk, the last President of South Africa's apartheid government, were jointly awarded the Nobel Peace Prize on October 15, 1993.

World War II

World War II served as a powerful stimulant to the African liberation quest. Many thousands of Africa's colonial "subjects" had been recruited into the armies of the European powers to fight on the respective far-flung war fronts. European states justified their engagement with World War II by appealing to the ideals of democracy in contrast to Hitler's ideological and political excesses. When African ex-combatants returned to their countries after the war, they were jolted by their awareness of a supreme irony: they had just been engaged in the defense of European colonial powers that were functioning collectively in Africa as an oppressive imperial presence. In other words, African combatants had fought as subjects of colonial powers, defending the democratic rights enjoyed by their colonial overlords, and not as citizens of independent countries. Subsequently, thanks to World War II exposure, many of these decommissioned combatants became activist nationalists, working for the political independence of the African continent.

Pan-Africanists

From these several beginnings, among others, Africa's liberation century developed a life of its own, punctuated by the dynamics of charismatic personalities, focused deliberations, and relentless activist resistance. Among the landmark deliberations was a series that became known as the Pan-African Congresses, the first five of which took place in Britain between 1900 and 1945. These congresses served as catalyzing focal points in which pioneering Pan-Africanists—including Afro-Caribbeans, African-Americans, and African nationalist leaders such as Nkrumah of Ghana and Kenyatta and Koinange of Kenya—brought together diverse strands of the African independence movement. Emerging directly from these deliberations came the initial realization during the late 1950s and throughout the 1960s of African independent countries. A second phase of the independence movement developed during the mid-1970s, when Portugal's African "departments" (in contrast to colonies) of Mozambique, Angola, Guinea-Bissau, Cape Verde, and São Tomé and Príncipe yielded to independence only after protracted resistance by armed rebel movements.

In the heat of the early independence movement, the minority European settler community in Rhodesia (Zimbabwe) defiantly announced on November 11, 1965, the formation of a government based, famously, on a unilateral declaration of independence. Beginning in 1923, Rhodesia had been ruled by a minority European settler government under the supervision of Great Britain. There followed a protracted armed rebel movement, countering Rhodesia's white minority declaration and resulting, after difficult and complex negotiations, in Zimbabwe's political independence in

1980. South Africa finally attained majority (black African) rule in 1994 following decades of organized resistance, supported by solidarity movements around the world. And then in 2011, in a kind of belated finale to Africa's liberation century, South Sudan became the newest independent nation state in Africa. An uneasy semblance of normalcy had been achieved after well over a half century of rebel wars, extensive negotiations, and eventual peace agreements. However, the "normalcy" of independence did not constitute a reinstatement of the continent's *ancien régimes*. Instead, the African continent had made its debut in the form of fifty-four politically independent nation states, patterned extensively on modern post–World War II statecraft championed by the United Nations. Long before the liberation century had reached fruition, Basil Davidson, the intrepid British historian, had referred to the newly minted independent African nation state as *The Black Man's Burden*.

Father Trevor Huddleston

Against the backdrop of the independence struggle of southern Africa generally and South Africa in particular, Father Trevor Huddleston must be considered a member extraordinaire of the African liberation movement's supporting cast. Thanks to his anti-apartheid activism in the South African township of Sophiatown, he was eventually expelled from the country and reposted by his High-Church Anglican missionary agency to the Diocese of Masasi in southern Tanzania. There he served as a diocesan bishop and continued his anti-apartheid activism—now on a more global scale—in collaboration with President Julius Nyerere of Tanzania. Subsequently, he was appointed bishop of a diocese in London and then Archbishop of the Indian Ocean, based in Port Louis, Mauritius. He was widely read as the author of *Naught for Your Comfort*, and was hugely pleased to be invited to and present at the inauguration of President Nelson Mandela in 1994. Huddleston was a member of the High-Church Anglican monastic order known as the Community of the Resurrection. Like many other British Anglican missionaries, he had been posted to Africa by the Universities Mission to Central Africa, which traced its beginnings directly to the missionary and anti-slavery ventures of David Livingstone, who had taken his cause—the "three Cs" of Christianity, commerce, and civilization for Africa—to the universities of Britain.

Bill Sutherland

Bill Sutherland was another remarkable member of Africa's liberation supporting cast. Defying ready category, he was an African-American who embraced, early on, the Quaker nonviolent tradition and spent more than five decades in and engaged with Africa as peace and independence networker par excellence. In his position as representative of the American Friends (Quaker) Service Committee, he nourished friendships with a generation of liberation leaders, including Nkrumah of Ghana, Nyerere of Tanzania, Kenyatta of Kenya, Kaunda of Zambia, Mandela and Tutu of South Africa, Nujoma of South West Africa (Namibia), Mondlane of Mozambique, Martin Luther King and du Bois of the USA, Padmore, Fanon, and James of the Caribbean, and many others. When Annetta and I arrived in Dar es Salaam in 1965, Bill Sutherland soon sought us out and became a friend. He proved himself an amicable interlocutor about town who was acquainted, it seemed, with everyone. He had long since become friends with the leaders of the Christian Council of Tanzania, to the staff of which I had been seconded by the Eastern Mennonite Board of Missions.

Behind the scenes, Sutherland facilitated all manner of interactions among Africa's liberation movers and shakers during a significant formative phase of Africa's liberation century. For example, Sutherland had arranged for Martin Luther King to be present at Ghana's independence celebrations in 1957. Everywhere in his interaction with African leaders he promoted nonviolence as an efficacious means toward genuine liberation. In his later years, he teamed up with Matt Meyer for an extended round of interviews with select African liberation leaders, some of whom (Nkrumah, Nyerere, Kaunda, and Nujoma) had become presidents of independent African nation states. The quest in those interviews focused on Sutherland's favorite topic, nonviolence, with particular reference to its realization, however fraught, during the protracted quest for the independence of the African continent.

The All Africa Conference of Churches

The All Africa Conference of Churches (AACC) ranks as one of the most important African church-related organizations that interacted with the continent's liberation movements. Established in 1963—two months before its political continental counterpart, the Organization of African Unity (now known as the African Union), was founded—the AACC is a continental Protestant Christian ecumenical membership organization. The year 2013 marked the AACC's fiftieth or jubilee anniversary. Its 173 member churches and organizations comprise mostly Protestant denominational churches, many, but not all, of which claim Western missionary origins. A number of AACC member churches can be identified as "African instituted" entities, while others are para-church organizations and national Christian councils. Typically, national Christian councils in Africa evolved from what were known earlier as "fellowships," which had been organized by missionary agencies for purposes of coordinating their common efforts in Bible translation/distribution and the provision of education and health services. Soon after its formation in the early 1960s, the AACC's collective ecumenical agenda on the continent became focused on the multiple dynamics of the independence movement. In this regard, Archbishop Desmond Tutu's tenure as chairman of the AACC from 1987 to 1997 added to the luster of the organization's public profile.

Early on, the AACC became deeply involved with the continent's burgeoning refugee population, a situation triggered in complex and distressing ways by the continent's liberation struggle. Its Ecumenical Emergency Action Program was intended to draw attention to Africa's refugee situation and to coordinate church-related programs throughout the continent in an effort to mitigate the refugee conundrum. By the mid-1960s, the ecumenical community was giving much attention to the recalcitrant countries and territories in southern Africa that were yielding most reluctantly to the independence momentum. Second-track diplomacy in this regard was undertaken by senior staff, and during its General Assemblies (convened every five years) plenary discussion and theological reflection focused on the issues of apartheid, racism, armed rebellion, nationalism, and political and ecclesial independence.

During the tenure (1971–78) of the Rev. Burgess Carr of Liberia as AACC General Secretary, the discourse on these core issues proved extraordinarily vigorous, as evidenced in the AACC's General Assembly reports and by high-profile collaboration with the World Council of Churches, also deeply engaged with the liberation movements of southern Africa. By this time it had become apparent that many leaders of liberation movements had much in common with the ecumenical church leaders of the day. They had studied in the same missionary schools, and siblings within the families of nascent nationalist leaders had made choices, some joining the independence dynamics as supported by the ecumenical community and others aligning themselves with the secular political liberation movements.

During Burgess Carr's tenure, civil war in the Sudan reached crisis proportions. It was a conflict between a rebel movement known as the Anyanya, comprising southern Sudanese (Christians), on the one hand, and the army of the independent (1956) "Islamic" Government of Sudan on the other. Following extensive field investigations, a staff member of the World Council of Churches compiled a summary report on the Sudan situation, identifying the contentious issues dividing the country. Thanks to its well-balanced analysis, protagonists agreed to submit to a negotiation process chaired by General Secretary Burgess Carr, with (the Christian) Emperor Haile Selassie of Ethiopia in attendance as witness.

This remarkable initiative resulted in the 1972 Addis Ababa Peace Agreement between the Anyanya rebel movement and the Government of Sudan. It was an agreement that prevailed for a decade and in its wake triggered a most remarkable outpouring of ecumenical support for the rehabilitation of war-torn southern Sudan. To this end, collaboration among the Sudan Council of Churches, the AACC, and the World Council of Churches created a rehabilitation commission headed by Bethuel Kiplagat, a Kenyan churchman seconded to the position by the National Council of Churches of Kenya and the Anglican Church of Kenya. At the time of his secondment, he had been serving as the deputy general secretary of the National Council of Churches of Kenya, a position to which he returned after a two-year stint with the Sudan Council of Churches. At this juncture, the Eastern Mennonite Board of Missions, in collaboration with Mennonite Central Committee, agreed to second me in 1973 to the Sudan Council of Churches Relief and Rehabilitation Commission, the first Mennonite foray into Sudan.

Kodjo Ankrah

Before resuming the narrative on subsequent developments in Sudan, it is appropriate to highlight two additional members of Africa's ecumenical liberation supporting cast. One of these persons was Kodjo Ankrah, a Methodist layperson of Ghana who served for extended periods with the World Council of Churches, the AACC, and latterly as the administrator of a development program promoted by the Anglican Church of Uganda. While deployed by the World Council of Churches and the AACC, he focused his energies on Africa's refugee situation. When the two organizations became engaged with the resolution of civil war in the Sudan, Ankrah served tirelessly in a liaison capacity amid the evolving relational dynamics that led eventually to the aforementioned peace negotiations and peace agreement.

For the greater portion of his professional life, Kodjo Ankrah worked as a devoted ecumenical layperson in the service of Africa's liberation. In his youth, Ankrah's faith journey had been nurtured by the Methodist Church of Ghana. In his formative years, he attended Goshen College (a Mennonite institution) for his undergraduate studies and was supported to this end by members of the Beachy Amish Mennonite community in the Goshen area. Many years later (during an active retirement), when Ankrah and his wife established a retreat and study center in Uganda, two of the seminar rooms were named after his Beachy Amish benefactor friends from Goshen, Indiana. In recognition of his years of service to the Anglican Church of Uganda, he was accorded the honorary title of "Canon."

The Rev. John Gatu

John Gatu, a Kenyan with a home base in the Presbyterian Church of Kenya, in which he served for years as moderator (the senior-most position in the church), was another distinguished member of Africa's ecumenical liberation pantheon. Gatu was gifted with an uncanny ability to act effectively within broad spectrums of church and society. In addition to his primary work as a minister in the Presbyterian Church, he served on a variety of pivotal committees within the National Council of Churches of Kenya, the AACC, and the World Council of Churches. He was also widely engaged with Christian evangelical groups that, among other ventures, sponsored the famous Lausanne (Switzerland) conference of 1974.

In his younger days he had served in the colonial armed forces (the King's African Rifles), but later endorsed Kenya's famous resistance movement known as the Kenya Land and Freedom Army (commonly referred to as the Mau Mau), dedicated to the recovery of land claimed by the British colonial power and an insistence on political independence. For much of his adult life he was an ardent member of the East Africa Revival Movement, through which connections he developed friendships with Mennonite missionary revivalists. In that context, he wrote a gracious foreword to *Ambushed by Love*, a book by Mennonite missionary Dorothy Smoker concerning Kenyan revivalist Christians who suffered at the hands of the Mau Mau movement.

In his engagement with the AACC, he became deeply involved in the liaison dynamics that led to peace initiatives resulting in the 1972 Addis Ababa Peace Agreement. In ensuing decades he sustained an interest in the fortunes of Sudan, an interest graciously acknowledged by the Government of Sudan, by officials of southern rebel movements, and, of course, by the church leaders of Sudan.

John Garang Mabior and the Sudan People's Liberation Movement

In 1983, after a ten-year period of relative peace, civil war in Sudan entered a second phase, this time between a southern rebel group known as the

Sudan People's Liberation Movement (SPLM), led by Col. John Garang Mabior, and the Government of Sudan, led initially by President Jaafar Nimeiri and after 1989 by President Omar al-Bashir. The war persisted for several decades, invoking protracted peace negotiations led by diplomatic instruments of the African Union, Sudanese church leaders, and peace groups, taking the shape of a Comprehensive Peace Agreement in 2005. During a public meeting of senior representatives of the Government of Sudan and the SPLM for a ceremonial signing of the peace agreement, Col. John Garang seized the occasion to make the point that Sudan, Africa's largest country at the time, was heir to multiple histories. From circa AD 500 to AD 1500, Nubia or northern Sudan—from Sudan's border with Egypt to the capital city, Khartoum—comprised three Christian kingdoms. Before the Christian era, multiple civilizations in Nubia had come and gone. Muslim Arabs from Egypt had slowly penetrated Sudan, guided by a famous *baqt* (pact) between the incoming Muslims and resident Nubian Christians after initial contacts in the middle of the seventh century AD, while southern Sudan was heir to a primordial African culture, more recently penetrated by European colonialism and Christian missionaries from north Atlantic countries. Throughout his career as a rebel leader of the SPLM, Col. John Garang had advocated for a unitary Sudan in preference to independence for southern Sudan. Obviously, a united Sudan would have called for an embrace by all parties concerned of Sudan's diverse history. Alas, at a critical moment during the early implementation phase of the Comprehensive Peace Agreement, John Garang died in a helicopter crash, and the vision of a revived unitary Sudan died with him.

In its wake, complex provisions of the Comprehensive Peace Agreement had pointed inexorably to the formation in 2011 of an independent state known as South Sudan. From the 1960s until the time of this writing in 2013, the World Council of Churches, the AACC, and the Sudan Council of Churches in its several guises had navigated an extraordinarily difficult ecumenical accompaniment of the churches and people of southern Sudan toward the much contested formation of South Sudan. Subsequently, the Rev. Samuel Kobia, former general secretary of the National Council of

Churches of Kenya and later general secretary of the World Council of Churches, was jointly appointed by the AACC and the World Council of Churches as ecumenical envoy to the Islamic Republic of Sudan with its capital in Khartoum and to the newly formed nation state of South Sudan with its capital in Juba as a continuing gesture of ecumenical solidarity. With the advent of South Sudan, the formal liberation project of the African continent, spanning more than a half century of sustained struggle, was in significant measure completed.

Liberation Metaphors

As noted at the beginning of this reflection, it was widely considered that if the thorn in Africa's toe was domination by colonial powers, the obvious antidote was political autonomy or independence for the continent. Thence emanated the liberation struggle and the fruits of liberation in the form of fifty-four independent African nation states. It was an understanding embraced by African Christians and by the ecumenical collectivity. During the formative and active years of ecumenical accompaniment with the liberation struggle, African theologians and church leaders had repeatedly invoked the Old Testament metaphor of "exile" (Israelites in Egypt); under colonialism, Africans found themselves in "exile." The liberation struggle as a way of being delivered or freed from exile, it followed, was located in the metaphor of the forty-year trek undertaken by Israelites in their move from Egypt to Canaan. During one of the AACC's pivotal consultations that took place shortly before Mandela became president of South Africa, Chairman Desmond Tutu waxed eloquent in his vision of the new Africa: "We are on the threshold of the promised land, but, alas, our operational theological metaphors are still bound up in language about exile and the forty-year-struggle toward the land of Canaan. We require fresh theological language to describe and to take account of where we are."

Reconstruction

It was in this context that Professor Jesse Mugambi of Kenya was commissioned to compose an exploratory paper in a quest for more appropriate language and a more appropriate theological metaphor to guide reflection on the way forward in a liberated Africa. Mugambi produced a paper (later a book) focusing on the metaphor of "reconstruction" as depicted in the Old Testament book of Nehemiah. Following that initiative, the notion of reconstruction was extensively discussed within Africa's fraternity of theologians. Guiding questions were raised and guiding questions persist: Upon which foundations is reconstruction to take place? Which are to be the guiding principles of such reconstruction? Who are we now? Who are we becoming (identity issues)? In which measure does the reconstruction process draw, if at all, on the African religious and cultural heritage?

African Theologizing

Long before Tutu's challenge, African theologians had engaged in vigorous debate regarding an appropriate African Christian identity. Indeed, it had become apparent early on that Christian theology as bequeathed by missionaries from the West was proving inadequate to the identity quest of the African Christian community. These "felt needs" had become ever more acute as the prospects of political independence became more certain. For an extended period before majority (African) rule came to South Africa in 1994, there had emerged contrasting emphases within the theological discourse in East Africa on one hand, and the discourse taking place among South African theologians on the other. In the former, the discussion focused on African theology, drawing heavily on African religio-cultural motifs. In South Africa, the theological discourse was focused on black theology, an identity inquiry guided by more strident ideological and theological discourse, inspired by the writings of African-American theologian James Cone.

Theological inquiry in Africa had long provided a compelling entry point to an examination of the pressing issues of the day. Already in 1958,

African churchpersons had convened a theology conference in Ibadan, Nigeria, that functioned as a precursor event to the formation of the AACC in 1963. In 1960, Tshibungu of the Congo had posed what was still considered at the time to be a troublesome question: "Could African Traditional Religion [later known as African Religion] serve as a contact point with Christianity in the quest toward the development of an 'African Theology?'" The formation in 1960 of the Association of Theological Institutions in Eastern Africa confirmed the existence of such an African theological quest. In 1969, the AACC produced a report titled *Biblical Revelation and African Beliefs*, reflecting findings gleaned from those earlier consultations undertaken by African theologians.

Then, in 1976, the Ecumenical Association of Third World Theologians was formed in Dar es Salaam, Tanzania, leading to the formation of a Kenyan chapter in 1993. With this evolution of theological inquiry and in its subsequent manifestations, male and female African theologians became increasingly systematic in their inquiry. The Circle of Concerned African Women Theologians quickly extended its quest toward issues such as gender violence, inter-faith dialogue, globalization, poverty, and societal conflict, among much else (parenthetically, according to the cumulative findings of the Circle, neither African culture nor the culture of the Bible had been kind to African women). In 1989, an additional theological initiative took form: the Ecumenical Symposium of Eastern African Theologians. True to its designation, this forum engaged both Catholic and Protestant—male and female—theologians. Following a disciplined pattern of reflection, writing, and exchange of papers and views, this group of theologians for a time produced publications (as part of a series) almost on an annual basis.

During the 1970s, 1980s, and 1990s, writings and publications by African theologians coalesced into a cascade. In that context and to this day, Mbiti's seminal book, *African Religions and Philosophy* (1969), serves as a major reference point. Among the remarkable developments since then has been the shift in the language or designation deployed in reference to Africa's belief systems. Writ large, the designations shifted over time from Edinburgh's "tribal religions" and "animism" to Mbiti's African religions to the widely used term African Traditional Religion, and eventually to an affirmation of the generic term African Religion.

In 1997, Tanzanian Catholic academic Laurenti Magesa published a remarkable book under the title *African Religion: Moral Traditions for Abundant Life*. An online description of the book affirms its import: "The book is the first comprehensive exploration of the moral and ethical imperatives of African Religion that treats the religious tradition of Africa as an equal among the world's religions."

In his book *Concepts of God in Africa*, John Mbiti refers repeatedly to African Religion, characterizing it as a corpus of understanding fully capable of conversation with Christianity at large and with the remarkable collection of writings on African Theology, also referred to as African Christian Theology. Going forward, several of the more venturous African theologians reflect on the theology of palaver, a theology of open-ended discourse, discernment, and engagement, moving toward an acceptable ethic (and identity) for life together on an extraordinarily diverse continent.

Political Ideology

With regard to counterpart reflection on political and ideological issues emerging during the century under discussion, two African political rhetoricians stand out: Kwame Nkrumah of Ghana and Julius Kambarge Nyerere of Tanzania. The former was a strident advocate for a United States of Africa, drawing heavily on Marxist/socialist ideology. Nyerere, by contrast, probed the foundations of the African communitarian (Ujamaa) heritage as an ideological basis for the modern African nation state. Other African statesmen and many African academics have written and probed extensively in this regard, among them Leopold Senghor, former president of Senegal, who developed the much-debated notion of Negritude. As of this writing, an African political ideology easily recognized or widely acceded to across the continent cannot be readily identified. Indeed, discussions on ideology have generally given way to discourse on the more efficacious ways of growing and managing modern (capitalist) African economies. During his tenure as chairman of South Africa's Truth and Reconciliation

Commission, Archbishop Desmond Tutu repeatedly championed the commonalities of African peoples by invoking the concept of ubuntu—the quality of being human, realizing oneself in community with others ("I am because we are"). In sub-Saharan Africa, the word and concept of ubuntu may be closer than any other to a common affirmation of African self-identity. Although cognates of ubuntu appear in many sub-Saharan languages, the concept has yet to be actively embraced as the generally accepted basis of a continental ethics.

In summary, the African "liberation century" as it played out between the years 1900 and 2011 produced three complementary and greatly intertwined results:

1. Fifty-four politically independent nation states with ubuntu as a promising, but not fully endorsed, common understanding of African identity.
2. A continent in which half of the population espouses the Christian faith, expressed in a myriad denominational and confessional forms, while the other half espouses various expressions of Islam.
3. An absolutely remarkable corpus of theological reflection on issues related to and engaged with liberation of the African continent: African identity, African Religion, missionary religions, African Christian Theology, and a broad range of issues related to the rapidly changing sociopolitical economic order in Africa.

Sources for this chapter have been included in the Chapter 3 sources.

3
Mennonites Accompany an African "Liberation Century"

Introduction

The following sketches of Mennonite engagement in Africa during this critical transition period toward liberation are abbreviated in the extreme. Multiple book-length summaries would be required to do justice to the complex, multifaceted Mennonite engagement on the continent during the tumultuous period between the years 1960 and 2011. Appended bibliographic references offer samples rather than comprehensive indicators of that experience.

Already in the late 1800s there had been forays by North American Mennonite and, later, Brethren in Christ mission boards into the Congo, Northern Rhodesia (Zambia), and Southern Rhodesia (Zimbabwe). Compared to mainline Protestant missions, the Mennonites and the Brethren in Christ were minor actors and among the later arrivals. But, like virtually all other Protestant churches across the African continent, these mission churches were touched in the 1960s by the dynamics of independence, subtly and overtly informing the related shift from expatriate missionary to African church leadership. As elsewhere, health and education services—formerly proffered by the missionary agencies—were expected in independent Africa to be made available, quite deliberately, to the service of the larger public by means of national government-imposed infrastructure. National missionary "fellowships," which had been established to coordinate health and education services, were now transformed into national councils of churches, with newly installed African leaders recruited on the strength of rapid change and new opportunities proffered or implied by the prospects of self-rule, both within political and ecclesial realms.

Like other North American service agencies, Mennonite Central Committee (MCC), the bi-national (American and Canadian), pan-Mennonite Christian service agency, was just emerging in the 1950s and 1960s from deep engagement with post–World War II relief activity in Europe and was now shifting focus to the African continent. Like other service agencies (widely referred to as nongovernmental agencies—NGOs), MCC had turned to Africa on an optimistic note, informed in some measure by the officially declared UN Development Decades (1960s and 1970s) and specifically by the findings of a UNESCO-sponsored conference (1961) convened in Ethiopia that identified education as a priority for the continent's newly independent countries. This declared priority was later reiterated in UN deliberations and coincided with a decision by MCC's Executive Committee to send a representative to Africa with the mandate to explore the possibilities of support for secondary education in central Africa.

Mennonite Central Committee's Teachers Abroad Program

Thus, in November 1961, Mennonite educator Robert Kreider visited North Rhodesia (Zambia), South Rhodesia (Zimbabwe), and Nyasaland (Malawi), where he explored the possibility of placing teachers in secondary schools. His immediate church contact for this purpose was Bishop David Climenhaga of the Brethren in Christ Church, with its far-flung mission infrastructure in the region and long-standing official relationship with MCC in North America. Another contact person was David Temple, serving as the education secretary for the Northern Rhodesia Christian Council and principal at a teacher-training institution. Temple served as a liaison person between the country's Ministry of Education and the governing councils of the respective secondary schools. Why this particular entry point for the MCC initiative? According to Kreider: "[It was] simply because in Africa the governments of the day, the Councils of Churches, and the Brethren in Christ all reported needs in this regard and all indicated a willingness to collaborate with the MCC program immediately."

MCC's ensuing teacher placement initiative in Africa was eventually christened the Teachers Abroad Program (TAP).

East and West Africa

Subsequently, the institutional/relational and teacher-placement model developed by Kreider was extended to other countries in southern Africa, to the three East African countries (Kenya, Tanzania, Uganda), to Congo in the middle of the continent, and to several countries in West Africa. According to a long-term MCC worker in Africa, the TAP model served as the initial entry point for collaboration between MCC and the respective national councils of churches in Africa. In part, these links represented relationships of convenience, for in the newly independent countries the government ministries of education generally relied on the emerging national church councils to facilitate relationships with church- or mission-related schools. But these links also facilitated MCC's determination from the beginning to relate to a broad range of churches and church institutions in Africa rather than developing its own institutional presence. In subsequent interactions with national councils of churches in several southern African countries, MCC's engagement agenda shifted toward a range of issues beyond the initial pattern of placing TAPpers in secondary schools.

Botswana

Botswana was one southern African country where MCC's support ministries took on a diverse character. Large in landmass, with a semi-arid climate and a population at the time well below a million people, featuring only a fledgling modern sector, Botswana was extraordinarily open to the presence and contribution of NGOs such as MCC. Mennonites embraced the country's openness by forging collaboration between MCC and several USA-based Mennonite mission agencies, resulting in a unique institutional configuration functional in Botswana known as Mennonite Ministries. Among the very first contacts made by Mennonites was with the Botswana Council of Churches.

Over subsequent decades, Mennonite agencies seconded more than three hundred people to a variety of positions in Botswana. Some personnel placements followed the TAP model, some were made in the context of Botswana Council of Churches member churches; one Mennonite worker provided financial and secretarial services directly within the Botswana Council of Churches administrative office. And, for an extended period, Mennonite Ministries served as a full-fledged member of the Botswana Council of Churches Executive Committee. In mid-2005, MCC celebrated and concluded forty years of service in Botswana.

If MCC's initial TAP foray into Northern Rhodesia (Zambia) was buoyed by postindependence optimism, the subsequent, more generalized attention to southern Africa was informed by "a bewildering complex of currents and crosscurrents which portend[ed] crisis." South Africa's apartheid system was widely recognized as an affront to the acceptable norms of human community, generally, and to the collective Christian conscience, in particular. Together with this general acknowledgment was the sense among many North American Mennonites in the late 1960s that any direct involvement within South Africa would be deemed a compromise of Christian conscience. It was considered best to avoid all contact with South Africa and advisable even to refrain from engagement in neighboring countries such as Lesotho, Botswana, and Swaziland. However, a few Mennonite leaders countered with an alternate vision. Following a visit to the region in May 1970, several Mennonite mission administrators began to formulate a Mennonite role in southern Africa: "While the international community holds apartheid in abhorrence, the windows and doors of the Republic [of South Africa] must be forced open from the outside so that the winds of change can blow through. This is Christian responsibility."

Southern Africa

Although direct MCC engagement within South Africa was ruled out both by the apartheid government and by general Mennonite sensibilities, engagement in Swaziland and other so-called frontline states was deemed to provide windows onto the changes which were virtually predestined to unfold in South Africa. The first Mennonite agency country representative in Swaziland spelled out the posture rather succinctly: "I have never really needed to question the rightness of our being here . . . I don't see Swaziland as an extremely needy country (by comparison), but there is plenty of scope for Christian concern . . . It is relevant for us to think of Swaziland in relationship to the whole of Southern Africa . . . So much is already being done in South Africa by intelligent, sympathetic, enlightened, committed Christians and humanitarians that I find it difficult to believe that we would have anything radically new to bring to the situation. Strengthening what is being done, yes."

Swaziland

In the spirit of "strengthening what was already being done," Mennonites in Swaziland forged relationships with a variety of agencies in the country, including the Swaziland Council of Churches, comprised at the time primarily of member churches with an evangelical hue. When a group of Zulu refugees escaped armed conflict in South Africa's Natal Province in the 1970s, the council did not consider response to the refugee needs as part of its mandate. In complex fashion, this incident gave rise, subsequently, to the formation of the Council of Swaziland Churches, with Catholic, Anglican, and Lutheran churches as members, and to a very unique ecumenical engagement with Mennonites.

During the formative proceedings of the Council of Swaziland Churches, a senior Mennonite worker in Swaziland was asked to serve as the first general secretary. When he protested initially, saying, "How can I as a foreigner take this position?" he was rebuked by the presiding Roman Catholic bishop: "Did you come to serve the churches in Africa?" "Yes I did." "Then you will do as you are told!" The Mennonite worker accepted the position in a council that would subsequently become affiliated with the World Council of Churches and the All Africa Conference of Churches.

Mozambique

Even as Mennonite workers were being placed in politically independent countries contiguous with South Africa, they were mindful of neighboring Mozambique, functioning till then as an overseas Portuguese "department," but now under siege by armed freedom fighters. In September 1964, the leading armed liberation movement of Mozambique, FRELIMO, fired the first ritual bullet in its quest for political independence. At the time, senior officials of the movement were being hosted by Tanzania, the country serving as secretary to the Organization of African Unity's Liberation Committee. From the mid-1960s to the early 1970s, two Mennonite workers were seconded to the Christian Council of Tanzania, located in the capital city, Dar es Salaam. They were assigned to programs supporting Mozambican exiles and refugees in camps hosted by the Tanzanian government, managed by the Lutheran World Federation and funded by the United Nations High Commission for Refugees. Coincidentally, the Mennonite workers in Dar es Salaam had as their nearby neighbors several senior FRELIMO officials, including Eduardo Mondlane, the movement's first president. Even to the casual observer, aspects of Mozambique's liberation war were played out on the doorsteps of this Dar es Salaam neighborhood, rendering the armed struggle for change in southern Africa a daily reality.

By 1975, Mozambique had achieved independence from Portugal in the wake of a long and vicious armed independence struggle. Thanks to the strong Marxist ideology nurtured during FRELIMO's struggle and thanks to the close collaboration between Portugal's Catholic Church and Portugal's colonial government, churches in Mozambique and the newly independent FRELIMO government of the day were mutually wary of each other. Church–state relationships, tenuous from the onset of independence, were rendered even more fragile when the new FRELIMO government proceeded, soon after assuming authority, to nationalize church-operated schools and hospitals throughout the country. It was in this charged context that MCC dispatched several senior Mennonites to visit newly independent Mozambique.

Meanwhile, the fledgling Christian Council of Mozambique was proceeding gingerly, seeking occasion to open dialogue with the government, but avoiding undue confrontation. By means of discreet engagement with select government leaders, the council carefully articulated its right and its perceived duty to participate in the reconstruction of the country. To this end, it was able, eventually, to mobilize considerable international support. In due time, the Christian Council of Mozambique emerged as the accepted link between the FRELIMO government and the Protestant churches. Just as a certain uneasiness characterized the church–state relationships within the country, so the Protestant churches in Mozambique were distrustful and cautious with regard to the prospect of overbearing interventions by international church-related service agencies.

Fully cognizant of these sensitivities on several fronts, the exploratory visits to Mozambique by senior Mennonites during the mid-1970s were focused on the Christian Council of Mozambique as the primary point of contact and guided by a carefully articulated relational posture:

"Our current stance of supporting [indigenous] church bodies rather than establishing our own in [southern] Africa is a thought-out and conscious missiological strategy, based on the assumption that we should strengthen rather than further fragment the Body of Christ and that we can share our understandings of what being a Christian means within other church groups."

These initial Mennonite contacts with the Christian Council of Mozambique were followed by MCC personnel placements in neighboring Swaziland with a mandate to provide material aid to Mozambican refugees in Zimbabwe in preparation for repatriation. They also had a mandate to provide material aid to needy people within Mozambique. Eventually it was determined that a Mennonite material aid consultant should be placed within the Christian Council of Mozambique secretariat to facilitate the logistical and administrative procedures related to the material aid being made available through MCC. From these beginnings, the relationship between MCC and the council progressed from strength to strength. Numbers of MCC personnel were subsequently appointed to auxiliary staff positions within the council's institutional structure and within its member churches in various parts of the country.

Transkei

Generally, MCC's declared strategy was to be present and engaged in countries and territories contiguous with South Africa, given that a presence inside the country was not feasible. In this regard, the Transkei was a special case. The Transkei had been designated by the apartheid regime as an African "homeland" or "bantustan," and was, according to official South African government policy, politically independent, though the independence was recognized by no other government in the world. This fictional political status imposed on the Transkei was rendered even more fragile when it became evident that the South African regime reserved and exercised the right to intervene in the affairs of the "independent" homeland at will. MCC's decision in 1978 to be present with the Transkei Council of Churches was therefore a decision to be present in a volatile frontline territory.

With origins dating to 1964, the Christian Council of the Transkei took on the status in 1969 of an affiliated regional council of the South African Council of Churches, at which point it became the Transkei Council of Churches. In 1978 MCC seconded staff to the council and in 1981 submitted a request for membership. Subsequently, both MCC and Mennonite mission personnel were variously seconded to staff positions within the council offices, to the council's field program positions, and to positions with its member churches. Several MCC workers served successively as development consultants to the council and, at one point in 1979, an MCC worker kept the central office operational when it was "closed down" during a particularly tense spate of interference by the South African government.

Within the Transkei Council of Churches and later in its placement of Mennonite personnel to a variety of positions within South Africa, MCC found itself interacting closely with South African anti-apartheid activists, both within and outside the church context. Even though the South African government kept a watchful eye on MCC activities, placement of MCC personnel within the country became a bit easier as the end of the apartheid period became inevitable. Among these host bodies was a dizzying variety of specialized study centers, church-related retreat centers, universities, street children programs, and welfare centers offering peace studies, training in a variety of skills, overseas sabbaticals for harried anti-apartheid activists, as well as general welfare services. Although MCC had provided a continuous flow of supporting funds to the South African Council of Churches and maintained close relationships with the organization over an extended period—both before and after Mennonite personnel were placed inside South Africa—the council did not serve as MCC's placement agency within the country. For these purposes, MCC placed and administered its personnel in South Africa from surrounding countries until the first MCC country representatives were placed in Durban, South Africa, in 1992.

Post-Apartheid South Africa

When in 1994 a relatively peaceful transition was realized, few solidarity actors, including MCC personnel, had anticipated that significant numbers of South Africa's church-related anti-apartheid activists would now be joining South Africa's newly formed government. Initially, the shift had the effect of crippling the South Africa Council of Churches and making visible an astonishing array of unresolved centrifugal dynamics. These included issues such as the viability of the prevailing nation state model in Africa, the relevance of the ongoing discussion regarding an "African renaissance," the rights and functional identity of ethnic and minority groupings, the control and deployment of natural resources, and the vicissitudes of urbanization, among others.

In an effort to engage with this array of issues in the post-apartheid context, MCC seconded a worker couple to Letsema, a program of the Wilgespruit Fellowship Center, located in Roodepoort, near Johannesburg. From the Wilgespruit base, MCC workers in 2001 established and subsequently supported a program known as the Africa Peace Institute, hosted by the Mindolo Ecumenical Foundation, located near Kitwe, Zambia. The institute developed a relationship with Eastern Mennonite University in Harrisonburg, Virginia, and from its inception received financial support from MCC. The Africa Peace Institute mounted intensive annual six-week courses in conflict resolution and peace studies from a Christian perspective, catering for students from across Africa pursuing academic certificates, professional enrichment, and personal development and growth. Instruction combined theory and practice for conflict resolution through applied study on topics such as peace building, nonviolence, intervention roles, trauma healing, and reconciliation.

Into Sudan

At the other end of the continent lies Sudan, until 2011 Africa's largest country, featuring a most remarkable history. Five of the ruling pharaohs of Egypt were Nubians (northern Sudanese). Pyramids, usually associated with Egypt, are also found in northern Sudan. People from northern Sudan (Nubia) had served in the armies of Egypt "from time immemorial," and trade within and beyond the Nile Valley had "always been there." Forty years after Pentecost, a Nubian man became the first African Christian (Acts 8:26–40). Centuries later, Nubia was evangelized jointly by the ancient Church of Constantinople and the Egyptian Orthodox Church, giving birth to a Nubian Christian community that survived for nearly a thousand years (circa AD 500 to AD 1500).

Following an initial assault in AD 642, Arab Muslims launched a series of incursions into northern Sudan, where they were met and restrained by the armies of Christian Nubian monarchies, whose soldiers were known as the "pupil smiters"—warriors with the ability to strike enemies in the eyes with arrows! In contrast to other successful conquests, including their conquest of Egypt, the Arab invaders were unable to gain control of Nubia. Faced with this unprecedented situation, they concluded a baqt ("pact") with their Christian Nubian counterparts shortly before the year AD 700. The pact provided guidelines governing Nubian Christian–Arab Muslim trade and restrictions regarding the settlement of Arabs in Nubia. Although Christian Nubia eventually succumbed to Muslim/Arab penetration, the provisions of the pact were adhered to in varying degrees by both parties for nearly six centuries. Extensive commentary and debate among Islamic scholars in successive centuries regarding this pact attest to its unique character.

Today's Christianity in Sudan traces its beginnings to the entry in the mid-1800s of European missionaries. Their endeavors suffered severely under the rule of the Mahdi (the Muslim revivalist, the "Sent One") in the 1880s, expanded under the joint Anglo-Egyptian rule (1898–1956), and chafed under successive independent Sudanese governments. Even before independence from the Egypto-British condominium government in 1956, aggrieved southern Sudanese had triggered an armed rebellion and a seventeen-year civil war, which ended in 1972 with the signing of the earlier noted Addis Ababa Peace Accord. Negotiations leading to this accord had been initiated and brokered by the World Council of Churches and the All Africa Conference of Churches. Following a ten-year period of more or less peaceful respite, civil war resumed and continued for another twenty years. This second phase of the war was resolved with the signing of a peace accord in 2005 between the Arab/Muslim-dominated Government of Sudan and the Sudan People's Liberation Movement/Army, brokered this time by the Intergovernmental Authority on Development, formed by governments in the Horn of Africa.

As in other African countries, missionaries to Sudan had been sponsored by a range of confessional traditions. And like elsewhere, they quickly found it necessary to collaborate on common efforts in the categories of health, education, and Bible translation; by the mid-1960s, this collaboration took the form of the Sudan Missionary Fellowship. In the late 1960s, the beginnings of the Sudan Council of Churches were taking institutional form.

Following the 1972 Addis Ababa Peace Accord, the Sudan Council of Churches was rendered a more formal institution and was supported by the global ecumenical community to undertake relief and rehabilitation activity, focused on war-ravaged southern Sudan. It was in this context that Eastern Mennonite Board of Missions, in collaboration with MCC, seconded personnel to the council's Commission for Relief and Rehabilitation, headquartered in Khartoum. Subsequently, MCC seconded personnel to a variety of field positions in both northern and southern Sudan. During the turbulent second phase of the civil war (1983–2005), MCC maintained its regional Sudan office in Nairobi, Kenya, enabling access to both rebel and government-held areas. From that base, MCC participated in the early 1980s with the establishment of the Nairobi-based New Sudan Council of Churches. Given the intensity of the prevailing civil war in Sudan, the Sudan Council of Churches was mandated by the member churches to be present to the government-held areas and the New Sudan Council of Churches to rebel-held areas. Another MCC window onto Sudan became possible through collaboration with the All Africa Conference of Churches. From 1989 to 1999, MCC seconded me to the International Affairs Desk of the conference. My mandate, among other briefs, was to accompany the ecumenical and political vagaries of Sudan.

During the following decades until the present, MCC personnel have participated variously and intensively in the respective ecumenical deliberations: annual general assemblies, partner round-table meetings, and field programs of the several manifestations of the two Sudanese councils of churches. Both councils—"two expressions of a single ecumenical reality"—enjoyed the full participation of Sudanese Catholic and Protestant member churches. At national and regional levels, MCC personnel were active, respectively, in the Ecumenical Support Program for Sudan, a solidarity initiative undertaken by the National Council of Churches of Kenya, and in the All Africa Conference of Churches Sudan Working Group, providing "second-track" diplomatic support for the official Sudan peace process. At the global level, MCC personnel participated in the so-called Sudan Ecumenical Forum, an innovative catch-all ecumenical forum bringing together support agencies from North Atlantic countries and representatives from select churches and Christian councils in Africa.

During the long-drawn-out process leading from the Comprehensive Peace Agreement of 2005 to the advent of independence for South Sudan in 2011, leaders of the Sudanese councils of churches were obliged initially to negotiate a merger between the two entities. When independence for South Sudan became a reality, church leaders eventually agreed to the establishment of separate national Christian councils, one based in Khartoum catering for churches in the Sudan, and one in Juba catering for the churches of the Republic of South Sudan.

Throughout the period, peace talks between the Government of Sudan and the rebel SPLM were variously underway, sponsored by the Intergovernmental Authority on Development. Churches in Sudan, supported by the aforementioned ecumenical apparatus, were relentless in their pursuit of peace within the south, for wartime was tension time, both among rebel fighters and within civilian communities. Churches and ecumenical partners also maintained close vigilance on the halting official peace talks, cajoling, commenting, advising, and mediating.

When the Comprehensive Peace Agreement between the SPLM and the Government of Sudan was finally signed on January 9, 2005, there was a huge sigh of relief and a vast sense of accomplishment across the East and Horn of Africa region. However, within six months after the signing, Col. John Garang, the charismatic leader of the SPLM, died in a helicopter crash. Meanwhile, provisions of the Comprehensive Peace Agreement called for continuing negotiations, which led, seemingly inexorably, to the formation of the independent country of South Sudan in 2011. In the wake of these developments, the churches of Sudan, including the Sudan Council of Churches, faced momentous challenges. Life for southern Christians in the Sudan was being made difficult, triggering a massive migration of southern Christians (resident for generations in the northern parts of Sudan) into the new country of South Sudan. As of this writing, these and many other transitional adjustments are ongoing and are extraordinarily challenging for the churches of Sudan and South Sudan, and for the ecumenical community in a continuing posture of Christian solidarity.

Conclusion

The emergence of the African continent in the form of fifty-four independent nation states and the emergence of the African peoples as self-governing participants in the global arena during the period considered in this reflection is significant beyond easy comprehension or exaggeration. Africa's social, religious, cultural, and economic richness calls for acknowledgment, appreciation, and engagement to reciprocal benefit in a globalizing world.

This reflection is an expansion of a presentation made to a group assembled by the Anabaptist Center for Religion and Society on the Eastern Mennonite University campus, Harrisonburg, Virginia, October 14, 2013.

Postscript

- As of this writing, Africa's newest nation state, South Sudan, is experiencing serious internal conflict, with IGAD mediating toward ceasefire and resolution.
- In 2013, the economic growth rates of several African nations states were among the highest in the world—"Africa Rising."
- Monetary contributions (remittances) from the African diaspora are among the largest sources of "foreign aid" to African nation states.
- The middle class in Africa is expanding rapidly, with African Christians as prominent participants.
- The economic gap between Africa's middle class and the low-income segments of society is growing.
- As a collectivity, African nation states experience persistent food deficits.
- China's presence in Africa is growing, manifest in infrastructure construction, trade, and resource extraction. In 2012, the Chinese government invited "all" African heads of state to China for consultations; in August 2014, President Obama, in a counter move, hosted more than 40 African heads of state for consultations in Washington.
- Among the most recognized/recognizable personalities globally are the following five Africans or people of African descent: Nelson Mandela, Desmond Tutu, Kofi Anan, Martin Luther King, Barack Obama.
- It is often observed that international and indigenous non-governmental organizations (NGOs) operational in Africa have assumed significant aspects of the agenda earlier pursued by missionary agencies.
- How do or should North American Mennonites reflect on their engagement [via MCC] with Africa's liberation century?

Sources

Alier, Abel. 1990. *Southern Sudan: Too Many Agreements Dishonored.* Reading, UK: Ithaca Press.

Ankrah, Kodwo. 1998. *Development and the Church of Uganda: Mission, Myths and Metaphors.* Nairobi: Acton Publishers.

Ashworth, John. *The Voice of the Voiceless: The Role of the Church in the Sudanese Civil War 1983–2005.* 2014. Nairobi: Paulines Publications Africa.

Assefa, Hizkias. 1987. *Mediation of Civil Wars: Approaches and Strategies—The Sudan Conflict.* Boulder, Colorado, USA: Westview Press.

Barrett, David B. 1982. *World Christian Encyclopedia: A Comparative Survey of Churches and Religions in the Modern World, AD 1900–2000.* Oxford/New York: Oxford University Press.

Bediako, Kwame. 1995. *Christianity in Africa: The Renewal of a Non-Western Religion.* Maryknoll, New York: Orbis Books.

Bertsche, Jim and Donald R. Jacobs. May 1970. "Southern Africa Study."

Blyden, Edward. 1887. *Christianity, Islam and the Negro Race.* London: Whittingham Press.

Bujo, Bénézet. 1998. *The Ethical Dimensions of Community: The African Model and the Dialogue between North and South.* Nairobi, Kenya: Paulines Publications Africa.

Byaruhanga, Christopher. 2015. *The History and Theology of the Ecumenical Movement in East Africa.* Kampala, Uganda: Fountain Publishers.

Chepkwony, Agnes. 1987. *The Role of Non-Governmental Organizations in Development: A Study of the National Christian Council of Kenya (NCCK) 1963–1978.* Uppsala, Sweden: Uppsala University.

Cone, James. 2010. *A Black Theology of Liberation.* (40th anniversary edition.) Maryknoll, New York: Orbis Books.

Davidson, Basil. 1993. *The Black Man's Burden: Africa and the Curse of the Nation-State.* New York, New York: Three Rivers Press.

Du Bois, W. E. B. 1903. *The Souls of Black Folk: Essays and Sketches.* Chicago, Illinois: A. C. McClurg and Co.

Fanon, Franz. 1961. *The Wretched of the Earth.* New York, New York: Grove Press.

Gatu, John. 2006. *Joyfully Christian—Truly African.* 2006. Nairobi: Acton Publishers.

Grant, Colin. 2009. *Negro with a Hat: The Rise and Fall of Marcus Garvey.* Oxford: Oxford University Press.

Hastings, Adrian. 1979. *A History of African Christianity 1950–1975.* Cambridge, London, New York: Cambridge University Press.

Hord, Fred Lee and Jonathan Scott Lee. 1995. *I Am Because We Are: Readings in Black Philosophy.* Amherst, MA: University of Massachusetts Press.

Huddleston, Trevor. 1956. *Naught for Your Comfort.* London: Collins.

Huddleston, Trevor. 1991. *Return to South Africa: The Ecstasy and the Agony.* London: Collins Fount.

James, C. L. R. 1939/2012. *A History of Pan-African Revolt.* Oakland, CA: PM Press.

Juhnke, James. 2011. "Botswana, 1971–1973" in *Small Steps toward the Missing Peace.* Garland, TX: Flying Camel Publications.

Kalu, Ogbu U. 2005. *African Christianity: An African Story.* Pretoria, South Africa: Department of Church History, University of Pretoria.

Kobia, Samuel. 2013. *Dialogue Matters: The Role of Ecumenical Diplomacy in the Run-up to the Independence of South Sudan.* Nairobi: All Africa Conference of Churches.

Kreider, Robert. 2012. *Coming Home: An Autobiography of My 1952–2011 Years.* Robert Kreider.

Lind, Tim. August 1989. *MCC Africa Program: Historical Background* (MCC Occasional Paper No. 10). Mennonite Central Committee.

MacMaster, Richard K. and Donald R. Jacobs. 2006. *A Gentle Wind of God: The Influence of the East Africa Revival.* Scottdale, PA: Herald Press.

Magesa, Laurenti. 2000. *African Religion: Moral Traditions for Abundant Life.* Orbis Books.

Makonnen, Ras. 1973. *Pan-Africanism from Within.* (Recorded and edited by Kenneth King). Nairobi, London, New York: Oxford University Press.

Mandela, Nelson. 1995. *Long Walk to Freedom.* New York, New York: Back Bay Books.

Mbeki, Thabo. 1998. *Africa: The Time Has Come.* Cape Town: Tafelberg Publishers Ltd.

Mbeki, Thabo. April 9, 1998. "The African Renaissance, South Africa and the World." Speech at United Nations University.

Mbiti, John. 1969. *African Religions and Philosophy.* Nairobi: East African Publishers.

Mbiti, John. 2012. *Concepts of God in Africa.* Nairobi: Acton Publishers.

Mennonite Central Committee Workbook editions 1964–2000.

Miller, Harold F. 1996. *Peace and Reconciliation in Africa.* (Occasional Paper.) Mennonite Central Committee.

______________January 18, 1989. "The Quest for Legitimacy: Church and State in Africa." Presentation in Winnipeg, Manitoba, Canada. [Unpublished paper.]

Mugambi, J. N. K. and Mary N. Getui. 1999. *Theology of Reconstruction.* Nairobi, Kenya: Acton Publishers.

Musser, Daniel. 1886. *Nonresistance Asserted: As Taught by Christ and His Apostles.* Cincinnati, OH: Inquirer Printing Co.

Nkrumah, Kwame. 1973. *I Speak of Freedom.* London: Zed Books.

Nyerere, Julius K. 1968. *Ujamaa: Essays on Socialism.* Oxford: Oxford University Press.

Odinga, Oginga. 1968. *Not Yet Uhuru—The Autobiography of Oginga Odinga.* Portsmouth, NH: Heinemann.

Odinga, Raila. 2013. *Raila Odinga: The Flame of Freedom.* Nairobi, Kenya: Mountain Top Publishers.

Orabator, A. 2008. *Theology Brewed in an African Pot.* Maryknoll, NY: Orbis Books.

Penner, Peter, and Leona Penner. 1992. "Southern Africa History Project Proposal." Prepared for discussion at Southern Africa Coordinating Group [MCC representatives' meeting].

Peterson, Derek R. 2012. *Ethnic Patriotism and the East African Revival: A History of Dissent.* Cambridge, UK: Cambridge University Press.

Regehr, Ernie. 1979. *Perceptions of Apartheid: The Churches and Political Change in South Africa.* Scottdale, PA: Herald Press.

Rudy, Jonathan. 1988. *Mennonite Committee Zambia: 35 Years—1962–1997.* Mennonite Central Committee.

_______________1996. *A Brief History of Mennonites in Swaziland: The First 25 Years.* Mennonite Central Committee.

_______________1996. *A Brief History of Mennonite Central Committee in Lesotho.* (For Mennonite Ministries in Lesotho and the Southern Africa Coordinating Group.)

______________ 1997. *History of Mennonites in Mozambique (Including MCC Involvement in Malawi Post-1981 Program Closure).* Mennonite Central Committee.

______________1999. *Mennonite Central Committee/Mennonite Ministries–Botswana.* Mennonite Central Committee.

______________2001. *Anabaptists and AICs: A Unique Paradigm for Mission in Southern Africa.* A thesis submitted to Eastern Mennonite Seminary in partial fulfillment of the requirements for a Degree of Master of Arts in Religion.

______________January 27, 2000. "Abstracts regarding African Christian Councils from MCC service histories." Personal communication.

Senghor, Leopold Sedar. See Wikipedia entry under the designation "Negritude." "What is Negritude" in C. G. M. Mutiso and S. W. Rohio (eds.), 1975. *Readings in African Political Thought.* London: Heinemann.

Smoker, Dorothy (compiler/editor). 1993. *Ambushed by Love: God's Triumph in Kenya's Terror.* Fort Washington, PA: Christian Literature Crusade–USA.

Stauffer, Carl. January–March 2002. "Nurturing the Tree of Peace." *MCC Peace Office Newsletter.*

Stauffer, Carl. "The Africa Peace-building Institute (API) – Zambia – Case Study" (undated brochure).

Sudan: Faith in Sudan book series (seventeen volumes). Nairobi: Paulines Publications Africa. [A treasure trove of Christian Sudanica, three volumes of which were published with MCC funding.]

Sutherland, Bill and Matt Meyer. 2000. *Guns and Gandhi in Africa: Pan-African Insights on Non-violence, Armed Struggle and Liberation in Africa.* Asmara, Eritrea: Africa World Press.

The Circle of Concerned African Women Theologians (see internet).

Thompson, V. B. 1969. *Africa and Unity.* London: Longman. [A definitive work on Pan-Africanism.]

Tolstoy, Leo. 2010 [1894]. *The Kingdom of God Is Within You.* Seaside, Oregon: Watchmaker Publishing.

Tutu, Desmond Mpilo. 1999. *No Future without Forgiveness.* London: Rider/Ebury Press, Random House.

Utuk, Effiong. 1997. *Visions of Authenticity: The Assemblies of the All Africa Conference of Churches 1963–1992.* Nairobi: All Africa Conference of Churches.

Vantini, Giovanni. 2009. *Rediscovering Christian Nubia.* Khartoum, Sudan: Collegio delle Missioni Africane.

Werner, Roland, William Anderson, and Andrew Wheeler (eds). 2001. *Day of Devastation, Day of Contentment: The History of the Sudanese Church across 2000 Years.* Nairobi: Paulines Publications Africa.

4
The Quest for Stability: Church and State in Africa

ACCORDING TO KENYAN professor Ali Mazrui, Africa has always managed to be at the center of the world, sometimes as facilitator of communications and commerce, sometimes as frustration to would-be traders and conquerors. Whatever one's opinion regarding the importance of Africa, its vital statistics are astonishing. Consider its physical size: the continent of Africa is larger than the whole of China, the USA, India, Europe, Argentina, and New Zealand combined, covering 11,706,166 square miles.

Consider its people: There are now an estimated one billion people in Africa. They speak approximately two thousand indigenous languages and a half dozen European languages. Africa is the only major area of the world in which human population growth continues unabated; in some places, such as Kenya, the annual growth rate in modern times has reached 4 percent, doubling the country's population in a matter of eighteen to twenty years.

By any measure, Africa is religious. As a continent, it is the font of primal religion, featuring vast diversity within general, overarching themes. African Religion has been and still is practiced as an un-codified, indigenous religious tradition that finds expression in everyday life, adapting itself to the changing needs of the populace and variously in tension with and complementary to the missionary religions of Islam and Christianity. Statistics regarding Africa's affiliation with Christian denominations are impressive. In the year 1900, the African continent contained 1.8 percent of the world's Christian community. Extrapolating from the present rate of growth, by the year 2000 Africa will represent 19 percent of the Christian population of the world. The comparable North American percentages have remained relatively constant during this time period, ranging between 12 and 14 percent.

Statistically, Christianity in Africa is growing more rapidly than anywhere else in the world. But Islam is also growing in numbers. By the year 2000, according to some statisticians, Africa would be more or less evenly divided between Muslims and Christians. While these two formal religions could be seen to have gained numerically at the expense of the practitioners of traditional religion, it cannot be assumed that indigenous religious practice has therefore disappeared. Indeed, as will be noted at the conclusion of these comments, such religious understandings are alive and well, providing important clues to Africa's future. "Church" in Africa is located within Africa's larger religious configuration, conspicuous as formal religious establishment and important as an actor within the modern body politic.

If "Church" enjoys a role within the body politic in much of sub-Saharan African, it has done so, in some measure, at the pleasure of the state. Against surprising odds, "Church" and the formally constituted state—whether of military or civilian character—comprise the two most important visible establishments in modern Africa. Their paths have criss-crossed in the most unlikely fashion, rendering them at times collaborators and at times antagonists. Together and separately, they are heir to both unhappy precedents and innovative initiatives.

From the earliest times Africa has been subjected by pirates and state-constituted trading companies to "looting," to borrow a term from the current writings of African political scientists. Over a period of several centuries, the African continent lost between twenty and forty million people to slavery. Of these, many were taken to the Arab Middle East and to the islands and littorals of the Indian Ocean, but the greatest portion went to the Americas—both North and South. Unspecified numbers were sacrificed to the logistics of the trade itself in the form of capture, forced marches, and voyages on high seas in impossibly cramped quarters—an exercise of holocaust proportions. Inasmuch as this pattern represented formal statecraft, it provided only a prelude to subsequent events.

In 1884–85, the great powers of Europe met in Berlin, Germany, to carve up the African continent among themselves. What had for centuries been informal looting became formalized domination, recognized now by international agreement. During the following seventy-odd years, European powers presided over Africa, profiteering wherever possible, gaining and losing their territories in war, but always on European terms. Anglophone Africa was governed by indirect rule, using for the purpose select indigenous ruling groups or establishments. Francophone Africa was ruled directly from France, emphasizing all along the supposedly superior character of French culture and permitting access to its cultural holy places such as the French parliament only on select bases. Lusophone Africa was from the beginning and without apology deemed to comprise an integral part of Portugal. Africans were selected to join the administration of the colonies, while those who qualified were set on a path toward assimilation—carefully selected and groomed to become Portuguese. For more than four hundred years, the Portuguese administrative structure in Africa prevailed, predating the 1884 ceremonies in Berlin and extending beyond the 1960s, when the larger portion of Francophone and Anglophone Africa had achieved political independence. In the mid-1970s, Lusophone Africa yielded, finally, to pressures of guerilla war and international opinion, giving birth to the modern African states of Angola, Cape Verde, Guinea-Bissau, Mozambique, and São Tomé and Príncipe.

But for most of sub-Saharan Africa, the great watershed was realized in the 1950s and 1960s, the decades of political independence that resulted in a total, eventually, of more than fifty-four independent states. The changes were swift and the results highly uneven; some of the colonies were more prepared than others for independent statehood. Tanganyika's (later Tanzania) transition from the status of UN trustee territory to independence was achieved without violence. Armed Mau Mau resistance to colonial Kenya and the factional wars in the former Belgian Congo were violent and protracted.

Whence the impetus for the explosion toward political independence? The antecedents were myriad, drawing on both internal and external dynamics. Of the external factors, one of the most important was initiative that came from the African diaspora, particularly from the Caribbean. For there the torch of African freedom had long been lit and the writings by intellectuals of African descent were well known, some among them having become classics. *The Wretched of the Earth* by Franz Fanon influenced a whole generation of youth, African and non-African alike. Walter Rodney's book, *How Europe Underdeveloped Africa*, provided compelling reading with regard to the Atlantic slave trade and the accompanying devastation. George Padmore became the personal assistant and ideological colleague to Kwame Nkrumah, the first president of independent Ghana, while the famous academic W. E. B. Du Bois, of African-Caribbean origin, invested a lifetime in Africa-related research.

Within the larger context of the African independence dynamic, the African-Caribbean initiative eventually took the formal shape of a series of so-called Pan-Africanist Congresses, beginning at the turn of the century, reaching a crescendo in 1945, and continuing into the independence period of the 1960s. African nationalists such Kenyatta of Kenya, Nkrumah of Ghana, and President Julius Nyerere of Tanzania participated in those congresses as formative members of the first generation of leaders in independent Africa.

Why was the vision of an independent Africa so clear among African-Caribbean intellectuals? Perhaps the longing induced by distance; perhaps inherited memories from the trauma of slave history; perhaps access to good education. In the event, much of the apparatus of modern statecraft and the accompanying administrative infrastructure also originated from outside Africa and was essentially bequeathed to the newly independent countries by the former colonial powers and only residually informed by the intellectual prowess of the African-Caribbean Pan-Africanist movement.

For all their ardor and persistence, African freedom fighters within the various independence resistance movements were frequently left out in the cold when the spoils of resistance were finally divided among the victors, pandering more to the needs and power of a new elite. Once established, the pattern of elitist state formation persisted, with few exceptions, throughout the independence decade of the 1960s. It was a trend facilitated by subsequent events. In the United Nations circles—where the newly independent nations of Africa and Asia now formed the majority—independence rhetoric quickly shifted to the rhetoric of "development." Indeed, the 1960s were declared by the United Nations as the First Development Decade and were followed during the Second Development Decade (the 1970s) by a series of international conferences on global issues such as food, water, population, women, environment, deserts, and energy, to note the themes of only a few of eighteen such conferences, together comprising essential elements of the emerging development agenda. Even the pope pronounced enthusiastically at a certain point that "the new name for peace is development."

Over the decades, the development enterprise focused on and mobilized massive resources. But such resources became available to a body politic that itself had not fully assumed the emotional ownership of the bequeathed independent state configuration and long before there was structured and widespread popular participation in the unprecedented change process underway in Africa. The result, according to a growing consensus among African political scientists, was that the development enterprise became lodged excessively in an elitist superstructure, rendering it vulnerable to abuse by power elites and reinforcing a state apparatus that has been enabled to live in relative isolation from the consent of the governed. In the opinion of caustic African academics, modern African states survive only because of the ability of their elite to loot the very economies over which they were intended to preside for the benefit of the whole of their respective populations.

The dire images from Africa that have dominated Western television screens over the years can be interpreted in a variety of ways. By some calculus, the starvation images are the logical outcome of development policies that catered precisely to the looting tendencies of Africa's modern elite, this by concentrating on production for export rather than on participatory mobilization of the general population toward equitable change. According to critics, this pattern is development gone awry, rendering Africa beholden to the dictates of the World Bank and the International Monetary Fund. African states have meanwhile become exposed routinely to debt defaults, to debt round tables (such as the Paris Round Table—an informal facility that services debt rollovers), and to the massive currency devaluations that align Africa's formal economy with the world economy, but often at the cost of popular resistance and social unrest. Such is the analytic rhetoric, excessively pessimistic perhaps, but commonly heard in critical development circles.

More direct are images of war in Africa. In Mozambique there is armed conflict between the established politically independent government and a resistance movement known by the acronym RENAMO, established originally during the independence war in neighboring Zimbabwe (then Rhodesia) and supported clandestinely by apartheid South Africa. A long-standing civil war in Angola is only now being resolved, but according to formulas tuned more to big power needs than to the requirements of local realities. In Sudan, civil war continues, between an Arab/Muslim-dominated national government with Khartoum as the capital city and a Christian/African rebel movement in southern Sudan. Citing numbers regarding the ensuing suffering serves merely to trivialize the respective tragedies.

Suffering in Sudan has already surpassed the effects of Ethiopia's 1984–85 drought. But until now the world knows of it only in part and responds only selectively. In the absence of an effective conflict resolution apparatus within the Organization of Africa Unity—Africa's continent-wide political forum—the resolution of Africa's woes are left to the whims of the big powers. Except for a ten-year (1972–1983) interlude of peace, Sudan had suffered internal armed conflict ever since the last century. At the time of this writing, a newly conjured peace plan had just collapsed, with the war proceeding full force, wreaking continued suffering onto the general populace. Africa's longest running war of resistance continues between Eritrea and Ethiopia, though nuanced in its intensity by winds of change in Kremlin policy. Ethnic and civil unrest in Somalia, Uganda, and Burundi have claimed thousands of lives, attracting only minimal international attention and hardly any outcry from Africa itself.

Where are the wars of Africa to be placed? How are they to be analyzed? What do they mean? Each conflict has its own rationale, yielding to analysis from many quarters, but rarely conclusively. Africa's wars and conflicts have been particularly resistant to easy resolution by the modern state. Long before its modern nation states appeared on the scene, Africa was highly diverse, but hardly pluralist. Pluralism bespeaks a collective commitment to cohesion in the midst of a relatively benign diversity. In the Western world, the modern state seeks to accommodate diversity, ideally catering more or less equitably for the needs of cultural diversity within specific state borders. In Africa, by contrast, the state has tended toward unitary, one-party systems, embodying in the political party a paradigm borrowed from the village or ethnic chieftain. During the early years after independence, the need for control and minimal national cohesion was deemed greater than the need for popular participation. Meanwhile, the control mechanisms over the intervening years have been strengthened while genuine pluralist facility has remained relatively underdeveloped, thus rendering potential stability fragile and tenuous.

Enter the church. The Christian Church penetrated Africa on a number of occasions and in various guises. Its origins in North Africa, in Egypt and Ethiopia, date to the early centuries AD. In Ethiopia the ancient church became bound to the state under the suzerainty of successive emperors. Interestingly, Ethiopia and Liberia were the only countries in sub-Saharan Africa that never bowed completely to a conquering colonial power. Despite its idiosyncrasies and abuses of power, the Ethiopian empire served for centuries as a spiritual and political reference point for Africa and for the Rastafarian movement within the Afro-Caribbean diaspora. Emperor Haile Selassie was revered by that movement as a manifestation of God, and even after his physical demise was believed by some to be alive, though in a hidden form. Across Africa, indigenous religious movements have frequently been characterized as "Ethiopian," providing oppressed peoples with the option of expressing allegiance to an African vision beyond the colonial or even the postcolonial experience. Interesting in the context of this reflection, the Ethiopian model firmly combined church and state.

On a less grand scale, but significant for its longevity, is the experience of Liberia. At the constitutional level, government in Liberia was from inception in 1847 essentially secular, but for many years the head of state was also conspicuously active in one or other of the prominent churches in the country. The Liberian elite, including the church elite, were slow to recognize and incorporate the indigenous population into the body politic (remember that Liberia was settled by freed slaves from the United States) of what was in effect a relatively benign church–state model. South Africa's racist government provided the example of a church–state configuration quite at the other end of the spectrum. Its history and wars were repeatedly compared to the biblical Exodus experience. While there is today some dissension in the laager, the South African state/church relationship is strong, articulating every vision except that of the majority African population. Stability—ever more tenuous—is for the time being presided over by the oppressor minority-led state, a state long informed by that remarkable church–state bridging instrument in South Africa—the Afrikaner *Broederbond*, a secret, exclusively male Calvinist organization dedicated to the advancement of Afrikaner interests.

During the colonial period, church–state alliances were in effect, both formally and informally. As early as 1906, Belgium had signed a formal concordat with the Vatican, granting the Catholic Church a position of privilege and ensuring that the great majority of missionaries within its African territories would be Belgian nationals. After 1940, Portugal forged similar agreements with the Vatican. At independence time—the early 1960s for the Belgian Congo and the mid-1970s for Portuguese territories—the Catholic Church fared badly. It was only through the thick fog of suspicion and protracted negotiation that an acceptable modus vivendi between church and state in these territories was finally achieved.

Thanks to the legacy of the liberal French revolution of 1789, Francophone Africa maintained a certain unease in its relationship with the established church. But in spite of this cautionary posture, Francophone colonialism attracted into its elite colonial administrative ranks a core of African leaders who had been educated in Catholic institutions. Among them were personalities such as President Leopold Senghor of Senegal, who excelled in religious and philosophical thought and contributed notably to creative encounter between Christianity and African cosmology. He was particularly attracted to the work of the French Jesuit paleontologist Teilhard de Chardin, whose writings such as *The Phenomenon of Man* provided an embryonic framework for the convergence of African and Christian understandings. Like President Nyerere of Tanzania, Senghor contributed to the church–state conversation at a level that generally avoided the petty political encounters so common to the Lusophone countries with their church–state concordats.

Anglophone colonialism never formally established the Anglican Church as an African state church. Nevertheless, links across the continent between the Anglican Church and the British colonial administration were cozy. Typically, the archbishop's manse was close to State House. In fact, State House in Khartoum, Sudan, was reportedly connected to the Anglican Archbishop's manse by an underground tunnel! Kenya's church–state links took the form of an old boys' network with its base in the Anglican-sponsored Alliance High School, which eventually provided a significant portion of President Kenyatta's cabinet. In his passionate commitment to education based on Christian principles for the students of (multi-church, including Anglican-sponsored) Alliance High School, headmaster Carey Francis became a legend in his own time and one of the most compelling examples of the colonial church informing the new independent state leadership by means of exceptionally well-trained government officers. In Nairobi the Anglican archbishop's manse is situated across the street from State House.

In Uganda, the British administration had chosen to govern (indirectly) through the Baganda ethnic community. As the Baganda community had long been united by a traditional monarchy, it soon became clear that its religious affiliation would prove pivotal to the life of the nation. Over the years, the successive Baganda kings (with the titular designation Kabaka) switched from Muslim to Catholic to Anglican allegiances, with each change evoking consequences of both political and ecclesial import. The national configuration was additionally complicated by the fact that major religious divisions (Catholic, Protestant, Muslim) within the country conformed to the geographic, political, and ethnic divisions as well. In Lesotho, a small Anglophone country completely surrounded by South Africa, the population had been ethnically homogeneous until the arrival of the missionary community. Their evangelization efforts resulted in a fundamental division within the population, separating the populace into Catholics and Protestants, and thus forming the basis for contending political parties. Long after the ecclesial rifts between Catholic and Protestant were healed, the political effects of the divisions continued to plague the country, rendering this politically divided country susceptible to manipulation by the neighboring giant, South Africa. With nuanced variations, Africa's body politic is replete with complexities of this kind.

Officially and unofficially, cross and flag accompanied each other during the colonial period. For many countries, the provision of superior education and health services by the religious establishment formed the supporting link between the colonial regimes and the newly independent countries. But these links for the most part did not survive the immediate postcolonial period. For the newly independent states, the easiest route to popular legitimacy was through the provision of expanded health and educational services. Churches were expected to expand their social services, but following now the policy guidelines of the newly independent governments. Tensions ensued. In some cases, churches were obliged to surrender all of their institutions to the governments of the day only to have them returned years later when the young state apparatus could no longer provide the requisite funds and administration. Meanwhile, demands for health and educational services in many African countries have outstripped all available resources—whether government or church sponsored—thus effectively shifting the church–state debate to other arenas of common concern.

Where is the church–state debate of the 1980s being conducted? To understand the answer to that query, one must take a quick glance backward to see what happened to the mainline missionary church establishment. As noted earlier, the formal and informal religious establishment in Africa is experiencing growth. During this period, many, if not all, methodologies regarding church growth have proven successful, but there have been perceptible differences of emphasis. In general, mainline Protestant churches in Africa pursued the goal, early on, of indigenizing the church leadership. That goal has been achieved in significant measure, while the counterpart Catholic establishment continued to rely heavily on expatriate clergy. In terms of institutional strength, Catholics have the edge. It is a configuration with political implications.

Africa's modern sector is for the moment dominated by two establishments: the church and the state. For a long time before independence, the trained leadership pool for staffing the modern sector came from a common source—from the church-sponsored educational establishment. Since independence, elite training has become greatly differentiated. Protestant seminaries experienced relative decline, both in terms of student numbers and quality. Catholic seminaries tended to attract gifted students, thanks to their more stringent academic standards, but the Catholic Church brought such students into the ranks of the clergy with some difficulty. However, those who graduated from the seminaries and stayed to work within the Catholic hierarchy were well trained. Today, when church and state encounter each other on controversial issues, Protestant leadership is likely to engage the debate with statements drawn on the basis of fraught consensus, while Catholic clergy, in contrast, will typically reflect deeply in common caucus and offer opinions in studied fashion on the basis of solid consensus. Governments tend to take Catholic contributions seriously, while playing the Protestant factions against each other.

But it is at the grass-roots level that the more substantive debate is taking place. The economic and social development activity of past decades has had dramatic effects on a great variety of groups and organizations that function at regional or local levels. Women's groups and savings and work groups typically enjoy some kind of indigenous base. Across Africa there are thousands of such groups. It is by now an accepted axiom that, for all practical purposes, every African woman belongs to an organized group of one kind or other, usually to several. Some of the more self-aware groups will deliberately seek to maintain distance from the grip of government by aligning with a church structure or by proceeding on their own entirely.

Multifaceted dynamic processes inform these many groups. Clearly "church" is one such source, while African religio-cultural heritage is another. Occasionally they come together. For example, the All Africa Conference of Churches' Development Department has been articulating a paradigm for the future in terms of "the village," drawing on values and images from the traditional village, not so much with the intent of replicating "village," but more for the purpose of acknowledging insights from the tradition and adapting them to current situations. In such cases "church" provides the forum and the praxis, while "village" provides the insight.

There has been borrowing from the Latin American Catholic experience: liberation theology, social analysis, Christian base communities, and "the pedagogy of the oppressed" are terms commonly heard in Catholic Church circles. There has been interaction with NGOs. As a category, NGOs now include, for certain purposes, the earlier category of "church." On a global scale, the proliferation is staggering: in 1905, by one estimate, 195 international NGOs were in existence; the figure today is an estimated 181,000. Their presence has been felt particularly within the development enterprise, both in terms of delivering official aid on behalf of bilateral or multilateral donors and in terms of articulating a wide range of alternatives to the generally accepted development paradigm.

In terms of general development strategy, NGOs are now major players on the international scene. They function within both institutional and power categories. Their far-flung presence and continuing proliferation is so new that formal-sector Africa has only begun to recognize the implications. For the time being, African governments see NGOs as some form of power configuration thrust upon them, in part, at the behest of donor governments. Having only just arrived at a modus vivendi with their chief rivals, the churches, governments are now asked to deal with a plethora of NGOs that conform to no common pattern.

What are the broad outlines of the NGO phenomenon in Africa? In general the NGO community can be divided into several distinct groups: (1) there is an army of international NGOs emanating from industrialized countries, acting as donors on behalf of their own constituencies or on behalf of donor governments, relating in the host country to counterpart NGOs, or relating to host governments or only to their own implementing programs; (2) within host countries there is a group of NGOs that acts as a mirror image or receptor to initiatives taken by the international NGO community; and (3) there are locally constituted NGOs within African countries, informed primarily by grass-roots dynamics and by insights from indigenous communities and the prevailing economic patterns.

Tensions abound. Both donor and host countries keep pressure on the NGO community to form coalitions, in the hope of rendering relationships more manageable. By far the most onerous challenge is the one faced by host governments. For a great variety of groups—including churches—that seek validity and exercise power, the NGO category may provide fresh access to funds and international linkages, and thus to a kind of legitimation that has otherwise proven quite elusive. Governments are hard pressed to anticipate the implications of this new category with appropriate legislation—with the strong legitimation provided by the international donor community, host governments in their effort to control the NGO community run the risk of invoking the ire of their most important donor governments. In short, a new power configuration is engaging the attention of the typical African government. By comparison, the simple category of "church" was easily managed.

While current independent African governments struggle to identify the most appropriate modus vivendi vis-à-vis the NGO phenomenon, theologians and political scientists reflect afresh on the multilayered power paradigm that has been emerging over the past more than three decades in Africa. In particular, political scientists and of course opposition activist groups talk of a re-legitimization of the state. According to one configuration—the one that informs much of this paper—the period from 1955 to 1965 in Africa was characterized by the lead concept of "trickle down": it functioned in the dominant central government mode, inherited from the colonial experience, and was passed on in various forms to the newly independent African governments, with policies and infrastructure constructed from the top down. The period from 1965 to 1975 was characterized by attempts toward decentralized administration and strategies promoted by the international development community, informed by the lead concept of "integrated development." From 1975 to 1985, the lead concept could be characterized by the phrase "small is beautiful." There emerged during this time a plethora of community-based organizations—later falling into the NGO category—pointing toward more participatory modes of development. From 1985 onward, these groups coalesced into or responded to intermediary NGOs with the facility of forging relational links in all directions.

In summary, this paradigm sees the development enterprise in Africa over the past three decades as having moved from centrally controlled, Western-style growth models of change toward greater equity and participatory modes. Over the same time period, perceptions and actions within the church have followed a similar trajectory. The church, like the colonial government, came with predetermined creeds to be enacted within structures that were largely transferred from other cultures and other situations. "Good News" as delivered by the church was exclusive, specific, limiting, and limited. By contrast, African response to the Good News has been largely inclusive. It was out of the vast heritage of African Religion that people of the continent were able to say "yes"—from many perspectives—to the Good News. Indeed, the answer to the Good News could only be yes—but just below or above the spectacular church growth charts—the answer was an African yes, answering African questions, many of which have eluded the Western observer.

Church, probably more than government, is taking African tradition seriously. This in part because the church—especially the institution-rich Catholic Church—can muster the necessary research and reflection tools. In the current configuration, those theological tools are augmented by a range of insights and action modes informed by the dynamics of the larger NGO community. The effect of the whole may over time prove to be paradigm changing. But the results are not just around the corner.

Several years ago a group of eminent African political scientists pooled their wisdom for purposes of divining the continent's future. They placed the beginning point of their scenario in 1957, the year when Ghana gained political independence, and then sketched an overview of the century, extending to the year 2057. Into this scenario they factored many ingredients, including a recognition of the myriad already noted grass-roots groups and NGOs across Africa that are analyzing, reflecting, acting, and changing—groups drawing on Christian values, on indigenous African values, on organizational modes borrowed from the past and, as it were, from the future.

According to this group's prognosis, the general situation in Africa will decline over the next thirty years, with pressures from all sides exacting their toll. Parenthetically—as if to justify such pessimism—an in-house World Bank historian has noted that the forces of the world's commodity markets easily overpower all other policy options that African countries can muster on their own. Indeed, if Africa considers its future in Western terms, there may be no future. But this group of academics considers that by 2035–40, things in Africa will begin to become more promising. A new generation of leaders will be in its prime; they will have experienced African realities in ways that eluded their compatriots during the colonial interlude and during the foreign-dominated development decades. A tidy church–state configuration or a tidy Western-style body politic will most likely not be precisely replicated. Africa's position in the world—as a human community and as a political economy—has long functioned in survival mode; of necessity, this has been the mode of innovation, of improvisation, of celebration of human life. Africa will survive; perhaps it will eventually thrive. But it will do so on terms neither entirely visible nor obviously beholden to the Western world.

—Kitchener, Ontario, 1989

Presented to a Midweek Development Seminar sponsored by the Canadian Mennonite Bible College and the Mennonite Brethren Bible College in Winnipeg, Manitoba, on January 18, 1989.

5
War and Peace in the Great Lakes Region of Africa

Introduction

Common usage of the term "Great Lakes region" is of fairly recent origin. It seems to have been spawned in the wake of the Rwanda genocide of 1994. That cataclysmic event rendered more obvious the linkages among the several points of conflict in the region, with the result that analysts referred to a regional conflict system. In general, changes in terminology reflected changes in the region's political fortunes.

Since colonial times, the term "East Africa" referred to Kenya, Tanzania, and Uganda, countries that were then and are now again moving toward the formation of an economic common market known as the East African Community. Intersecting with the East African Community countries was the Intergovernmental Agency for Development (IGAD), encompassing the seven countries of Djibouti, Somalia, Kenya, Uganda, Sudan, Ethiopia, and Eritrea, stimulating fresh awareness of a region referred to as the Horn of Africa. Since 1993, IGAD shifted from its original mandate of regional locust control to some measure of peace diplomacy, this with reference to the long-running civil war in Sudan and later the border war between Ethiopia and Eritrea. While the Democratic Republic of the Congo was a member of the Southern African Development Community, it was also included under the informal cluster of Great Lakes countries.

Thus had the political alliances and collectivities in the Great Lakes region shifted significantly from the earlier rather more simplistic matrix of the Anglophone and Francophone colonial heritage or the subsequent configuration of independent African nation states. On their own, many

African states could not be deemed economically viable. Global market pressures were stimulating the formation of regional or common markets in Africa. Similarly, interlocking regional conflicts were stimulating the formation of regional conflict resolution initiatives as well as the search for longer-term regional security structures. In the Great Lakes region, these dynamics could be observed among both governments and ecumenical organizations.

"Peace" and "War"

Africa's "un-peace" was often contrasted with the relative peace "enjoyed" during the Cold War era and the relative unity of the continent experienced in its protest against South Africa's apartheid governance system. The combination of a Western victory in the Cold War and the end of South Africa's apartheid regime in April 1994 set the stage for the overt manifestation of many simmering tensions in Africa generally and in the Great Lakes/Horn of Africa region in particular. Ironically and tragically, Rwanda's genocide also took place in April 1994. The great shame of apartheid gave way to the shame of genocide; the former a matter of injustice writ in "black and white," and the latter a witches' brew of complex history and difficult social dynamics. A number of strands leading to and connecting the present conflicts in the region can be identified, cited for purposes of sketching a general overview of the immediate situation rather than an in-depth analysis.

On January 26, 1986, Yoweri Museveni overthrew the military government of Uganda, following a five-year civil war. In consolidating his power, Museveni mobilized the discontent among people of the traditional kingdoms earlier governments in Uganda had disrupted. As a means of attracting their loyalties, these kingdoms were "reinstated" by Museveni, but restricted to the exercise of cultural rather than political powers. Also among the discontented were Rwandans who had settled in Uganda as refugees following the 1960 Rwandan civil war. Many of these (mainly ethnic Tutsi) Rwandans were recruited into Museveni's government and army, whence they (known as the Rwandan Patriotic Front or RPF) launched an attack in 1990 on Rwanda, at the time featuring a Hutu-dominated government.

Reeling under this rebel assault, the Rwanda government became overextended and accepted the provisions of the 1994 Arusha Peace Agreement, essentially a peace that incorporated the demands of the rebel Rwandan Patriotic Front. The provisions of the Arusha agreement were rendered mute with the death of the Rwandan president in a plane crash that triggered the well-planned genocide of April 1994, during which nearly one million Rwandans perished. Those events provided occasion for the Rwandan Patriotic Front to complete its assault on Rwanda and establish a new government. Two million Rwandan refugees and significant remnants of the Rwandan Army fled into eastern Zaire, where they were given protection under President Mobutu.

Meanwhile, eastern Zaire had become a cauldron of tensions involving Rwandans (Banyamulenge) who had migrated to the region in colonial times, Rwandans (Banyarwanda) who had come following the 1960 civil war, Rwandans newly arrived as a result of the Rwandan Patriotic Front victory in Rwanda, as well as Zairians chafing under Mobutu's despotic rule. In the absence of decisive international intervention, the Rwandan Patriotic Front Government of Rwanda joined forces with Museveni. Together with the Democratic Alliance Forces of Zairian rebel leader Laurence Kabila, they successfully overthrew Mobutu, who had dominated Zaire for more than thirty years, having served as a dutiful client of the West during and after the Cold War. However, by August 1998 President Kabila's new government in Zaire—rechristened the Democratic Republic of Congo—was fraying. Kabila made a tenuous situation worse by expelling from the new government those Rwandan and Ugandan contingents that had helped him oust Mobutu, a maneuver that effectively ended his alliance with the governments of Uganda and Rwanda.

After August 1998, rebel factions in the Democratic Republic of Congo—under shifting umbrella structures comprising disgruntled elements in eastern Congo and former members of the Kabila government—launched armed resistance against Kabila's government. They did so with the support of the governments in Rwanda and Uganda, while Kabila garnered armed support for his effort from the governments of Zimbabwe, Angola, Namibia, and Sudan. Sudan became involved because of its long-standing conflict with Uganda, while the other three countries represented support from the Southern African Development Community. The rather too eager support for Kabila from Southern African Development Community member countries such as Zimbabwe triggered tensions. For the community had officially announced its preference for a negotiated peace. This official position represented the view of President Mandela of South Africa, one of the strongest member countries. These seemingly contradictory dynamics reflected as well a personal power contest between President Mandela and President Mugabe of Zimbabwe.

The long-running civil war in Sudan functioned as a major conflict element in the Great Lakes region. Since its independence in 1956, there had been war between Sudan's Muslim/Arab government and the rebel southern Sudanese (Christian) minority, relieved only by a ten-year period of relative peace that came with the signing of the Addis Ababa Peace Agreement in 1972. Prior to that agreement, the southern rebels were known as the Anyanya. When the Addis agreement was breached in 1983, the war resumed under the leadership of Colonel John Garang and his Sudan People's Liberation Movement/Army (SPLM/A). In 1992, the SPLM/A experienced a major split, several contingents of which chose in subsequent negotiations to form an alliance with the Sudan government. SPLM/A proceeded to prosecute a civil war against the central government, working for this purpose with northern dissidents within a configuration known as the National Democratic Alliance. In this war Garang enjoyed the support of President Museveni in neighboring Uganda, just as the Sudan government supported anti-Museveni dissidents in northern Uganda and in the Democratic Republic of Congo.

Since 1993, IGAD has served as the officially designated forum for peace negotiations between the Sudan People's Liberation Movement/Army and the Government of the Sudan, with the member states of Uganda, Ethiopia, Eritrea, and Kenya designated as lead facilitators. When the border war between Eritrea and Ethiopia broke out in 1998, the IGAD negotiation forum was greatly compromised. As of this writing, the Khartoum government announced a postponement of the IGAD negotiation session that had been scheduled for April 1999. Apart from these scattered inconclusive IGAD negotiations, there was scant sustained initiative from any source working for peace in the Sudan, even while there was the sense on the part of all protagonists that military solutions were not feasible. A major peace process was successfully concluded between the Dinka and Nuer communities in southern Sudan. In complex ways, this rather localized peace agreement was seen by some observers as an initial step toward a more comprehensive peace process for the Sudan.

Burundi provided yet another element of the conflict system in the Great Lakes region. Burundi's many organized political groups (at one point the figure was nineteen) were committed to an all-party negotiating process under the chairmanship of the former president of Tanzania, Julius Nyerere. The path to this rather promising possibility was strewn with much tragedy and intense negotiations.

Similar to Rwanda, Burundi featured an ethnic mix comprising 85 percent Hutu, 14 percent Tutsi, and 1 percent Twa. And, like all of the countries in the Great Lakes region, Burundi had had a disruptive, volatile colonial experience that rendered many of the latent tension points visceral and overt. Ethnic strife and killing in Burundi had long featured as an integral element in its history. On October 21, 1993, the Burundi Army killed the incumbent, democratically elected President Melchior Ndadaye, together with other senior government personalities. Ndadaye was succeeded by two other presidents. The first died in a plane crash with the president of Rwanda and the second was overthrown in a military coup on July 25, 1996, by military strongman Pierre Buyoya. In response to this military coup, countries in the region imposed economic sanctions on Burundi beginning July 31, 1996.

During the whole of this period, dissident groups as well as the government's armed forces kept the country on the boil through widespread arbitrary killings. Thousands of people died, thousands fled to neighboring Tanzania as refugees, and additional thousands were displaced within the country. Precise figures are disputed and serve only to trivialize the suffering of the people of Burundi, a suffering not easily exaggerated. As of this writing, thanks to the persistent chairmanship of Nyerere amid extreme odds, Burundi is in the process of negotiating a new political order.

Church Response to Conflict

Mainline churches—generally those affiliated with national Christian councils and the All Africa Conference of Churches—were long associated with a sustained quest for political independence from colonial rule. They have been identified as "African nationalism at prayer," similar to the so-called African Instituted ("independent") Churches serving as custodians of indigenous religious and cultural heritage. Like African member states of the Organization of African Unity, mainline churches in ecumenical circles enjoyed a certain unity of purpose on the issue of apartheid in South Africa. After the collapse of the apartheid regime in South Africa, the churches were momentarily disoriented, and in some instances divided on critical national issues much as the larger body politic was divided. However, with regard to conflicts in the Great Lakes–Horn of Africa region, substantial church initiative for conflict resolution was soon realized. Such initiatives could be separated into at least two general categories.

First, during the immediate aftermath of the 1994 genocide in Rwanda, there was a virtual explosion of response from the international and ecumenical communities. Hundreds of NGOs converged on Rwanda, offering every imaginable version of first aid relief and trauma counseling, supported by all manner of workshops on peace and reconciliation. In the process, important concepts and processes were propagated, but also in some measure trivialized and devalued. People who attended multiple workshops were at times referred to as those who "ate ice cream," i.e., those who enjoyed good food in upscale hotels as professional workshop participants. In retrospect, this remarkable, well-intentioned response from the international church community was recognized as a form of "compassion overkill."

On the other hand, much genuine one-on-one peace-and-reconciliation work was accomplished during this time. Among many other initiatives in the region, a small contingent of Mennonite Central Committee workers became engaged as a "peace presence" in Burundi. Others became available in both Burundi and Rwanda as hands-on peace teachers and liaison persons, connecting and encouraging people who were traumatized and scattered by unspeakable atrocities. Indeed, such work persisted in many forms initiated by many people—representing both local and international churches—undertaking low-profile initiatives for the healing of broken people.

On another level, churches in the ecumenical tradition began planning early on for a long-term, more structured response to conflict. For it was recognized that international responses—even appropriate responses—would quickly dissipate, leaving the general populace to deal with unresolved problems. It was also recognized that long-term responses could not be initiated in the absence of at least minimal institutional infrastructure. Hence the rather remarkable series of deliberations described below.

In an August 1996 meeting of the All Africa Conference of Churches' Great Lakes Working Group, it was recommended that a consultation for church leaders from Burundi, Rwanda, the Democratic Republic of Congo, Kenya, and Tanzania be convened to consider the effects of sanctions imposed on the new military government of Burundi by governments in the region. These sanctions were intended to register disapproval of a government that had come to power by means of a military coup and to press for a continued peace process between the Burundian government and the several armed dissident groups.

Following the recommendation, an initial consultation was held in Johannesburg, South Africa, in November 1996, sponsored jointly by the World Council of Churches and the All Africa Conference of Churches. Subsequently, follow-up meetings were held in Entebbe, Uganda (March 1997), and Kigali, Rwanda (August 1997), and then a joint meeting in Geneva, Switzerland (September 1997), with representatives from the Great Lakes region as well as North American and European ecumenical partners. Out of this series of meetings developed the Great Lakes Core Group, for which the National Council of Churches in Kenya served as the first "chair," a position that was intended to continue on a rotation basis among the respective participating agencies.

Apart from the purely organizational development during these successive gatherings, it quickly became clear that they served as a forum in which church leaders, estranged by conflicts in the region, could begin to rediscover each other as "brothers." For it had become painfully clear that among their number several had identified strongly with the "rightness" of their respective national political postures. Indeed, the initial meeting in Johannesburg nearly floundered precisely because of such conflictual and strongly held "nationalist" views. However, overall there was growing consensus that the exercise had evolved into a useful ecumenical peace forum.

As a continuation and expansion of this process, a consultation was convened in Nairobi (April 1998) by the All Africa Council of Churches, the New Sudan Council of Churches (serving the churches of south Sudan in areas under the control of the rebel Sudan People's Liberation Movement/Army), and the National Council of Churches of Kenya, the latter serving as convener of the evolving Great Lakes Core Group. This consultation brought together representatives from Christian Councils and churches in the Democratic Republic of Congo, Rwanda, Tanzania, Kenya, northern and southern Sudan, Ethiopia, and Eritrea, as well as officials from the Kenya government in its capacity as the secretariat of the IGAD peace process for the Sudan, officials of the Government of the Sudan, and senior representatives of the Sudan People's Liberation Movement/Army. This convocation provided occasion for the churches to listen collectively to the protagonists of the long-running civil war in the Sudan and its deleterious effects on countries in the region. And it provided occasion for the representative of the Kenya government (and its IGAD secretariat) to present an update on the performance of the IGAD peace negotiating forum.

In March of 1999, this process continued with the formation of a regional ecumenical facility with the unwieldy name Fellowship of Churches and Christian Councils in the Great Lakes/Horn of Africa (known as FECCLAHA). This development was understood as an initiative by churches and Christian Councils from the countries of Eritrea, Ethiopia,

Kenya, Uganda, Sudan, Rwanda, Burundi, the Democratic Republic of Congo, and Tanzania. Like its two parallel regional ecumenical fellowships in southern and western Africa, FECCLAHA was intended to provide a forum for periodic sharing of information and concerns of regional and common import. Subsequently, a modest secretariat was established under the umbrella of the National Council of Churches of Kenya in Nairobi, where the shape and function of this fellowship was being formulated. Soon after its launch, FECCLAHA staff joined representatives of the World Council of Churches on a peace mission to Ethiopia and Eritrea, where the churches had unfortunately taken positions identical to the positions of their respective governments with regard to the current border war.

Conclusions

Conflict in Africa is explained in many ways and at many levels. In this brief review, only the most cursory observations have been made within a particular regional setting. A more careful consideration of African conflict would require a detailed examination of the political, cultural, and religious dynamics on the continent. It would need to consider the weakness of Africa's modern state structures, the relative strength of religious and cultural factors, and the current dysfunctional relationship between the two. It would need to consider the meaning and function of "church" on the continent and its complex relationship with the African body politic.

This recounting of regional ecumenical formation and structure must be placed and understood in context. As noted at the outset, the context comprises an interlocking conflict system spread over a huge area of Africa. This conflict system feeds on weak or non-performing governments and on important sociopolitical changes currently underway. While the embryonic regional ecumenical networks newly in place are clearly not sufficient to the resolution of the region's conflicts, it can be argued that they are in fact necessary. They provide a structured ecumenical context within which and from which long-term peace initiatives can be undertaken. The formation gives expression to the principle that peace in Africa is first and foremost a challenge to African peoples and African churches. But it also serves as an invitation to churches in Europe and North America that would support the peace of Africa by supporting African peace initiatives. For how long? Until war has ceased, wounds are healed, and each community is at peace with the other.

—May 1999, Nairobi, Kenya

A version of this article entitled "War and Peace in the Great Lakes Region of Africa" appeared in the *MCC Peace Desk Newsletter* of July–September 1999.

6
Peace and Reconciliation in Africa

AFRICA DOES NOT yield easily to common, overarching descriptions. From some perspectives, Africa is the center of the world. Its position on the globe is strategically central; its unitary peninsular shape suggests a formidable geographic whole. However, for centuries the political and economic realities of this vast continent have defied cohesion. Initially, European explorers encountered Africa as barrier to the treasures of the east; later they focused their wiles on what were considered to be Africa's treasures of slaves, gold, minerals, and ivory, among much else. For these purposes, the continent was divided and subsequently ruled by imperial European powers. Imperial greed was rendered formal in meetings of the great European powers held in Berlin, Germany, in 1884–85. Since then the quest for a cohesive African whole has proven elusive, but not for want of heroic efforts.

Partly as a consequence of the current shifts and partly as a consequence of its beleaguered history, Africa is experiencing considerable disarray. African politicians and intellectuals have long aspired to some form of continental unity. But always the rhetoric has exceeded the grasp of those aspirations. Today, the dream of a united African continent lives on, though in truncated fashion. Among the effective dreamers were those of the African diaspora, particularly those of the Caribbean islands. The dream they worked for came true—Africa gained political independence from the colonial powers.

Thirty years beyond its initial independence experience, Africa is experiencing what has been widely touted as a second liberation; a political and economic reordering, the dimensions of which elude ready analysis. While global political and economic dynamics provide much of the context for the current changes, other active elements can be discerned. These include large numbers of national, regional, and international nongovernmental agencies that took shape during recent decades. Together, these actors and the supporting dynamics are effecting a restructuring of the body politic in Africa, releasing enormous centrifugal forces in their wake. In this context, which actors and whose visions possess the power of constituting and articulating an African "whole"?

This reflection is focused on the perspectives and initiatives of one of the continent's actors, the All Africa Conference of Churches (AACC). Established in 1963, the AACC provides institutional and ecumenical expression for the Christian Protestant community scattered across Africa. The AACC has a mandate from its constituency to think and act continentally. As might be expected of a church-related organization, the AACC's vision of Africa is informed by theological, pastoral, and metaphysical considerations. Given the diversity and wealth of Africa's religious heritage, the AACC is well placed—at least in theory—to articulate a multidimensional vision of the continent. In an effort to test the AACC vision against the demands of a changing continent, this essay traces the theme of peace and reconciliation as it coursed its way through the organization's deliberations and programs. The ecumenical vision has offered much. But the AACC's contribution is still in formation; it articulates its vision sometimes in concert with others and sometimes as a lone voice, but always aware of the continental context.

For centuries, Africa had been acted upon by aggressive European powers; today its presence is felt globally in diplomatic forums, in music, in sports, and in all manner of north–south debates. For purposes at hand, Africa has been preoccupied over the past four to five decades with three principal enterprises: (1) political independence, (2) development/modernization, and (3) religious formation. All three were driven by and informed on the one hand by dynamics exogenous to the African continent, and on the other by a primordial African cosmology engaging with many aspects of a globalizing world. These projects have meanwhile interacted and cross-fertilized each other in ways that are yet to be fully understood. Moreover, the composite results are being subjected to ideological and economic shifts in the world, of paradigmatic proportions.

Pan-Africanism: Continental Political Independence

Shortly after 1897, Henry Silvester-Williams laid the intellectual foundations of what later came to be known as the Pan-Africanist Movement. As an ideology, it took shape initially within the African diaspora in the Caribbean and eventually attracted a train of articulate intellectuals and ideologues. Personalities such as Du Bois, Garvey, Padmore, James, Kenyatta of Kenya, Nkrumah of Ghana, Sobukwe of South Africa, Makonnen of Guyana, and Nyerere of Tanzania were associated with the movement. Beginning in 1900, the Pan-Africanist Movement organized a series of congresses that effectively led the way toward the political independence of Africa in the 1960s and beyond. While only the last of these conferences was convened on African soil, the founding in 1963 of the Organization of African Unity gave embryonic continental institutional form to the original Pan-Africanist vision.

Pan-Africanism was premised on the understanding that the emancipation, development, and prosperity of African peoples everywhere could only be achieved by an appeal to the African sense of a "unitary whole." Latter-day Pan-Africanists note that Africa's potential for unity is even today frustrated by the colonial legacy. Examples are myriad and pronounced: Since the 1960s the Somali people have been living in five different nation states, the Bari-speaking people of Sudan spill over into several neighboring states, and the Herero people of southern Africa are found in multiple countries. Some advocates of Pan-Africanism insisted that continental cohesion could be successfully achieved only through an aggregate embrace of Africa's languages. How, they ask, can Africa move forward on the basis of adopted imperial languages?

If the Pan-Africanist vision left troubling questions in its wake, it must nevertheless be conceded that the whole of the political independence saga is to a significant extent a fulfillment of that original vision, however partial or truncated its accomplishments. The Pan-Africanist project unfolded in dramatic sequence, with the largest number of African countries achieving political independence in the 1960s. In the mid-1970s it was the turn of the former Portuguese colonies; Zimbabwe's statehood was achieved in 1980;

Namibian independence was realized in 1990. Then in 1994 South Africa underwent radical change toward more equitable forms of governance.

By any comparison, the Pan-Africanist Movement proffered a remarkable vision. No other continental vision has been so carefully planned and so successfully executed. Both the All Africa Conference of Churches and the Organization of African Unity are in some sense heirs to the Pan-Africanist vision, but both are now challenged by events in the world and in Africa to imagine continental visions commensurate with the demands of the times.

Development Nemesis

If political independence was perceived as a necessary condition for the attainment of some form of eventual continental unity, economic development was believed to be its handmaiden. Thus were the 1960s and 1970s designated respectively by the United Nations as the First and Second Development Decades. With the perspective offered by subsequent years, the development decades are now remembered as Africa's golden age. It was a time of hope; national economies were growing, and there was a sense that the modern sector was delivering on the development promise. However, by the 1980s disillusionment had set in. From 1980 to 1990, Africa's debt to donor countries and agencies—a widely accepted economic indicator—more than doubled. In the sub-Saharan region and on a continental basis, the debt represented, respectively, 112 percent and 90 percent of Africa's gross national product. At the time, few other regions of the world came close to these debt ratios.

Western analysts offered a variety of explanations for the apparent failure of the modernization effort in Africa. The analysts and their explanations have been separated into several categories: (1) those within the so-called mainstream model, (2) those who supported the basic needs/structuralist alternative, and (3) those who endorsed the transforming institutionalist critique.

Mainstream analysts explained Africa's economic straits as a result of constraints emanating from government policies that blocked the optimal functioning of competitive forces, both in domestic and international markets. Unimpeded or shifted substantially toward the private sector, such policies, they believe, would provide incentives for improved efficiencies and higher productivity. They cite industrial, agricultural, administrative, and fiscal policies as particularly pivotal to any International Monetary Fund or World Bank restructuring processes. Meanwhile, the importance of the human dimension and the need for popular participation in the short term mitigated mainstream analysis. But for the long term, the World Bank continued to support basic restructuring of African economies, bringing them into harmony with the global economic order.

Analysts who endorse the basic needs/structuralist alternative identified the causes of Africa's crisis as structural impediments imbedded in the economies of the developing world economies, thus distorting their relationships with the industrialized world. They point out that the absence of domestic capital leaves foreign firms in control of key sectors of respective African economies; at the international level such impediments force African governments toward an expansion of exports and into further debt. According to this analysis, African governments should take specific action to redirect human, physical, and financial resources to a more balanced, integrated national and regional people-centered development.

Finally, transforming institutionalists asserted that in the context of the changing international division of labor, "African class formation and state institutions combine with transnational corporate behavior to cause Africa's poverty and oppression." Only a fundamental change in African institutions and patterns of economic development can achieve self-sustainable development. They believe that an alliance of trade unions, church groups, intellectuals, professionals, and small businesses should support African liberation and development, and that only the interaction of such allied groupings can point the way toward mutually beneficial peace and trade.

Revisions now underway in the structure and function of the European common market promise to effect important changes in the famous Lomé Conventions—the successive economic trade and aid agreements contracted between the European Economic Community and the so-called ACP (African, Caribbean, and Pacific) countries. There is a real fear that the fragile gains realized by the Lomé Conventions will be lost or severely compromised during the anticipated consolidation of the European common market.

As if to add political insult to economic injury, the recent shift from a bipolar to a unipolar ideological world has only exacerbated an already difficult situation for African countries. In a reordered ideological climate, it is now possible for the major industrial powers to attach new and more stringent conditions to already diminishing flows of development aid and declining commodity prices. Pressures from industrialized countries on African countries to shift toward multiparty democracy, open markets, and the privatization of the huge parastatal sectors have been strong and less than subtle.

In its attempts to adjust to these diverse and powerful forces, Africa has for all practical purposes forfeited the tenuous gains achieved during its "golden age." Despite the talk of an African Common Market by the year 2000 and the formation of supportive regional trading blocs—such as Preferential Trade Areas and the Economic Community of West African States—there is little possibility that Africa's hopes for economic development will be realized. Additionally, Africa's quest for Western-style economic development has proven profoundly divisive—the more than fifty African countries compete with each other for assistance from the same pool of donor countries. With the exception of the collective negotiations related to the Lomé Conventions, many of the encounters between Africa and donor countries take place in the context of round-table talks, an arrangement in which an individual African country meets a collectivity of well-coordinated donor communities, constituting, essentially, another process of divide and rule.

Still, the counter discussion by African planners on economic direction for the continent has not been totally absent. In April 1980, the Organization of African Unity adopted the Lagos Plan of Action, a plan emphasizing the objective of continental self-reliance in Africa, calling for an all-Africa economic community by the year 2000. This plan viewed self-reliance as both the means and the goal by which the region would eventually mobilize its resources, its development, and its future.

For purposes of continental integration, it was considered that complementary relationships must exist among regional African organizations such as the Southern African Development Coordination Conference, the Preferential Trade Area, the Intergovernmental Agreement on Drought and Development, and the Economic Community for West African States, among others. It was considered, finally, that if an African economic utopia was eventually to be realized, the continent's political systems would need to evolve toward full democracy, with full participation by all sectors of society.

The tenth Preferential Trade Area summit for heads of state provided yet another occasion for the region's senior politicians to dream about a more cohesive African future. President Chiluba of Zambia, then chairperson of the Preferential Trade Area, dreamed of a common market in the region as an answer to the choking debt problem. He spoke of a "common market with common sense for the common man." Like others before him, he was appealing to the dream of an Africa "united." Others would argue that a politically stable, economically active South Africa provided the only possible alternative for kick-starting Africa's moribund economies.

The Religious Enterprise: African Faith Expressions

Thirdly, there was the African religious enterprise. Professor John Mbiti had famously insisted that "Africans are notoriously religious," a much noted and variously interpreted assertion. There was in fact debate about the nature and the efficacy of the changing religious character of Africa. According to one researcher, Africa's religious heritage was rapidly succumbing to the missionary advances of Christianity and Islam. According to him, by the end of the century, Africa would be divided more or less evenly between adherents of Christianity and adherents of Islam. Whether in traditional or current terms, Africa was meanwhile being portrayed as one of the most religious continents in the world.

But was such deep-seated religiosity necessarily good news at a time when the world media projected Africa as a continent in deep crisis from which no ready recovery in the foreseeable future was expected? In addition to the already noted debt crisis, Africa was the hungriest continent in the world, generating half of the world's refugees. Was there some perverse relationship, it was posed at the time, between Africa's religiosity and its dire economic and political circumstance? The question was troubling. Answers were sought, in part, in a continuing quest to understand and situate African Traditional Religion, or as more recently designated, African Religion.

Apart from its apparent demise under the advances of Islam and Christianity, how is African Traditional Religion understood today? Within ecclesial and academic circles, it was being accepted increasingly as an autonomous religious system, quite distinct from Christianity. Moreover, it was not part of vanishing Africa. Despite the enormous diversity of African Traditional Religion practice in sub-Saharan Africa, its generic characteristics, according to one author, are easily identified: there is everywhere on the continent a spiritual view of life; within community and family, there exists respect for human dignity; there is an accepted communion of the living and the dead; there is a heritage of ceremony and ritual related to age-group initiation rites; there is a close relationship between the religious and the physical sense of well-being; and there is an understanding of the unity of matter and spirit, to name only a few of its characteristics. Today, African Traditional Religion is visible in aspects of cultural practice and in religious values and beliefs that inform every human community on the continent. Additionally, it was perceived to be acquiring many new external forms, manifest in both creative and academic writings and as mythmaking among new religious movements and even within mainline Christianity.

Explanations for the formal and informal presence of African Traditional Religion varied widely. One missionary author argued that Christianity had acted as a catalyst in African Traditional Religion's acceptance on a theological level; that it was now difficult to conceive of a future for it without reference to Christianity in one form or other. An African writer insisted that the staying power of African peoples in the face of massive influences from outside the continent could only be attributed to its cohesive metaphysical constructs—referred to now as African Traditional

Religion by theologians and as paganism by neo-traditionalists. Paganism, he insisted, had demonstrated exceptional resilience and innovative capacity. According to him, religions (Christianity and Islam) of the conqueror were accepted in the African sense; they were accepted as new elements to reinforce local paganism in the age-old tradition of deploying all forces to confront the routine problems of survival. Conversion among Africans could be explained on one level as a tactical move on their part to appropriate and domesticate the new spirit from outside the realm of the familiar. Finally, it also served as a means by which to come to terms with the demands of new political and economic forces.

Commenting more sympathetically on the integrative functions of the Christian enterprise, another African writer noted: "By the mid-1960s, the (Christian) initiative [had become] African and, generally speaking, integrated the essential theses of a new model of conversion. The emphasis [was] put on new premises; on negritude, on blackness, on the African heritage and experience. It tend[ed] to present conversion in terms of critical integration into Christianity; that is, on the one hand, asserting cultural autonomy and, on the other, defining Christianization as a way of accomplishing in Christ a spiritual heritage, authentically African" (Mudimbe, 1988).

Academic and theological encounters between the claims of Christianity and the counter or complementary claims of African Traditional Religion represented the formal, articulate pursuit of a process that began with the arrival of the first Western explorers and missionaries. Today, that encounter continues under the rubric of constantly shifting language, common within which are concepts such as adaptation, indigenization, contextualization, and, latterly, enculturation, all terms intended to describe the process by which Christianity becomes variously rooted within African culture and African cosmology. As the language implies, many of Christianity's claims—particularly the cultural trappings—had their origins outside the continent and were expected, particularly by mainstream Catholic theologians, to function authentically as they become firmly rooted over time within African realities. Some African theologians would contend that the continental vision was better served with a counter understanding, namely, that African Traditional Religion was integral to the continuum of revealed religion; that it was responded to and acted upon by African peoples; that only when African Traditional Religion was recognized as seminal and authentic to the whole of the religious enterprise would any holistic vision for the continent be articulated.

Like economic visions, ecclesial visions for the African continent were informed, still, by strong overseas relationships. In every African country, the church looked for resources to the lands from which the missionaries had come. This was true both of mainline Protestant churches and, especially, of Catholic churches. Early on, the former sought to transform the missionary heritage by indigenizing church leadership. In their formation of clergy and theologians, however, Catholics were more deliberate and thorough. If current theological writings provide reasonable indicators, Africa's Catholic theologians are the better trained; they have been bold and competent in their theological and metaphysical explorations, testing—perhaps more than their Protestant counterparts—the claims of Christianity against both the counterclaims and complementarities of African Traditional Religion.

For some years, the Catholic Church was preoccupied with planning for a continent-wide African Synod, intended to address, if not to totally change, what was perceived by some African theologians as an excessively dependent relationship with Rome. According to advocates of the proposed synod, the church in Africa had in fact changed; African missionaries were now scattered across the continent, evangelizing people in countries other than their own. Among Catholics there was a growing continental ecclesial awareness. An African Synod was intended to bring the scattered efforts together into focused conversation on the unique needs and characteristics of African Christianity. In such a forum, the African church would be expected to set its own priorities, strategize its own evangelization, and think continentally and in cohesive fashion on issues related to the soul of Africa.

Even while preparations for an African Synod were underway, there was much on the African religious scene that militated against the requirements of a common religious vision. According to studies carried out by an All Africa Conference of Churches researcher, Africa was being inundated afresh by a great variety of religious movements. With roots in the North American fundamentalist-revivalist tradition, these groups were capitalizing on the vulnerability of a continent contending with economic challenges and major political transition. And although they promoted basic Christian truths, theirs was a gospel which diverted attention from prevailing social conditions; it was a gospel which insisted that God had decreed the miseries of the poor; a gospel that perceived the situation in the world becoming only worse. For true believers, resolution would be realized through wealth bestowed by God, by miracles performed among the faithful, or, finally, by entry into heaven.

Together with many other Western initiatives, this particularly fundamentalist form of Western Christianity made its appearance during a time when the ecumenical vision was regrouping, as it were, discovering and coining language deemed appropriate to the challenge of a holist African vision. As Pan-Africanists had long insisted, it was considered quite impossible to develop on the basis of someone else's language, whether that language was ethnic, political, philosophical, theological, or religious. Indications were that the change dynamics in Africa had obliged mainline church people—as well as politicians—to come closer "home," to speak more directly and more self-consciously to African realities and more particularly within the African context.

Global Ecumenicity: Toward a Household of Life

The Christian ecumenical movement attributes its formal beginnings to the 1910 missionary conference in Edinburgh, Scotland. But inspiration for the movement can be traced to learnings derived from the worldwide missionary enterprise on which the conference was premised. From those undertakings came early glimmers of what is now referred to as the global village. Hence the question: How are we together in a worldwide fellowship? And the answers were typically informed by certain assumptions about creed and institution. Christian ecumenism had, among other things, embodied the search for a more comprehensive understanding of the meaning of the *oikos*—the household of God. A general secretary of the World Council of Churches provided a stimulating overview of that quest, pointing toward shifting paradigms of understanding.

He traced the emergence of the ecumenical movement from the disintegration of a Christian world order that had succumbed to insights from the enlightenment and eventually to the devastation of the world wars. An early enthusiasm for progress was reflected in a parallel understanding of God's universal plan of salvation: "God sends forth the church to carry out his work to the ends of the earth, to all nations and to the end of time." The whole world was understood within the perspective of the coming kingdom of God; it was a preoccupation with salvation history. The ecumenical movement was seen as an expression of Christ-centric universalism, involving the whole inhabited earth, preparing for the emergence of a "planetary world." As paradigm, it served as a quest for unity, with reference points transcending all differences and divisions.

Christianity's claim on the world through its embrace of an exclusivist understanding of "salvation history" had slowly been obliged by circumstance to embrace a more inclusive understanding of an emerging pluralist world. For rather than succumbing to Western Christian civilization, the major religions of the world—notably in Asia, and to varying degrees in Africa—were experiencing rejuvenation. It had become incumbent on the Christian ecumenical movement to understand salvation history in new, increasingly pluralist terms. A sense of transition toward a new paradigm had been further stimulated by an understanding of the integrity of creation, on the one hand, and justice, on the other. It had become increasingly evident, reflecting on such key considerations, that the history of humankind was embedded in the history of nature. Reducing history to an exclusive concern only with human—anthropocentric—initiatives was becoming a problematic abstraction.

Obviously, the biblical view of justice included the protection, the right to life, of all living beings. Thus the sustainability of all life—including human life—was becoming a sacred concern. An authentic understanding of history had to do with the relationships among all living things. The history of human action, with all its conflicts, was taking place within the divine *oikonomia* (economy); within the divinely protected household of life. God's action within human history served to contain violence and was directed toward protecting the lives of its victims. The self-surrender of Jesus Christ to the violence of the cross provided an indication that God would ultimately overcome humankind's history of violence—both the enmity among human beings and the enmity between humankind and the created order. In the Christian understanding, it was in the person of Jesus Christ that God was placed at the point where life's relationships are resolved, thus bringing about reconciliation.

Such a view of history rendered the *oikumene* a household, an oikos. As metaphor, this understanding of the oikumene had provided much of the paradigm around which ecumenical understandings were focused. What was being referred to here was not one global extraction, as in the whole human race, one world, or one united world church. Rather, the reference was to "relationships between churches, between cultures, between people and human society in their infinite variety; between the world of humankind and creation as a whole. All human beings, their living, knowing and acting, was from the very beginning related to the world, to other people, to the living environment, to those things necessary to life" (Raiser, 1991).

Human knowledge and survival is accompanied, constantly, by the quest for connections. Radical changes over past decades have been accompanied by an awareness of the inhabited earth as an interrelated whole, a totality of relationships. There is a growing certainty that God has established a covenant with the whole of creation, thus rendering the earth habitable. In the metaphor of oikos, the ecological, social, political, and ecclesiological dimensions become inextricably intertwined. The new paradigm begins to take shape.

With the collapse of Corpus Christianum, the ecumenical movement acknowledged the provisional nature of the church in its diasporic existence. The transformation of the whole human race, of the creation as a whole, into the "household of God" was becoming the promise by which the church lived. As always, the church is to live as a light of the world, as salt of the earth, and thus as a visible witness to the new community in the "household of God." It is to live for the world to change the world.

The discerning reader will recognize that this paradigmatic shift within the ecumenical community constituted, inadvertently, an affirmation of African metaphysical and religious understandings of the world, and also acknowledged the influence of the contemporary science of ecology. It represented a shift from a linear to a spherical vision of life, coinciding with the conversation of scientists who recognized the biosphere—that integrated living and life-supporting system comprising the surface of the earth. The more speculative among them referring additionally to the *noosphere* (global mind) as the human sphere, the sphere of reflection, of conscious invention, of the union of spirits. Here the vision is one of a growing, expanding sphere of life in which the parts are supported and enlarged into an ever more self-conscious whole.

On this level of abstraction, traditional African wisdom, the more speculative forms of Western scientific wisdom, and now the theological reflections on the essential unity of the world seemed to coalesce. Among African academics, Kenyan philosopher Odera Oruka was one of the few who had attempted a connection among or a comparison of these elements. He broached the problem in a discussion on eco-philosophy, citing approvingly the relevance of traditional African sagacity to the concerns of environmental ethics. Generally, however, the commonalities and continuities between African cosmologies and post-Newtonian science remained largely unexplored.

Ecumenicity in Africa: All Africa Conference of Churches Deliberations

Two meetings held in 1958 provide major points of reference in Africa's ecumenical story. Before its integration with the World Council of Churches, the International Missionary Council held its first meeting on African soil in Accra, Ghana. Deliberately coinciding with the meeting of the world body was the first All Africa Church Conference convocation in Ibadan, Nigeria. In retrospect, the two meetings provided windows, respectively, onto the end of the missionary era and the beginnings of an indigenous ecumenical journey on the African continent. A cursory comparison of the deliberations only emphasizes the contrasts.

Representatives of missionary societies meeting in Accra were admonished neither to revel in past achievements nor to declare victory. They were reminded, instead, of the urgent need for an expansion of social services—education and health care, in particular—and they were urged not to depart the African continent at that critical moment. Whereas ecumenical meetings in the past and in other parts of the world had been attended by African church leaders, the Ibadan meeting was hosted by them. Missionaries were asked to observe in silence the unfolding of a new world before their eyes! Both missionary and African postures at the meeting portended a changing order.

Ibadan's agenda came face to face with many of the issues that subsequently focused the attention of African churches, among them monogamy versus polygamy; female circumcision; bride price; church versus nationalist sentiments; the role of traditional African religion, not yet understood in generic terms; and indigenous churches versus missionary churches. All the issues reflected the far-reaching implications of serious encounter between Christianity and African culture.

In a review of the significance of Ibadan, one author detected the embryonic shape of the All Africa Conference of Churches' reconciliation mandate. Even if the missionary enterprise was now seen to have been too closely associated with the colonial enterprise, it was, he suggested, inappropriate for the conference to ignore the impulses emanating from that period. For, during the colonial past, African cultural aspirations had been based more on the sentiments of "Ethiopianism" than on the promise of nationalism as a nascent form of the nation state. Whether seen as boon or bane, the partition-like function of the nation state in Africa was believed to inject enormous complications into the African ecumenical picture. Separatist and nationalist claims, together with the conditions externally imposed, promised only to create conditions of instability in both church and national life.

In successive general assemblies—mandated to be held every five years—the All Africa Conference of Churches reflected on the forces dividing Africa and on its mandate as a continental reconciling agent. The inaugural General Assembly of 1963, convened in Kampala, Uganda, was preoccupied with the nature and function of nationalism. Nationalism was perceived at the time as the obvious and legitimate response to repressive colonialism and as the vehicle by which Africa would move toward liberation. There were questions about the virtues of violence and nonviolence in the mobilization of nationalism: "Should we not remind ourselves that the church ought to present itself to the world as the messenger and the witness of that revolution which began in accomplishing that supreme act which reconciled man to God?" The church, it was reaffirmed, was called to witness to the reconciliation already effected in Jesus Christ; this affirmation was to be declared in the midst of those situations where political leaders, parties, nations, and power blocs were in conflict.

Similar sentiments were expressed in the 1969 General Assembly held in Abidjan, Ivory Coast, reflecting difficulties already evident in newly independent countries. Among the many recognized reasons for tension in Africa were the artificial boundaries set by colonial powers, tribalism, and racial differences. In this context, the assembly reasserted its mandate to minister in God's name as an agent of reconciliation. Concern was expressed regarding the number of coups d'état taking place in independent Africa, noting especially the tendency toward authoritarian and oppressive rule. Churches reminded themselves of the need to identify with the oppressed: "Christians are peacemakers, they must endeavor to bring together in peaceful negotiations those who are in conflict. In the tragic conditions of violence, oppression and conflict, Christian love and compassion must extend to both sides."

In his penetrating and wide-ranging presentation during the 1974 Lusaka General Assembly, All Africa Conference of Churches General Secretary Canon Burgess Carr called on Christians to come to terms with the "radical character of the Gospel of Jesus Christ." That gospel impels Christians to "struggle for cultural authenticity—acceptance of Christian faith has too frequently meant outright rejection of Africa's soul, human development, justice and reconciliation." He distinguished between the "selective violence" employed by the liberation movements and the "collective vengeance" perpetrated by South African, Rhodesian, and Portuguese regimes. "We must give our unequivocal support to the liberation movements because they have helped the church to rediscover a new and radical appreciation for the cross. In accepting the violence of the cross, God, in Jesus Christ, sanctified violence into a redemptive instrument for bringing into being a fuller human life." Recommendations from the work groups did not elaborate on the rather daring and controversial theological themes invoked by Carr, but they did encourage the strongest support for the liberation of southern Africa from the oppressive political regimes still in place.

The 1981 General Assembly report included an extensive and well-articulated section on the church as God's agent for reconciliation: "Through his church [God] wants to restore wholeness and bring healing to his broken world." Agonizing about the denominational divisions bequeathed by the colonial era and the inherited Western emphasis on the individual, the assembly affirmed "the indigenous African model of reconciliation." That model assumes a holistic view of reconciliation—as a renewal of relationships—between individual and God, with neighbors and social reality. "We must be free to practice the holistic approach to reconciliation because it embraces the Christian model and goes beyond it."

Christians were admonished to reconcile themselves to African culture "from which we have become estranged, so that we may discover our identity and authenticate our Africanness. By doing this we will be able to become coworkers with God in the development of our culture as a particular expression of God's creation." Additionally, there were specific recommendations with regard to reconciliation as a tool for securing God's liberation, as a means of nation building, as a way of structuring an equitable society, and as a way of enhancing a holistic gospel.

The 1987 General Assembly report from Lomé, Togo, included a section on human rights. African countries were enjoined to "devise ways and means to eliminate conflicts and divisions resulting from the colonial past and present links with different (ideological) blocs." Partner agencies and churches were encouraged to press for human rights, while African governments were encouraged in their embrace of the Organization of African Unity's African Charter on Human and Peoples' Rights. Churches and Christian councils in Africa were encouraged to establish human rights desks in order to "discourage dependency and the paternalistic syndrome to promote national unity and identity through reconciliation of conflicting ethnic groups."

A quick review of the All Africa Conference of Churches' assembly deliberations on the theme of peace and reconciliation provides a profile of varying emphases, but always a clear witness to the mandate of reconciliation, reflecting clearly the immediate demands of the political and social realities in Africa. Throughout, there was the quest for a holist African cultural identity, cited repeatedly as the basis for a peaceful Africa. The excesses in independent Africa of political parties and military governments and the socioeconomic inequalities were noted and duly denounced, while the church was consistently challenged to function as a reconciling agent in the world.

When African theologians formulate the theological basis for any particular category of concern, they are prone to draw analogical parallels between the perceived claims of African Traditional Religion and the Christian biblical tradition. Insights from the tradition are frequently associated with the practices and beliefs of a particular community of people. Throughout the All Africa Conference of Churches' deliberations, reconciliation as a specific function of African ecumenicity was appealed to theologically rather than programmatically. This can be attributed in part to the pressure of other urgent action agendas in a rapidly changing Africa, but also to the fact that African theologians understood Christian truth more as metaphor than as a plan of action. Thus one theologian acknowledged the ecumenical task of reconciliation by appealing analogically to the nature and function of the African extended family.

According to her, "The traditional African family is an ever-expanding, outward-looking community, structured as concentric circles in which relationships are moderated by convention. Bifocal and parallel systems of authority for male and female ensure participation of all. The cohesion of the African family and the quality of relationships expected has become the basis of the whole society" (Oduyoye, 1989). Family constitutes community where members feel at home, a collectivity in which to grow. It is the perspective from which the physical needs of people are met and the perspective from which the memory of the departed is maintained. To sustain family means to care for the whole of life support systems that surround family.

Family functions as the sustainer of life. When family is understood as a metaphor of the oikos, the reference point for peace and reconciliation becomes clear; in the African extended family symbols, rituals and a shared memory provide the impulse for cohesion. Church is called to model such cohesion on a macro scale, providing reference points and functioning as a living, communal ritual toward reconciliation.

Whereas people from the Western world have much to say about individual rights, African religious and social traditions appeal to collective "well-being," salvific concepts about being at rest, about peace and contentment with oneself and harmony with the world beyond oneself: "Salvation consists of liberation from all that endangers the life of the individual and the community." In the Akan community, this well-being (salvation) was spoken of in terms of seven blessings, wished onto every person of the community: *nkwa*—long life, good health; *adom*—favor with the spirit/ancestor world; *asomdwee*—peace of mind and peace with society; *abawotum*—power of procreation; *anihutum*—good eyesight; *asotatum*—power of hearing; *amandoree*—prosperity of the community. Well-being for the Akan—and by extension, for Africa generally—was at once material and spiritual, internal and external, human and nonhuman, individual and communitarian, functioning as a household of life.

In the Hebrew tradition, *shalom* was the word used to describe well-being, that harmonious order in which people proceeded with their lives and their relationships with neighbor and the larger world. From New Testament writings, African theologians cited the cosmic reconciliation effected in the crucifixion and resurrection of Jesus Christ—all things are reconciled, all walls are down. There is the promise and the possibility of community, in which each offers talents to the whole, in which wisdom is exercised as the reconciliation of divergent views in an atmosphere of free expression.

Visions of community and wholeness were deemed relatively easy to recall from the past or conjure for the distant future, but difficult to implement in the present. In an attempt to marry reconciliatory metaphor and praxis, the All Africa Conference of Churches, under the guidance of a trained mediator, launched an exploration of both the theoretical and methodological categories of peace and reconciliation. Much was learned; much remained to be explored.

Any attempt toward programmatic implementation of peace or reconciliatory values immediately raised questions of definitions and assumptions. Even the word *peace* conjured a great variety of understandings. There were notions of "peace as maintenance of law and order," "peace as a quest for tranquility," or "peace as resolution of conflict." In this regard, it was considered helpful to emphasize peacemaking and reconciliation not as a series of isolated events, but rather as dynamic process requiring continuous nurture. On a personal and social level, reconciliation implied problem-solving, release from frustration and anger, and a commitment to positive relationships. At the macro levels, peacemaking and reconciliation had to do, ultimately, with a shift from oppressive dependency toward the liberation of independence to the security of interdependence.

In reconciliation praxis, the peacemaker was to assist contending parties in their search for enduring solutions to conflicts that divide and alienate. Solutions, if they were to be helpful, would need to appeal to commonalities of the protagonists, resolving the grievances of all concerned. Moreover, the goal of a peace process was understood as the healing of emotional (spiritual), physical, and social wounds suffered by the respective parties, and as building long-term and mutually enriching relationships between adversaries, fostering collaboration instead of confrontation.

Peace and reconciliation were intended to function within a network of relationships. Those values in turn were concerned with the maintenance and nurture of life in community. However, in the real world, the absence of conflict could never be taken for granted. Indeed, it was not a matter of eliminating conflict; it was more a matter of "managing" tensions as potential conflict. Conflict management already suggested methodology and technique, as well as social and analytical skills. A brief examination of the several requisite components and dynamics follows.

One of the most common peacemaking roles is that of the third party, the mediator. Generally, mediators exercise leverage on at least three levels: (1) as communicators, they function as catalysts providing information and communication to which the disputant parties on their own do not have access; (2) as formulators, they suggest alternative ways of resolving the conflict at hand, and (3) as manipulators, they deal with incentives and alternative outcomes. By definition, mediators are not power brokers, nor do they identify with power blocs. Instead, their strength resides in personal and institutional integrity, exercised by means of suasion, compassion, and religious or humanitarian concern.

Another actor common to peace initiatives is the peace advocate: a person or a collectivity of persons or organizations focusing on the creation of an environment conducive to the resolution of conflict by means of negotiation and mediation rather than through the pressure of armed violence. A committed peace advocate, like an effective mediator, views conflict as a problem to be solved, not a battle to be won. She or he functions on the basic premise that the interests of the protagonists and their constituencies are better served by peaceful rather than violent processes.

Those with a calling to peacemaking are challenged to imagine and organize incentives for a process that renders the peace option attractive to protagonists in the midst of intractable conflict. Peace is not secured simply by signing a static agreement; it is best perceived as a continuous dynamic. For these purposes, the peacemaker becomes peacekeeper, facilitating a guarantor process which ensures that negotiated peace is sustained.

As an approach to the resolution of conflict, the All Africa Conference of Churches' peace and reconciliation praxis was understood as an expression of faith in the possibility of new beginnings. Mediation, as described above, offers a process approach to such initiatives, with Christian forgiveness functioning as a concomitant element. Forgiveness is a theme central to the biblical story and foundational to the nature of Christian community and to all new beginnings. Legitimacy for church initiatives in peace and reconciliation was understood to be lodged in its commitment to incarnate the forgiving community.

The whole of the dynamic just described is captured under the general rubric of mediation. As a tool for conflict resolution, mediation was identified in Africa by Western anthropologists who, together with other social scientists, parlayed the concept into methodology, with wide application in a great diversity of conflict situations. In its work on peace and reconciliation, the All Africa Conference of Churches was testing the applicability of then current mediation theory, modifying and augmenting as the several situations required or permitted. Clear conclusions could not be drawn, but on the basis of the limited data available, it seemed apparent that carefully crafted adaptations of the mediation method offered means of expressing aspects of the Christian ecumenical mandate for peace and reconciliation.

Peace and Reconciliation: All Africa Conference of Churches Praxis

The experience of the All Africa Conference of Churches (AACC) in specific reconciliation work was fairly substantial. Indeed, its record conformed more nearly to the grand reconciliation mandate generally articulated in the several assemblies than it did to the daring endorsement of violence, as proposed in the 1974 Lusaka speech by the AACC's general secretary. What can now be referred to as the classic AACC reconciliation initiative took place in 1972, an initiative related to the conclusion of a fifteen-year civil war in the Sudan between the dissident Anyanya rebel movement and the Sudan government, led at the time by President Jaafar Nimeiri.

With Emperor Haile Selassie of Ethiopia serving as host and the general secretary of the AACC as chairman, an extensive peace process was concluded in a formal peace accord. While the accord did not answer all outstanding grievances of southern Sudanese, it did bring relative peace to the country for a ten-year period. More than was appreciated at the time, the Sudan peace process parlayed the issues of church and state, religious diversity, ethnic and cultural diversity, formal mediation methodology, and personal charisma into a definitive reconciliation experience.

Taking initiative in a new direction, the AACC's International Affairs Desk organized the African Church Leaders' Human Rights Summit in Cairo, Egypt, during September 1986. An extensive report on the Cairo summit included several excellent papers outlining the biblical basis for a concern with human rights. The Cairo initiative greatly influenced deliberations at the AACC's 1987 General Assembly in Lomé, Togo, generating a special mandate for the desk to focus on human rights as an implementation of the reconciling mission. To this end, the AACC established a Human Rights Commission that functioned essentially as the advisory committee to the International Affairs Desk.

Meanwhile, in addition to participation in many international and ecumenical forums, the International Affairs Desk organized a conference in Lesotho entitled "The Debt Question as It Affects Human Rights." Recommendations from an extensive report stimulated at least one national Christian council in Africa to undertake a serious study of the African debt question. These several efforts ensured that the twin themes of human rights and the African debt issue became integral to the general awareness of the ecumenical community in Africa.

At an immediate practical level, the churches in Angola and Mozambique requested the AACC to organize a consultation on the theme of peace and reconciliation. The consultation was held at a time when prospects for an eventual ceasefire in Angola were becoming visible. It was considered that churches from the several divides could play supportive, reconciling roles during the transition period toward the end of Angola's civil war. A similar workshop was conducted in Liberia at the request of the Liberian Council of Churches. Both of these consultations were conducted primarily for the orientation and education of church leaders on the principles of peacemaking and conflict resolution. More than could have been anticipated, churches in such situations undertook specific peacemaking initiatives, identifying with the search for longer-term stability.

By contrast, an initiative from the Christian Council of Rwanda brought together representatives of churches in Rwanda and neighboring countries, representatives of the Rwandan government, and the Organization of African Unity, as well as unofficial representatives from the opposition, the Rwandan Patriotic Front. This consultation was carefully structured as a layered, sequential process in which estranged parties were able to meet and discuss their differences. Action-oriented suggestions were generated for each of the participating groups, including the AACC. Subsequently, the AACC pursued a number of activities ensuring that contact between the parties continued. In follow-up activity by the churches, new collaborative relations between Roman Catholic and Protestant churches were forged. Together they undertook reconciling roles, initiating and maintaining conversation with the contending parties.

The AACC was also involved—through its consultants—with ongoing peace negotiations between the factions of the Sudan People's Liberation Movement. The chair of these proceedings was assumed jointly by the National Council of Churches in Kenya and the Catholic-affiliated People for Peace in Africa group, with church people from southern Sudan participating as witnesses to the process. These inordinately complex negotiations involved many competing interests and communities. In addition, there were troublesome questions of principle related to mediation between rival factions of the same liberation movement. Eventually, agreement was achieved on all but the most fundamental leadership questions. A two-month monitoring and cooling-off period was agreed to by all parties in the hope that the remaining differences could then be revisited and satisfactorily resolved.

Meanwhile, AACC staff pursued any number of promising and sometimes not-so-promising leads toward resolution of conflicts. In Togo, AACC staff provided support for public personalities during the country's partially successful change of government. Representations were made to Burundi, Zaire (now the Democratic Republic of Congo), Liberia, and Angola to assess reports of actual or potential conflict. In one novel initiative by the AACC Youth Desk, a youth group with participants from all over Africa was organized to visit Rwanda. By means of low-key exchanges of concern and experience, youth in Rwanda were able to voice tensions that had been studiously avoided until then. At the insistence of the involved youth, Rwandan church leaders were drawn into a discussion of covert and overt conflict situations in Rwanda. There were indications that the exercise may have established a model for the discussion of difficult conflict issues.

AACC's forays into specific conflict situations brought numerous contentious issues into focus. First, there was the matter of local church participation and initiative. Typically, churches in Africa experienced divisions in much the same way as the general body politic. Thus, if church was to carry out a reconciliation ministry, it would need to be reconciled first of all within itself. Second, experience suggested that the third-party mediator role was conceptually not an easy one for African church leaders. In terms of theological, social, or ethnic considerations, where, precisely, is the church located within the African body politic when it undertakes peace initiatives? Do the apparent conceptual difficulties reside in the African awareness of an undifferentiated, unitary metaphysic? Is the successful deployment of mediation initiatives a matter of coining new and more specific language to negotiate the transitions at hand? While the answers remained tentative, several initiatives were carried out precisely in the context of these continuing questions.

In a March 1993 meeting held in Geneva, Switzerland, the Sudan Council of Churches and the New Sudan Council of Churches declared themselves representatives of one Christian community in the Sudan, whether in the Muslim-dominated north of the country or in new, purportedly liberated areas of the south. It was resolved in that meeting that the AACC would serve as a convening forum, bringing together representatives of the two councils on a regular basis as a way of strengthening the church in Sudan and as a way of continuing the exploration for peace in this war-torn country. In a similar venture, the AACC hosted church representatives from the Horn of Africa region (Ethiopia, Sudan, Kenya) in an attempt to strengthen church-to-church solidarity and to equip churches to play reconciliatory roles within the larger society.

Finally, as the continent of Africa moved toward multiparty democracy, misunderstandings were expected to increase exponentially. For it was not at all self-evident that party politics alone were capable of providing formulas sufficient to a peaceful future. The reconciliation task in Africa would be concerned not only with the resolution of differences among opposing views, but with the creation of alternative options.

Actors and Paradigms in Transition

"When the history of Africa of the twentieth century comes to be written, the most dominant theme will have been liberation." As noted at the outset of this essay, the continental project since the turn of the century had been political liberation from oppressive colonialism. This project was supplemented by projects on religion and, latterly, economic development. As Africa approached the close of the twentieth century in the throes of a so-called second liberation, its dimensions were being discerned only slowly. But clearly, the profile of the continent's major projects was being recast.

Political independence was from the beginning perceived by the pioneering Pan-Africanists as a response to colonial hegemony. However, both the religious and economic projects had been profoundly influenced by the hegemony (stability) of East–West ideology. Hardly any element of modern Africa had been untouched by the rise and the subsequent ignominious fall of modern East–West (Cold War) ideology. Indeed, it is fair to say that modern Africa was premised on the stability offered by that ideological paradigm. In the ensuing vacuum, Africa faced its own fractured hegemony of ethnicity, which, rather than functioning as a unifying factor, promised to keep alive that most vexing of the continent's "strengths."

Against this backdrop, which were the most promising prospects for an African future? If African Christian theology was to speak effectively to twenty-first-century requirements, it would be characterized, according to one theologian, by an emphasis on social transformation and reconstruction. According to him, already in the early 1990s, this paradigm shift was discernible: "This shift involves discerning alternative social structures, symbols, rituals, myths and interpretations of Africa's social reality by Africans themselves, irrespective of what others have to say about the continent and its people." If African societies were to enjoy a promising future, such a future would need to be constructed, eventually, on the foundation of Africa's own utopian visions.

But how were such visions to be conceived and birthed? Within which institutions were they to be articulated and carried to fruition? In modern Africa, two of the most conspicuous institutional players within the greater body politic have been organized religion and the state. For the foreseeable future, these two institutions—separately and in collaboration—are destined to play major formative roles in determining the shape of Africa's future. As subsequent comments indicate, much remains to be understood about the relationships between these institutions.

Formal religion (for purposes at hand, primarily Christian, though Islam is prominent in much of Africa) and government (the bureaucratic manifestation of the modern nation state) are everywhere present in Africa. They have remained while trade unions, ethnic welfare organizations, and even political parties disappeared from the public scene. Relationships between organized religion and the state call for special attention, if only because of the alternating collusion and tension between the two since they first met. In pre-independence days, African church leaders chafed under missionaries who were generally perceived to be compliant to colonial regimes.

Typically, it was these African leaders who risked their positions and Christian reputations to team up with nationalist leaders in the quest for independence. During the 1960s, independence had about it a seamless politico-religious aura, expressed in words such as *freedom*. While political parties offered ideological slogans in support of liberation, religion—whether Christianity, Islam, or African Traditional Religion—in its own strange way had provided sanction for both the most colonial as well as the most revolutionary dynamics in African society.

During the heat of independence fervor and into the 1960s and 1970s, African church leaders and nationalist leaders—later, leaders of independent nations—simply assumed that a profound collegiality bound them in common cause. It was difficult for either group of actors to draw a clear line between the political and the religious realms. The rifts between church and state—increasingly apparent during the 1980s—only underscored the absence of a clear articulation as to how they had been together in the first instance or why they were now suddenly estranged. By this time the honeymoon was over: Africa's independent governments were increasingly perceived by select church leaders as oppressive; church leaders spoke out against the evils perpetrated or tolerated by governments of the day. In response—sometimes in self-defense—government leaders exercised their superior power, relating to churches on the basis of divide and rule.

In the considered opinion of one writer, the church in Africa, like the church elsewhere, had failed to achieve all that it sought to accomplish. There were inherent difficulties involved in being both pastor and prophet to young nations—not least when such nations were part of a continent that had until recently existed not for itself, but for the benefit of predator nations who accepted Africa as no more than a repository of raw materials. The debate on the function of the church in independent Africa was no more than several decades old. Nor was there a widely accepted model guiding church–state relationships. Many of the current and traditional church–state doctrines in Africa were exercised through the persistence of a variety of Christian denominations and Western traditions. Only the beginnings of an African articulation of church–state relationships could be discerned.

In Africa, both church and the modern nation state were perceived to be patterned, structurally and institutionally, on Western models. In some sense, both continued in the quest for legitimacy, particularly in relation to the largest portion of society, the "uncaptured peasantry." Interaction between church and state had been informed to some extent by the issues of the day. During the honeymoon period of church involvement in the postindependence development project, church had been readily perceived as an ally of government. In the later political restructuring, church was frequently perceived by African governments of the day as the not-so-loyal opposition.

Churches had been involved in the change process from the bottom up and from the top down. Wherever the church laid claim to large constituencies and wherever those constituencies were deeply involved with development and social change, there the church could claim grass-roots legitimacy, with some ability to mobilize people from the bottom up. At the other end of the spectrum, some churches in Africa were conspicuous because of their hierarchical apparatus. Where such an apparatus was entrenched by tradition and convention, church survived and thrived, even when its government counterpart collapsed.

During the so-called second liberation, relationships between church and state were not seen as a contest between the two. Rather, both were being tested for their respective legitimacies. It was understood that legitimate government was one that assured rule by the people and for the people. Legitimate church was recognized by its ability to inculcate religious and public values, rooted in biblical tradition, enculturated into African society, and open to service in the world: "The church is the church only when it exists for others." Still, the manner in which church and state interacted ideally in modern Africa remained a matter of continuing discussion.

Professor Omari detailed the antagonisms that plague church–state relations. After a review of the classical relational formulations, he likened the interaction of the two to the human body with its two hands, each carrying out different tasks but attached to and serving the same body. In the African context, it proved very difficult to speak of the relationship in completely distinct categories.

During the so-called United Nations Development Decades (1960s and 1970s), churches in Africa became deeply involved with and, according to some observers, seduced by the development agenda. In the context of the development enterprise, churches lost their near monopoly identities as nongovernmental actors; they were now increasingly competing with or included within the larger category of nongovernmental organizations. In that context, secular development literature offered comment on the respective functions of church and state in terms as realist and current as the collective comment from Africa's theologians.

David Korten, one of the respected contributors to the alternative-development discussion, assigned to government the task and the ability to requisition resources by means of power or coercion. While such authority was preferably exercised with the consent of the governed, still it was only the government that rightfully claimed such authority; indeed, it constituted government's essential and distinctive role. But it was precisely this authority that was most readily perverted and abused, threatening the liberties of the civilian populace. In an idealized view of government functions, such powers were to be exercised in defense of the law and to protect minorities while maintaining social justice by transferring wealth from the rich to those in need. In fact, of course, the political marketplace—managed by those who controlled political access—determined the allocation of resources.

Thus was government an imperfect but indispensable instrument within the body politic. In some contrast, voluntary organizations—including, for purposes of the immediate discussion, churches—specialized, ideally, in activating the power of consensus in support of integrative values that motivated actions not usually associated with personal gain or political power. The church traded on and elicited value commitments and drew others into such commitments, defining and functioning as a primary influence in the "marketplace" of social values and ideas.

The noted political scientist Goran Hyden took the discussion further by means of analytical cognates not at all alien to categories understood by theologians. He defined the key word *governance* as the "conscious management of regime structures with a view to enhancing the legitimacy of the public realm." Effective governance was expected to produce legitimacy. And which were the components of effective governance? He described the governance realm by contrasting the concepts of power and exchange; compliance and innovation; trust and accountability; authority and reciprocity.

These concepts were understood in the context of continuums, including, on the one hand, coercive power postures and, on the other, participatory and innovative postures. According to his definitions, governance was meta-politics: more than the sum of party politics, government, and collective or individual actors and actions. It was the combined and dynamic interaction of the whole of a nation (or continent) in pursuit of an ordered and innovative body politic.

The church was no stranger to these concepts. For had not the Christian Gospel enjoined the church to function as light, as yeast, as salt, as discerner of the times, leading the way toward abundant life? Was not the church called to build and exemplify trust, to become the caring—the giving and receiving—community? Hyden's categories and the categories within which church functioned called for a focus on the building of relationships, on the building of wholes rather than the segmentation of the parts. While Hyden spoke of the governance realm, in the scriptures God was committed to saving the world. In this context, church was called upon to articulate a vision of what ought to be, and in its life together, to demonstrate what was possible and beneficial for the whole of the social order.

The All Africa Conference of Churches shared with both church and state all the ambiguities of modern Africa. It commanded a continental overview and, to some degree, laid claim to a continental mandate. But much of its institutional life was maintained on the basis of resources from overseas. Member churches in Africa and affiliated Christian councils were not in the position, in any foreseeable future, to sustain the institutional life of the AACC. Thus much of the AACC's strength lay in its ability to nurture the worldwide network of partner relationships.

If in the restructuring of the African continent the AACC was to play a meaningful Christian role, it would be important to deploy that which kept African issues in constant dialogue with African values. Despite all the rhetoric in favor of an economically self-reliant Africa, such a condition was not readily imagined for the near future. For the AACC, it would be a matter of coming to terms with a less than optimal situation, deploying resources toward the articulation of an African future in which the prevailing interdependencies would at the very least be understood and processed, if not optimally just.

For the AACC laid claim to a Christian legacy from around the world, on the one hand, and functioned as heir, on the other, to the religious tradition of the African continent. From the former, there was available the wealth of institutional and recorded precedent; systematic theology and methodologies attuned to quite diverse initiatives. From the latter, the AACC drew on the still-unexplored wealth of African Religion and on the precedents set and lessons learned from the postindependence period. From this vast and diverse perspective, the AACC was called upon to participate in the imagining of a continent that was at once new and a composite of all that had formed the past. So far, the instincts have been clear: consciously and unconsciously, however slowly and painfully, Africa's future was developing around elements of a common vision. The AACC was in a privileged position to share in the pursuit and articulation of that vision.

—Nairobi, Kenya, 1996

A version of this essay first appeared as "Peace and Reconciliation: An AACC Vision of Africa Renewed" in Perspectives on Africa, published by the All Africa Conference (Nairobi) in 1996. It was also published as "Peace and Reconciliation in Africa," Occasional Paper No. 19, by Mennonite Central Committee.

Sources and Further Reading

General All Africa Conference of Churches Documents

Achebe, Chinua, Goran Hyden, Christopher Magadza, and Achola Pala Okeyo. 1990. *Beyond Hunger in Africa: Conventional Wisdom and An African Vision.* Nairobi, Kenya: Heinemann.

"African Debt: What about Debt Today?" *Peace Courier,* December 1991.

All Africa Conference of Churches. 1969. *Engagement, Abidjan.* Nairobi, Kenya.

All Africa Conference of Churches. 1975. *The Struggle Continues, Lusaka 1974.* Nairobi, Kenya.

All Africa Conference of Churches. 1982. *Follow Me—Feed My Lambs, Nairobi 1981.* Nairobi, Kenya.

All Africa Conference of Churches. 1986. "African Church Leaders Human Rights Summit." AACC report on a meeting held in Cairo, Egypt, September 8–13, 1986.

All Africa Conference of Churches. 1988. *You Shall Be My Witnesses, Lomé 1987.* Nairobi, Kenya.

All Africa Conference of Churches. 1990. *Africa Challenge Series.* Nairobi, Kenya.

All Africa Conference of Churches. 1990. *The Debt Crisis as It Affects Human Rights.* AACC report on a conference held in Maseru, Lesotho, September 26–30, 1990.

All Africa Conference of Churches. May 1991. *A Proposal for Reflection.* General Secretariat/Information Office. Nairobi,Kenya.

Chipenda, Jose, Andre Karamaga, J. N. K. Mugambi, and C. K. Omari. *The Church of Africa: Towards a Theology of Reconstruction.*

The Right Time for Change: What Hope for Crisis-Stricken Africa?

United Society for Christian Literature. 1963. *Drumbeats From Kampala.* London: Lutterworth Press. Published for the General Committee of the All Africa Conference of Churches.

Angola and Mozambique

Assefa, Hizkias. 1987. *Mediation of Civil Wars: Approaches and Strategies—The Sudan Conflict.* Boulder, Colorado: Westview Press.

Assefa, Hizkias. 1991. "Conflict Resolution and Reconciliation," notes from presentations to AACC staff conference, January 8–14, 1991, Mombasa, Kenya.

Assefa, Hizkias. May 15, 1991. "Humanitarian Activity and Peace-Making: Challenge for NGOs." *Mimeo.* Nairobi, Kenya.

Bainton, Roland H. 1960. *Christian Attitudes toward War and Peace: A Historical Survey and Critical Re-evaluation.* Nashville, Tennessee: Abingdon Press.

Barrett, David B. 1982. *World Christian Encyclopedia: A Comparative Survey of Churches and Religions in the Modern World AD 1900–2000.* Nairobi, Oxford, New York: Oxford University Press.

Chepkwony, Agnes. 1987. *The Role of Non-Governmental Organizations in Development: A Study of the National Christian Council of Kenya 1963–1978.* Sweden: University of Uppsala.

Cliffe, Lionel, Martin Doornbos, Abdel Ghaffar, and John Markakis, eds. 1992. *Beyond Conflict in the Horn: The Prospects for Peace, Recovery and Development in Ethiopia, Somalia, Eritrea and Sudan.* Khartoum, Sudan: Khartoum University Press.

Curle, Adam. 1992. "The Power of Non-violence." *Life and Peace Review*, Vol. 6, No. 2.

Dag Hammarskjold Foundation. 1992. *The State and the Crisis in Africa: In Search of a Second Liberation.* Uppsala, Sweden: Dag Hammarskjold Centre.

Dahlen, O. 1988. *Governmental Organisations in the International System.* Uppsala, Sweden: Communications Department.

Deng, Francis and William I. Zartman, eds. 1991. *Conflict Resolution in Africa.* Washington, DC: The Brookings Institute.

Erickson, T. H. 1992. "Ethnicity and Nationalism: Definitions and Critical Reflections." *Bulletin of Peace Proposals,* Vol. 23, No. 2.

Friesen, Duane K. 1986. *Christian Peacemaking and International Conflict: A Realist Pacifist Perspective.* Scottdale, PA: Herald Press.

Frost, Brian. 1991. *The Politics of Peace.* London, UK: Dartman, Longman and Todd.

Gifford, Paul. *Christianity: To Save or Enslave.* Harare, Zimbabwe: Ecumenical Documentation and Information Centre of Eastern and Southern Africa.

Grinevald, Jacques. 1987. "Development of the Biosphere." *L'homme Inacheve.* Cahiers de L'IUED. Geneva, Paris: Presses Universitaires de France.

Gwyn, Douglas, George Hunsinger, Eugene R. Roop, and John Howard Yoder. 1991. *A Declaration on Peace: In God's People the World's Renewal Has Begun.* Scottdale, PA: Herald Press.

Hastings, Adrian. 1975. *A History of African Christianity 1950–1975.* London: Cambridge University Press.

Hyden, Goran. 1980. *Beyond Ujamaa in Tanzania: Underdevelopment and an Uncaptured Peasantry.* London: Heinemann.

Hyden, Goran and Michael Bratton, eds. 1992. *Governance and Politics in Africa.* London, UK: Lynne Rienner Publishers, Inc.

Ibrahim, J. 1991. "Religion and Politics in Nigeria." *The Journal of Modern African Studies,* 29, I.

Karamaga, Andre. September 1991. "The Christian Presence in Africa" in *The Church of Africa: Toward a Theology of Reconstruction* by Chipenda, Karamaga, Mugambi, and Omari. *African Challenge Series.* Nairobi, Kenya: All Africa Conference of Churches.

Korten, David C. August 8, 1991. "People Centered Development: Alternative for a World in Crisis", based on a paper presented to the APDC/ANGOC Regional Dialogue on GO-NGO Relations: Prospects and Challenges for Improving Policy Environment for People-centered Development. Manila, Philippines.

"Peace and Reconciliation in Angola and Mozambique", Lusophone Consultation. Limuru, Kenya, September 20–27, 1990. A communiqué from consultation participants.

Liberia

All Africa Conference of Churches. "Preliminary Report: Workshop on Reconciliation and Conflict Resolution, July 31–August 2, 1991."

Liberian Council of Churches. "Workshop on Conflict Resolution" (undated).

Liberian Council of Churches. September 1991. "Plan of Action Package." Conflict Resolution Sub-Committee.

Mazrui, Ali. 1990. *Cultural Forces in World Politics.* Bloomington: Indiana University Press.

Miller, H. F. January 18, 1989. "The Quest for Stability (Legitimacy?): Church and State in Africa." Paper presented to a mid-week Development Seminar at the Mennonite Brethren Bible College in Winnipeg, Canada.

Mshana, Rogate R. 1992. *Insisting Upon People's Knowledge to Resist Developmentalism: Peasant Communities as Producers of Knowledge for Social Transformation in Tanzania.* Frankfurt, Germany: Verlag fur Interkulturelle Kommunication.

Mudimbe, V. Y. 1988. *The Invention of Africa: Gnosis, Philosophy and the Order of Knowledge.* London: James Currey Publishers.

Mugambi, J. N. K. ed., 1990. *The Church in African Christianity.* Nairobi, Kenya: Initiatives Ltd.

Mugambi, J. N. K. November 9–16, 1991. "Problems and Promises of Churches in Africa", paper presented at AACC Symposium, Mombasa, Kenya.

Mugambi, J. N. K., ed. 1992. *Ethics in African Christianity.* Nairobi, Kenya: Initiatives Ltd.

Munene, Pauline. February 2, 1992. "PTA Role Towards Unifying Africans." *Kenya Times.*

Nairobi Peace Group. March 30, 1992. "Activity Report: Workshops on Reconciliation and Conflict Resolution," conducted in Monrovia and Buchanan.

Ndumbu, Abel, ed. 1991. *Africa in the Debt Yoke.* Nairobi, Kenya: Development Horizons Trust (for the National Council of Churches in Kenya).

Nkiwane, S. 1992. *The Churches' Role as Agents of Peace and Development, Case Study: Zimbabwe.* Life and Peace Institute.

Nyamiti, Charles. 1988. "The Naming Ceremony in the Trinity." *African Christian Studies,* No. 1. Nairobi, Kenya: The Journal of the Faculty of Theology of the Catholic Higher Institute of Eastern Africa.

Oduyoye, Mercy Amba. October 1989. "The African Family as a Symbol of Ecumenism." *The Ecumenical Review,* Vol. 43, No. 4.

Okri, Ben. 1991. *The Famished Road.* London: Jonathan Cape.

Okullu, Henry. 1974. *Church and Politics in East Africa.* Nairobi, Kenya: Uzima Press Ltd.

Okullu, Henry. 1984. *Church and State: In Nation Building and Human Development.* Nairobi, Kenya: Uzima Press.

Okure, T. and Paul van Thiel. 1990. *Inculturation of Christianity in Africa.* Nairobi, Kenya: AMECEA Publications.

Oruka, Odera H. March 1992. "Eco-philosophy: An Essay on Environmental Ethics." Nairobi, Kenya: Africa Centre for Technology Studies.

Pobee, John. "Theological Basis of Liberation and Human Rights," in a report on an African Church Leaders Human Rights Summit held in Cairo, Egypt.

Prah, K. K. November, 1991. "Vision for the Year 2000: Insights from the Pan-Africanist Experience," Paper prepared for AACC Symposium.

Rwanda

All Africa Conference of Churches. "Report on the Rwanda Consultation, August 19–22, 1991." Nairobi, Kenya.

All Africa Conference of Churches. January 1992. "AACC Rwanda Consultation Follow-up Action Report."

National Council of Churches of Kenya. 1992. *The Cursed Arrow: A Report on Organized Violence against Democracy in Kenya.* Nairobi, Kenya.

Raiser, Konrad. 1991. *Ecumenism in Transition: A Paradigm Shift in the Ecumenical Movement.* Geneva, Switzerland: World Council of Churches Publications.

Seidman, Ann and Fredrick Anang, eds. 1992. *21st Century Africa: Towards a New Vision of Self Sustainable Development.* Trenton, NJ: Africa World Press.

Shenk, David W. 1983. *Peace and Reconciliation in Africa.* Nairobi, Kenya: Uzima Press.

Shorter, Aylward. 1991. *The African Synod: A Personal Response to the Outline Document.* Nairobi, Kenya: St. Paul's Publications.

"The Missionary Calling of the Church." 1952. *International Review of Missions,* Vol. 41, No. 164.

Utuk, Efiong. 1991. *From New York to Ibadan: The Impact of African Questions on the Making of Ecumenical Mission Mandates.* New York, Paris: Peter Long.

Van Beek, Walter E. 1992. *Religion in Africa: Experience and Expression.* USA, Canada: Heinemann.

Villa-Vicencio, Charles. 1986. *Between Christ and Ceasar: Classic and Contemporary Texts on Church and State.* Grand Rapids, Michigan: William B. Erdman's Publishing Co.

Waliggo, Crollus, Nkeramihigo, and Mutiso-Mbinda. 1986. *Inculturation: Its Meaning and Urgency.* Nairobi, Kenya: St. Paul's Publications.

Yarrow, C. H. M. 1978. *Quaker Experience in International Conciliation.* New Haven, Connecticut: Yale University Press.

Yoder, John Howard. 1972. *The Politics of Jesus.* Grand Rapids, Michigan: William B. Erdman's Publishing Co.

7
Christian Councils in Africa: Whence? Whither?

Introduction

In mid-1965, I accepted the staff position of Secretary for Relief and Service in the Christian Council of Tanzania, headquartered in the coastal port city of Dar es Salaam. A more idyllic physical locale could hardly be imagined. A statuesque Lutheran cathedral graced the picturesque harbor front. Close by, State House, with its coastal colonial architecture, graced the banks of the harbor entrance.

Several streets inland from this placid scene, President Julius Kambarage Nyerere was at the height of his powers, proclaiming the virtues of *Ujamaa*, popularly referred to as "African socialism" or "familyhood," not to be confused with Marxism or Communism. A prominent building on Lumumba Street served as a favored venue for lectures on topical issues, open to the public virtually every day of the week. Scattered throughout the city were the tiny offices of liberation movements from countries to the south, including Rhodesia (later Zimbabwe), South West Africa (later Namibia), Mozambique, Angola, South Africa, and Guinea Bissau, among others. In Dar es Salaam, the respective (often rival) would-be representatives from those countries presented their credentials to the Liberation Committee of the Organization of African Unity, of which President Nyerere was chair, thus seeking recognition as leaders in their hoped-for independent countries. Independence from colonial rule in sub-Saharan Africa had been launched in Ghana in 1957 and was sweeping across the continent. Countries to the south of Tanzania were among the recalcitrant latecomers.

Within the Christian Council of Tanzania's Relief and Service Department, a pastor to representatives of liberation movements and the related plethora of urban refugees was posted. As it happened, he was extraordinarily knowledgeable about Africa's independence dynamic and the multiple related movements and personalities. A tripartite agreement between the United Nations, the Lutheran World Federation, and the Government of Tanzania had birthed an organization known as the Tanganyika Christian Refugee Service, mandated to administer refugee settlements scattered in western and southern Tanzania. It reported in dotted-line fashion on its activities to the churches of Tanzania through the "good offices" of the Christian Council of Tanzania's Relief and Service Department. In these direct and indirect ways, the council served as midwife to the high drama of transition. Liberation was in the air—geopolitically at state level, but also within the ecclesial establishment: everywhere missionaries were being replaced by indigenous African church leaders.

Following a six-year stint with the Christian Council of Tanzania, I was seconded to the Sudan Council of Churches, with its head offices in the capital city of Khartoum. In the wake of an eighteen-year civil war, the 1972 Addis Ababa Peace Agreement had just been concluded between the "Muslim Arab" government of Sudan and the "African Christian" Anya'nya rebel movement of southern Sudan. Both the World Council of Churches and the All Africa Conference of Churches had been deeply involved as mediators and brokers in the peace process. The secondment was a follow-up to the peace agreement, for purposes of administering the Sudan Council of Churches' relief and rehabilitation program in war-ravaged southern Sudan. After nearly two years with the Sudan Council of Churches, I was seconded to the National Council of Churches of Kenya Rural Development Department for an eight-year stint. And then from 1989 to 1999 I was seconded to the All Africa Conference of Churches' Department of International Affairs.

This exposure to several segments of the African ecumenical community during a time of intense and often conflictual transition offered entry into an alternate world. My own Mennonite faith community was rooted in the "historic peace churches," marginally conversant on select issues with the ecumenical community in which I now found myself undertaking several staff positions for a quarter of a century and informally engaged for additional decades. My understandings regarding the African ecumenical dynamic, as well as the global ecumenical story, developed piecemeal, not as the result of focused research, but as an accumulation of select impressions amid programed activity. Apart from specific self-identity descriptors of individual national Christian councils, relatively little was written—then and now—regarding the character and function of national councils of churches in Africa. In this regard, the personal impressions comprising this reflection must be considered an exceedingly modest contribution. An exhaustive inquiry into the rich African ecumenical lode must await an exercise much more vigorous than the one on offer here.

Christianity in Africa

Christianity in twenty-first-century Africa cannot be understood without taking account of the modern, largely Western missionary movement with its beginnings in the middle of the nineteenth century. Today its tentacles and effects are felt across the whole continent. Nevertheless, it is a mistake to overlook the existence and significance of the ancient churches of Africa, namely, the Egyptian Orthodox Church and the Ethiopian Tewahedo Orthodox Church, respectively founded in AD 62 and AD 331. Today these churches are considered part of the larger "oriental" as opposed to the "Eastern"' Orthodox Church tradition. Leaders from Africa's ancient churches—such as Origen, Tertullian, and St. Augustine—are widely claimed and are included within the common Christian heritage. During the period from AD 1050 to 1948, the ancient or Orthodox Churches were quite separated and "hidden" from their Western counterparts. However, since 1948, when Orthodox Churches joined the World Council of Churches, Western Protestant and Catholic churches have become well acquainted with Orthodoxy, thanks to prolific and articulate writings by its theologians. Today, both Western missionary-founded churches in Africa and the continent's ancient churches claim membership in the World Council of Churches and in the All Africa Conference of Churches.

For purposes of this reflection, Africa's Christian councils are best understood as Western ecclesial institutions, lodged within the global ecumenical movement, which in turn is heir to the global Christian missionary tradition. One of the early reference points for the modern ecumenical movement was the advent of the historically significant Edinburgh Mission Conference, convened in 1910, which led in turn to the formation of the International Missionary Council in 1921, a forerunner institution of the World Council of Churches. Christian councils were recognized in their institutional form within the context of the establishment of the World Council of Churches in 1948. Thus is the genealogy of Christian councils in Africa marked by these several reference points.

While it is beyond the scope of this brief review to comment on the efficacy of the global missionary experience, it is important to cite some of the underlying assumptions generated by it. Already in 1910, and certainly by 1941, there was a strong sense among Western church leaders and missiologists that the Christian Church now constituted a global phenomenon. Given the wisdom of the day, which called for this newly established global church to function as a self-supporting, self-administering, and self-propagating entity, the corollary assumption that called for large Western missionary establishments to be phased out eventually is easily understood. It was envisaged by missiologists of the day that the global, Western-initiated mission apparatus would be replaced by ecumenical institutional structures and relationships, reflecting a significant degree of parity among the respective churches scattered around the world.

At the end of the great missionary century, marked by the Edinburgh convocation, there was little sense among those gathered that Africa would someday—even before the close of the century—become one of the centers of world Christianity. Indeed, there was the contrary sense that Islam would probably become the dominant "missionary" religion in Africa and that the continent's strong religious and cultural heritage would not yield readily to Christianity. However, it is now widely acknowledged that Africa is home to a virtually unprecedented expansion of the Christian faith, recognized as a significant locus of world Christianity in the twenty-first century.

African Christian Councils

From 1900 to the 1960s, the direct antecedents of Africa's Christian councils took the form of missionary councils or "fellowships," which had been formed as a response to the need for coordinated approaches to Bible translation and its concomitant literature publication and distribution, to medical care, and to education, activities deemed integral to the process of evangelization. In select situations, missionaries expressed "political" concerns with regard to the oppressive relationships between the respective colonial governments and their African subjects. At other times, missionaries were identified as collaborators with colonial regimes: in popular secular parlance, the colonialist and the missionary were the same. Beginning in the 1960s and coinciding dramatically with the political shifts of the day, leadership in churches across the continent was transferred from expatriate missionaries to indigenous African church leaders, a transition also effected in the leadership of African Christian councils. This shift took place within the context of far-flung continental African "nationalism," taking the form, eventually, of more than fifty politically independent states. Its ecclesial counterparts were taking the form, ideally, of self-governing, self-propagating, and self-supporting churches, though various dependency and reciprocal ties with erstwhile "mother churches" in the West persisted.

Development

It will be recalled that the 1960s and 1970s were designated, respectively, by the United Nations as the First and Second Development Decades. This designation can be understood in the context of the post–World War II period characterized by massive American aid (the Marshall Plan) to a devastated Europe and the return to their homelands of African soldiers who had fought against European totalitarianism on behalf of colonial powers! The promise of political independence and the prospects of economic development provided powerful stimuli to the African imagination, not least the imagination of African church leaders.

The basic assumptions supporting the expectations of the development decades were upbeat: it was assumed that, given sufficient support of the right kind, Africa, like the industrialized world, would also develop. These assumptions and expectations took shape against the backdrop of a series of United Nations–sponsored global conferences (a total of eighteen between 1972 and 1982) on subjects as diverse as environment, food, water, population, women, and health. Each of these conferences resulted in global surveys and prescribed coordinated global action in efforts to achieve acceptable standards for people living in the so-called third world. With the coming of independence to peoples of Africa, it was widely assumed that the sky was the limit for possibilities now unfolding; there was the sense that Africans with their strong survival abilities would be released to realize their true potential. This optimism flourished even as the UN's global conferences defined Africa as grossly underdeveloped. At best, these contrasting views could be interpreted as complementary; at worst they constituted a shift from initial optimism to protracted remedial initiatives, the fruits of which were mixed but ongoing. In retrospect, it can be queried whether the "global" development standards advocated at the time and the concomitant specter of the West's excessive and wasteful affluence could rightly be advocated as a measure of sustainable lifestyles for all peoples on this planet.

Refugees

In the midst of this remarkable momentum, the All Africa Conference of Churches, in collaboration with the World Council of Churches, initiated a massive refugee-cum-development program under the rather complex rubric of the Ecumenical Program for Emergency Action in Africa. With an initial budget of ten million US dollars, the program addressed the continent's growing refugee population, triggered by the massive transition from colonialism to independence that was underway. For this purpose, the field staff collaborated closely with All African Conference of Churches member churches, with African Christian councils, and with a range of non-church, quasi-nationalist institutions (e.g., the Dar es Salaam–based Mozambique Institute, the education wing of FRELIMO, struggling at the time for the political independence of Mozambique).

Altogether, the ecumenical program initiative was an attempt to address the most pressing fallout (refugees) of a rapidly changing continent and to strengthen the leadership and institutional capacity of the churches in Africa, the former an acknowledgment of Africa's acute problems and the latter an investment in hope for the future. In contrast with significant portions of subsequent ecumenical and partner funding processes, the monies supporting the Ecumenical Program for Emergency Action in Africa were genuinely ecumenical, solicited from churches in the West through the good offices of the World Council of Churches. Meanwhile, Western humanitarian agencies, including church-related service agencies—many of them birthed during or immediately after World War II as relief agencies—metamorphosed into development agencies and thus identified new leases for their institutional lives by shifting programmatic operations to Africa.

For Western church-related humanitarian agencies, Christian councils in Africa provided precisely the kind of partner linkages required in an emerging but still relatively under-institutionalized African continent. This partnership was supported by mushrooming funds, initially from purely ecumenical sources, but later from the coffers of donor governments, funneled through ecumenical institutions. During the 1970s and 1980s, Christian councils in Africa developed substantial budgets, expanded personnel rosters, and launched extensive development programs. Some Christian councils became program implementers in their own right, sometimes in competition and sometimes in collaboration with their own member churches. It was, at macro-level, a shift from the generic missionary rubric of "evangelism" to the Ecumenical Program for Emergency Action in Africa agenda on refugees and thence toward the promotion of "development," including many overlapping continuities and discontinuities, to broad-based education and leadership training, all within the context of Africa's enthusiastic ecclesial and political development.

With the dawn of the 1990s, new relational configurations within the ecumenical community took shape, triggered by, among other factors, the remarkable changes in eastern Europe. Churches in Africa, like churches in the West, had been strongly influenced by the post–World

War II East–West ideological divide. Some portion of the financial largesse available from North Atlantic ecumenical donors to Christian councils during the 1970s and 1980s rested on Africa's "pawn value"; Western aid to Africa was not without strings attached. When it became apparent that communism in its monolith "soviet" form had lost the Cold War, Western aid shifted conditionalities. Now Western aid—meanwhile significantly reduced—became available under the rubric of support for "democratization," an emphasis readily adopted by Christian councils. Funds for "democratization" activities augmented Christian council budgets, but for a relatively brief period. Indeed, the democratization venture brought several Christian councils to the brink of financial collapse, in part because the ready availability of funds had bloated staff and budget figures in ways that could not be sustained.

The achievement of majority rule in South Africa was realized as the culmination of the struggle for continental independence, championed already in the late 1800s and early 1900s by activists among the Afro-Caribbean diaspora. By the mid-twentieth century, the South African Council of Churches was championing the anti-apartheid cause with great intensity, fully supported by the global ecumenical community. And rightly so, for South Africa's official apartheid governance policy was recognized by the modern democracies and churches around the world as a heretical relic from another age, based as it was on highly questionable ideological and theological foundations.

Post-Apartheid Era: Councils in Turmoil

With the advent of majority rule in South Africa on April 27, 1994, the South African Council of Churches virtually collapsed. Approximately half of its staff joined the new majority government (catalyzed by the powerful African National Congress party), while ecumenical funds quickly dried up. Subsequently, the council was slowly reconstructed around new realities prevailing in the country and region. Additionally, it was adjusting afresh to the changed international donor climate. If the struggle against apartheid toward majority rule had consumed the South Africa Council of Churches and the wider ecumenical community for more than three decades, the agenda of reconstruction and reconciliation soon came into focus.

Apart from the dramatic happenings in South Africa, April 1994 was significant for another reason. It was the month during which a genocide in the tiny central African country of Rwanda took place. Between 500,000 and 800,000 people were killed by hand during that tragic month. In consequence, the whole of the church structures in Rwanda for all practical purposes collapsed, including the Conseil Protestant du Rwanda (Christian Council of Rwanda). Only after protracted efforts to reconstitute the ecumenical life of the church in Rwanda was it possible, finally, in 1996, to reestablish the council. In its first General Assembly following the genocide of 1994, the Conseil Protestant du Rwanda was able to elect officers and appoint a general secretary. In one of his first communications to the All Africa Conference of Churches, the new general secretary requested assistance with the formulation of a proposal that would bring together leaders of the Rwanda Church from both inside and outside the country. The council's reconciliation task proved to be herculean; as the most pressing agenda, reconciliation engaged all its creative powers, with substantial support from the All Africa Conference of Churches and councils in the region.

During the 1980s, in another troubled arena, Sudan featured two Christian councils, together giving shape to a single ecumenical reality. The Sudan Council of Churches head office was located in the capital Khartoum; the New Sudan Council of Churches offices were at the Nairobi headquarters of the All Africa Conference of Churches. Registered in Kenya as a nongovernmental organization, the latter served the needs of the churches in the war zones of southern Sudan. In collaboration with the World Council of Churches, the All Africa Conference of Churches provided an ecumenical forum within which the two councils could articulate and sustain their common vision for the church in the Sudan, a country torn by forty years of civil war, a recent segment of which had extended from 1983 to 2005.

From 2005, when the Comprehensive Peace Agreement was signed between the Sudan People's Liberation Movement and the Government of Sudan, until 2011, when South Sudan's independence made it the youngest country in the world, the fortunes of Sudan's ecumenical institutions were mixed. Today there is a Sudan Council of Churches with headquarters in Khartoum and a South Sudan Council of Churches with headquarters in Juba, the capital of South Sudan, each actively involved with their respective demanding circumstances.

During the 1997 All Africa Conference of Churches General Assembly convened in Addis Ababa, Ethiopia, the Desmond Tutu Peace Prize was awarded to two Liberians, one a Muslim and the other a Christian. In the context of initiatives by the Liberian Council of Churches, representatives of the two faith traditions had launched an interfaith initiative to heal a country fractured by civil strife. In an earlier All Africa Conference of Churches General Assembly in Harare, Zimbabwe, the Desmond Tutu Peace Prize was awarded to two Mozambicans, one a Catholic bishop from an area dominated by the RENAMO rebel movement and the other an Anglican bishop acting from a Mozambique Christian Council base, located in an area controlled by the ruling party, FRELIMO. Amid complex political and ethnic divides, these church leaders had worked for the peace of the land. Sometime after Nelson Mandela was installed as president of post-apartheid South Africa, he appointed Bishop Desmond Tutu, former general secretary of the South African Council of Churches, as chair of the government-initiated Truth and Reconciliation Commission. In his book *No Future Without Forgiveness*, Tutu recorded emotive episodes in the quest for national reconciliation. Betwixt and between these and other undertakings by church leaders in Africa, Christian councils played significant direct and indirect midwifery roles in the quest for a peaceful African continent.

April 1994 stands out as a pivotal turning point for the African ecumenical/conciliar community. With the achievement of majority rule in South Africa, the 1960s liberation agenda was finally "fulfilled." Rwanda and other points of tension across the continent gave expression to an altered agenda for the future. Much was written, subsequently, in an attempt to understand the past, to understand the meaning of April 1994 and its implications for the future. As indicators of the times, Christian councils engaged with diverse agendas: war and peace, forgiveness and reconciliation, church–state relational issues, Muslim–Christian relations, and traditional religious understanding vs. Christian faith as introduced by missionaries. Conciliar structures and conciliar relationships as they became known and as they functioned in Africa were poised to engage with these and other dynamics. As they embraced emerging mandates, they were working to reconstruct an African world both comfortable with itself and communicating at par with the global ecumenical faith community. In the words of Jesse Mugambi, these initiatives called for an embrace of *reconstruction* in contrast to the Exodus *liberation* metaphor, the latter having for decades inspired ecumenical discourse and action in Africa in its accompaniment of the dramatic shift from colonial and missionary tutelage to political and ecclesial independence.

Meanwhile, African ecumenical institutions have acquired a remarkable profile. Today there are thirty national councils of churches in Africa, twenty-four of them claiming associate membership in the All Africa Conference of Churches. Although initiative for the formation of national councils of churches emanated primarily from the Protestant church community, thirteen of Africa's councils include Roman Catholic churches as members. Beyond the respective national councils of churches, four regional collectivities of national councils have taken shape: the Fellowship of Christian Councils and Churches in Central Africa, the Fellowship of Christian Councils and Churches in the Great Lakes and the Horn of Africa, the Fellowship of Christian Councils and Churches in Southern Africa, and the Fellowship of Christian Councils and Churches in West Africa. Issues these regional configurations address include climate change, agricultural policy, and a broad range of societal issues.

In 1963, the All Africa Conference of Churches (AACC) was established several months prior to the establishment of its political counterpart, the Organization of Africa Unity (now the African Union). Since then, the two agencies have initiated and nurtured discourse on a range of issues, commensurate with the general transition dynamics of the African continent. For its part, the AACC has for some years maintained a liaison office with a full-time representative in Addis Ababa, Ethiopia, nurturing relationships with the African Union on matters of both common and special interest. In 2014, African Union representatives met with African religious (Christian, Muslim, Baha'i, Hindu, Sikh, etc.) leaders in meetings convened by the AACC to consider "the Africa we want in 2063," the centenary anniversary year of both organizations. Since then, leaders of the African Union have approached the AACC to provide guidance with regard to moral and ethical foundations for the future of the African continent. It is a challenge which the leadership of the AACC has accepted and acted upon with alacrity.

Christians in Africa are articulating new understandings of the Christian Gospel, understandings long imbued with Western biases. If the ecumenical journey in Africa is to be authentic, it will need to be leavened and enriched with the "corrections" offered by Africa's dynamic engagement with Christianity against the backdrop of its immensely rich religious and cultural heritage, now widely acknowledged as African Religion. Growth points in collective ecumenical understandings will become manifest in a variety of ways, not least by the nature of the engagement through and with Africa's conciliar communities and institutions, such as Christian councils. Clearly, Christian councils are not ends in themselves. They function merely (imperfectly, always) in ecclesial midwifery roles through which and around which common learnings can be shared and, to a greater or lesser extent, acted upon within an ever-expanding ecumenical faith community.

Sources

All Africa Conference of Churches Team. 2014. *African Agenda* 2063. Consultation with the African Faith-based Organizations on African Agenda 2063 (organized by the African Union Commission in partnership with the All Africa Conference of Churches). Nairobi, Kenya.

Assefa, H. 1987. *Mediation of Civil Wars: Approaches and Strategies—The Sudan Conflict.* Boulder, Colorado: Westview Press.

Byaruhanga, Christopher. 2015. *History and Theology of the Ecumenical Movement in East Africa.* Kampala, Uganda: Fountain Publishers.

Chepkwony, Agnes. 1987. *The Role of Non-governmental Organizations in Development: A Study of the National Christian Council of Kenya (NCCK) l963–l978.* Sweden: University of Uppsala.

McCullum, Hugh. 2004. *The Angels Have Left Us: The Rwanda Tragedy and the Churches.* Geneva: World Council of Churches.

Mugambi, Jesse. 1991. *The Church of Africa: Towards a Theology of Reconstruction.* Nairobi: All Africa Conference of Churches.

National Council of Churches of Kenya. 2013. *A Century of Ecumenism and Mission: The Story of National Council of Churches of Kenya 1913–2013.*

Okullu, Henry. 1974. *Church and Politics in East Africa.* Nairobi: Uzima Press Ltd.

Tutu, Desmond. 2000. *No Future without Forgiveness.* Image Publishers.

Utuk, Efiong. 1997. *Visions of Authenticity: The Assemblies of the All Africa Conference of Churches 1963–1992.* Nairobi: All Africa Conference of Churches.

8
Ecumenical Sharing Beyond Frontiers

Introduction

The comments offered in this chapter will be very general, for they are informed by only a moderate acquaintance with the language and practice of the ecumenical community with regard to the "ecumenical sharing of resources." I did some background reading on the previous National Council of Churches of Kenya roundtable meeting, deliberations astonishing for their diversity and complexity. I had the impression, after reading the materials, that almost every possible angle on ecumenical sharing has been explored. Additionally, I had the sense that when changes or innovations become possible, they come only in incremental stages—small steps at a time.

These reflections are not intended to debate the inner workings of current ecumenical sharing patterns. Rather, they are intended to reflect in cursory fashion on the nature of the frontiers that "bind" or "loose" the creativity of our life together. We are considering, in the broadest sense, the prospect of life together in a disparate world, a world unevenly endowed with natural resources and divided into gross inequalities of many kinds.

Two questions will in a general way guide the remainder of this reflection:

1. Where have all the frontiers gone?
2. How do the current frontiers—or our perception of them—influence our life together?

Prospects for Alternative Frontiers Language for Change

Dr. Walter Brueggemann, a noted American Lutheran theologian, makes much of the language chosen and deployed by the church community. According to him, one of the primary tasks of the church (however defined) is to create or identify language for the future. Stated just a bit differently, it is incumbent on the church to create language that leads toward creative futures. Brueggemann writes of "languaging our way into the future." It follows that those with no ready language for the future may in fact be handicapped in laying claim to meaningful futures.

Let us consider aspects of the language we deploy in our life together. Consider the word *oikumene*. As defined in the dictionary, oikumene refers to "the inhabited world." With its Greek origins, one can assume that the word referred originally to the then-known inhabited world. Like all peoples, the Greeks were prone to assume that the world as they knew it was in fact the extent of the real world. It could be argued that over the past several thousand years the meaning of the word oikumene has expanded, commensurate with the growth of knowledge about the peoples who inhabit planet earth. As will be indicated later in this presentation, human habitation may well include more than meets the eye.

If we stay with the original meaning of oikumene as the inhabited world, it becomes clear that we have diminished its basic intent. When we talk in this context of the "ecumenical movement," we are in fact talking only about Protestant Christian relationships as symbolized by the World Council of Churches, the All Africa Conference of Churches, and, in this case, the National Council of Churches of Kenya. Professor Jesse Mugambi reminds us that there are in fact numerous Christian oikumenes. There is the Catholic oikumene, which lays remarkable claims to a worldwide community of believers—the word "catholic" itself is defined as "universal." (Christians insist on large visions!) And then there is the worldwide Orthodox community of Christian believers.

For purposes of comments coming later in this reflection, it is worth noting here that the Orthodox community has always articulated a more holistic view of the world than have its Catholic or Protestant counterparts.

Today there are various groupings of evangelical Christians that can also rightly be referred to as oikumenes. Current religious writing refers to the Islamic oikumene (the ummah), and to the Hindu, Buddhist, and other oikumenes of faith. Thus it becomes obvious, in the most cursory examination of one of our definitive concepts, that the language we use to describe ourselves and our task may be less than accurate, or it must be recognized, at the very least, as changing, just as our perception of the world changes. As a preliminary conclusion, let us accept that our use of the word "ecumenical" no longer refers to "wholes." It refers in fact to a very narrow band of activity and to only one of several faith communities.

Some of the most powerful language for the future comes from the past, from the Bible. Consider, for example, the biblical notion of "unity" or "one-ness." In his famous prayer, recorded in John 17:21, Jesus pleaded for his disciples: "May they be one, so that the world will believe that you sent me." In the centuries since the time of Christ, Christians have claimed that prayer as both promise and as command: a promise that we are all accepted by God and a command to always seek for unity within the believer community.

Similar language is used by the Apostle Paul. In Ephesians 2:14 he writes of the unity between estranged peoples: "For Christ himself has brought us peace by making Jews and Gentiles [estranged peoples] one people. With his own body he broke down the wall that separated them and kept them enemies." Even more astonishing is the claim by Paul in Colossians 1:20, where he declares that "through the Son, God decided to bring the whole universe back to himself. God made peace through his son's sacrificial death on the cross and so brought back to himself all things, both on earth and in heaven." It is tantalizing to speculate on the meaning of the phrase "all things." If we accept it at face value, we are clearly well set for the future, as subsequent comments will demonstrate.

As far as the New Testament message is concerned, all walls are down. Those who claim to be Christians are already living in a world redeemed and a world open to the future. In the "real" world of every day, we are appalled by the divisions that separate us on the one hand, and left breathless by the prospects for change on the other. One African theologian lays claim to those prospects by defining salvation in broad terms. According to him, Africa understands salvation as liberation from all that attacks the individual and all that disturbs life in community. It is liberation from physical, mental, and spiritual illness, from hunger and poverty. It is, in short, the restoration of harmony "disrupted or broken by a certain evil."

On the same subject, another theologian from Africa writes of the restoration of "health" to our life in community. According to him, health implies balance, just as illness would be defined as imbalance. Christians in general and the African Christian community in particular lay claim in religious language to vast complexities and to all-encompassing "wholes." The daring demonstrated by our life together is dwarfed by powerful, yet-to-be-realized visions articulated in the language we use. If there is a gap even now between our vision language and the realities of our life together, the future promises to be even more daunting. For the language that beckons from the future is exceedingly strong. We are left with the choice of participating both in the creation and use of such language or being guided by those more courageous than ourselves.

The Language of Political and Economic Realignment

Within the past five years, our vocabularies have been enlarged by the words *perestroika* and *glasnost*, Russian words connoting, respectively, "restructuring" and "openness." The effects of the policies associated with these words have overwhelmed even Mikhail Gorbachev. During the past weeks, an anxious world has been monitoring the fortunes of the Soviet empire, which is teetering on the brink of chaos and held together by the thin prospects of a new order. Changes in the Soviet Union particularly and in eastern Europe generally may provide indications of shifts on a global scale.

We seem to be moving rapidly from a bipolar to a multipolar world order. For more than forty years, we have been accustomed to thinking about a world divided: between "East" and "West," between socialism and capitalism, between communism and organized religion. Even for non-Marxists, the Marxist ideology has for decades provided an alternative to the perceived ravages of colonialism and capitalism. With the apparent demise of Marxism, it would seem that one of the world's ideological lobes has been excised. The void is rapidly being filled with alternative configurations: nationalisms of many kinds are on the rise and organized religion is being articulated afresh, while the political and economic power centers rearrange themselves. Already it is easy to imagine a future in which Asia is dominated by Japan or, perhaps later, by China; in which North and South America reconfigure relationships with the USA; in which Europe will realize its common market, but featuring still a towering German economy; and, finally, in which the African continent has South Africa and Nigeria playing leading roles. It was in the context of such changes that the American ambassador to Kenya noted recently: "The Cold War is over." And with it, the political value of Kenya (Africa) to the purposes of the United States declines accordingly. Conditionalities of Western aid to Africa, as manifested in the Fourth Lomé Convention, the Bretton Woods institutions, and the bilateral aid from the USA and France, have generally and subtly become more stringent. Across the continent, African countries are reeling from the cumulative effects of micro and macro changes in the world.

Science Language for Change

For this section of the presentation, let us again consider the importance of two key words: *biosphere* and *noosphere.* Neither of these is widely used by laypersons or nonscientists. But they are effecting a revolution in the world of scientific and metaphysical reflection. Let us consider the history and the meaning of these concepts, for they have already played important roles in shaping our common future.

Within the past the past 130 years, scientists have coined language describing, increasingly, the basic unity of the world. In Newton's time they were laboring under the image of the world as a large-scale factory comprised of interacting but discrete parts. Scientists assigned themselves the tasks of managing the factory, replacing or manipulating the parts as demanded by the needs and, at times, by the whims of humankind. As already noted, the biblical record is replete with metaphors of "wholes." However, in 1875 scientists were beginning to think more seriously in "holist" terms. An Austrian by the name of Suess coined the term biosphere, defining it as "the sphere of the influence of life." In 1926 a Russian scientist by the name of Vernadsky for the first time popularized the word in a formal paper. In his understanding, the word biosphere referred to "the integrated living and life-supporting system comprising the periphery of the earth." Like others after him, he was reaching for an understanding of the globe as a "single living organism."

Later on in his scientific quests, Vernadsky incorporated into his lexicon the word noosphere (*noo* = Greek for mind, *sphere* = globe; together = global mind). The current dictionary definition of noosphere is given as "the conscious or unconscious effect of human activity on the biosphere." The word was coined in 1925 by the French Jesuit priest, Teilhard de Chardin. He was trained in theology as well as paleontology. His lifetime work was carried out in China, but he frequented the universities of Paris, where he encountered Vernadsky. With reference to the noosphere, Teilhard was more ethereal: he spoke of the "human sphere, the sphere of reflection, of conscious invention, of the union of spirits."

While Vernadsky for many years played the role of a senior scientist within the Soviet Union, he frequently found himself at odds with the Stalinist (dialectical materialist) establishment. Gorbachev, however, embraced Vernadskian understandings, referring to them in his speeches. He is not alone. There is evidence that large sections of the Soviet scientific community shared such understandings. Indeed, the word noosphere became a centerpiece concept within Soviet intellectual circles. A general Soviet definition of the word refers to "the epoch when further development of the planet will be guided by reason" (i.e., reasonable action by humankind). In recent years, Western "green" (i.e., ecologically inclined) scientists have enthusiastically joined the Soviet scientific community in the quest for an understanding of the globe as a single living organism.

The implications of these concepts for the future of the world are only slowly coming into focus. For the Soviet Union, accustomed as it was to more than half a century of materialist ideology, the break was very sharp.

It was considered by the Soviets during this time that the world operates and history moves according to clearly identifiable objective laws. With that understanding, humankind was left with the task of discovering those laws and behaving accordingly. Hence the need in the Soviet experience for guidance by an all-knowing, avant-garde political party. In the Western world it was simply assumed that people were to take charge of nature: to dominate, to control, to manage. In both cases people were somehow perceived to be separated from or "above" the processes of nature.

A prominent Soviet scientist distilled astonishing conclusions from those understandings of the biosphere/noosphere concepts. According to him:

1. The most important change factor operative in the world is human activity. What we do collectively has greater impact on the biosphere, on this living global organism, than any other single change factor.
2. We are responsible. There are no observers, no bystanders. Humankind no longer exercises the option of playing passive or dominating roles in the world, reacting to or acting upon forces of a benign or hostile "nature."
3. All of us have something to contribute to the well-being of the "living" world. No people are devoid of gifts to be shared with the larger community.
4. The world can only move ahead on a sustainable basis if we together identify and live by conflict-free or nonviolent models.

Parenthetically, during the 1960s a friend in Dar es Salaam confided that Tanzanian President Julius Nyerere was reading for his edification the famous book by Teilhard de Chardin, *The Phenomenon of Man*. According to the informer friend, Nyerere was convinced that few Westerners, with whatever intent, had come as close to an understanding of the African cosmos as had Chardin. This sentiment was echoed by President Senghor of Senegal.

Chardin referred repeatedly in his writings to our collective "co-creator" and "co-developer" roles in the world. In his December 1988 speech to the United Nations General Assembly, Mikhail Gorbachev used precisely those words in outlining the task toward a common future. As human beings we stand in awe of ideas whose time has come. If as Christians we do not fully understand all the implications of these powerful concepts, there is nevertheless about them a familiar, reassuring ring, exciting our faith and our vision.

Whither Africa's Future

In the wake of the momentous changes in eastern Europe during late 1989 and early 1990, fear was expressed in Africa regarding the continent's possible marginalization. Salim Salim, the Tanzanian General Secretary of the Organization of African Unity, speculated that eastern Europe would capture the attention of donor countries at the expense of ongoing aid to Africa, a sentiment frequently repeated in East Africa's press. Despite assurances to the contrary, both the fears and the possibilities of marginalization are real. For a community like this one of so-called ecumenical partners, the challenge is a particularly strong one.

A number of issues call for attention. Within what might be called the development fraternity—both within the ecumenical and the larger NGO communities—there is an understanding that, while Western countries occupied themselves with the east–west divides, the so-called third world has become concerned about the north–south disparities. The former was seen as an ideological divide, the latter as an economic divide between the rich and the poor. With the aforementioned shift from a bipolar to a multipolar world, there is cause for reassessing the divides by which we live or die. This roundtable discussion is concerned, among other issues, with the north–south divides, from both ideological (theological) and economic points of view. It has centered on how and on what basis available resources are shared.

Where in a multipolar world will the debate be focused? More specifically, will this round table continue to engage primarily Europeans and Africans in a process matching northern money with southern projects, or will the discussion eventually shift its attention to the deployment of resources within Africa on a continental basis? Which are the ready models providing guidance for such a shift? Until now, the ecumenical pattern of sharing has not seriously taken a continental form. National and, to some extent, regional roundtable formats are still in formation, competing to a greater or lesser extent for access to northern donor communities. An Organization of African Unity model of sharing against the larger Pan-Africanist backdrop may offer some helpful nuances.

An Organization of African Unity Model of Sharing

In April 1980, the Assembly of Heads of State and Government of the Organization of African Unity adopted the Lagos Plan of Action. The plan was complemented by the so-called Final Act of Lagos, the primary objective of which was to overcome the handicaps created by the extreme balkanization of Africa through the promotion of subregional economic cooperation and integration. The Lagos Plan of Action places particular emphasis on the objective of achieving collective (continental) self-reliance in Africa, calling for the establishment of an African Economic Community by the year 2000. According to this plan, Africa views self-reliance as both the goal and the means through which the region will eventually find its true identity, full dignity, and historic strength. It is also perceived as the goal and the means by which the region will find the capacity to master its resources, its development, and its future.

In moving toward these goals, several considerations must be entertained: (1) the integration of the physical, institutional, and social infrastructures; (2) the integration of the production structures; and (3) the integration of African markets. For these purposes, the Organization of African Unity will need to assess the potential complementary relationships among regional African organizations such as the Southern African Development Coordination Conference, the Preferential Trade Area, the Intergovernmental Agency on Drought and Development, and the Economic Community of West African States. Finally, it is considered that if this model is to succeed, Africa's political systems will need to evolve toward full democracy and participation by all sections of society. Because of the sequence and the timing of events, the proposal does not take account of the potential role of a post-apartheid South Africa within the continent. Meanwhile, the idea of an African economic community is at this stage only in the form of a proposal. Nevertheless, the ecumenical community could do worse than to compare its own concerns with the rationale and major components of the Organization of African Unity proposal.

Pan-Africanism

Still alive is an older vision for sharing Africa's continental wealth. It functions under the rubric of Pan-Africanism, with some portion of its roots in the African diaspora of the Caribbean region. Pan-Africanism, as articulated by Du Bois, Padmore, Fanon, James, Nkrumah, and Nyerere, among others, was carried along from the turn of the century by a series of congresses. They functioned to identify and rally the spirit of political independence for Africa. Currently, plans are underway for the convening of the Seventh Pan-African Congress. Dr. Kwesi Prah, a Pan-Africanist academic, explains its purpose.

Prah is passionate and eloquent in his defense of Africa's cultural and potential economic prowess. According to him, the intent of the Pan-Africanist Congresses was to awaken the continent to political realities and possibilities, which led to the drive for independence from colonial powers. The continuing agenda for Pan-Africanism concerns itself with the liberation of the continent's cultural and economic wealth. He is doubtful that Africa will ever develop using other peoples' languages and other peoples' expertise. His doubts are premised on an understanding that Africa's wealth lies (largely unexplored and unexploited) in its family of languages. He contests the research findings of colonial social anthropologists, insisting that they were given to excessive disaggregation of the family of African languages. According to him, Africa is more correctly explained as a family of a relatively small number of major language aggregations. By emphasizing the smaller number of language groups, he is underlining the essential unity of the continent and thus a major strength to be deployed.

Pan-Africanism as an ideal or as an ideology is identified, frequently, with a particular generation of Africans and with a particular political task. Its golden age extended roughly from 1900 to 1960. Writings and personalities from that period provide formidable reference points for any in-depth discussion of Africa's potential. Unfortunately, Pan-Africanism's visibility and its power to interpret Africa's potential have for the past two or three decades been eclipsed by the continent's lone unifying factor—a common abhorrence of apartheid. Whether Pan-Africanist understandings of the continent are sufficiently articulate or relevant to capture the imaginations of the coming generation of African leaders is a point to be tested, perhaps during the forthcoming Seventh Pan-Africanist Congress. Among the resource-sharing or resource-generating models noted in this paper, Pan-Africanism offers a high view of the continent's spiritual, cultural, and economic potential.

Summary Comments

The world order has been convulsed by the changes taking place in eastern Europe. World War II is coming to an end, finally, as statespersons from various quarters negotiate the unification of Germany, the contested borders of Poland, the introduction of market economies in erstwhile socialist countries, and new security arrangements reflecting the needs of a "common European home." Coming as they do at the time of rapid movement toward a European common market by a 1992 target date, these changes collectively have the effect of ushering in a new world order.

Changes have taken place at a bewildering pace, providing scant opportunity for leisurely reflection on their primary causes and on the driving forces. There seems little doubt that economic constraints and contradictions catapulted already uneasy situations in eastern Europe into explosive demands for change. Gorbachev as a key figure in the drama has managed to stay a step or two ahead of the unfolding events, which can lay no claim to clear direction. How long he will be able to stay atop this maelstrom is a point being watched the world over. Meanwhile, Marxism as expressed in eastern Europe over the past decades has been disgraced. Whether it will survive as an ideology is being debated, with some observers arguing that the current lapse is temporary. They argue that Marxism is experiencing corrections and refinements for another day. On the other hand, it is not at all clear that the West has "won" in the current upheaval. Sustained military competition has severely strained the American economy, rendering it unable to preside over the "spoils" as an undisputed victor.

From the world of science, powerful concepts have been unleashed, making their way toward new understandings of the future. Although they were known and articulated for the greater part of this century, they have only now come to the fore, thanks to the growing awareness of environmental degradation and the massive political and ideological shifts in the world order.

Brain Drain and Languaging

Africa perceives itself to be on the periphery of the change scene, but very much influenced by it. Economically there is fear of marginalization and an awareness of the difficulty of maintaining a continuing flow of aid and investment from abroad. A second wind of political change in Africa seems to be inspired partly by events in eastern Europe and partly by policy changes within Africa's traditional donor communities, the two factors being not unrelated.

As a process and as an ongoing relationship, the ecumenical sharing of resources between north and south is situated within this matrix and profoundly informed by the unfolding changes in the north. Until now, round tables of the kind we are attending have devoted the smallest portion of their energies toward imagining African futures based partially or wholly on African resources. The time for such a consideration may have come.

A Modest Proposal

There is no doubt that Africa's wealth and potential has yet to be fully realized and enjoyed by African peoples. The history of this continent is the history of plunder, exploitation, slavery, and domination by exogenous forces. Of this there is on every hand abundant evidence. Note the example of Namibia. In the years leading to its independence, Namibia was the victim of massive unscrupulous and illegal exploitation of its mineral resources. There is some hope that a UN-initiated legal suit will eventually provide for a measure of compensation from the offending mining companies and the consenting governments.

At another level, Africa is still exporting its most valuable resource: trained minds. Some of the continent's strongest resources are subject to what has been called a brain drain. The brain drain has several dimensions. Europe and North America beckon with their job opportunities and strong salaries—thus the external brain drain. Meanwhile, an internal brain drain is also at work: large numbers of African academicians make their financial ends meet only by means of consultancies carried out in Africa on behalf of multilateral and bilateral aid and development enterprises. Even though Africa may benefit indirectly from such consultancy work, it is nevertheless true that the "language" of consultancies is foreign. As the Pan-Africanists would say, Africa has been trying to develop by means of other people's languages, with mixed consequences.

The change forces affecting Africa are formidable. Obviously there are no single solutions promising to shift the course of these changes in Africa's favor. Nevertheless, a modest proposal might address in preliminary fashion the need to mobilize Africa's wealth for Africa's benefit.

Documentation presented at this round table provides ample evidence of the diversity of the ecumenical experience, and more particularly the experience of the National Council of Churches Kenya. You will be discussing the need for adjustments and perhaps redirection of aspects of council activities. But there is no denying the wealth of experience generated by the council over the past decades. It is my view that much of that experiential wealth has functioned largely under categories dictated by the development enterprise, the language of which has emanated primarily from the north.

Perhaps this is the time to restate the learnings of that collective experience in language coined on this continent. Perhaps a renaming of what has been done and learned into categories more tuned to African realities would itself render the learning more potent. To this end it might be useful to deploy on a permanent basis within the National Council of Churches of Kenya one or more academics without the burden of specific programmatic portfolio. Such a person or persons would be present not so much as the expert(s), but more as the trained listener(s), distiller(s), subject precisely to the process that has generated the unique experience of the council, but given now to the coining of new language to describe it.

In this way the National Council of Churches of Kenya might be able to understand and name more precisely what has transpired over the years, while at the same time identifying language for the future. As noted earlier in this chapter, the future belongs to those who command the language for it.

—May 1990

Presented to the National Council of Churches of Kenya Round Table, Kanamai, Mombasa.

Sources

Africa Recovery. "Lome IV Grapples with Aid Conditionality." October 1989.

Byaruhanga, Christopher. 2015. *The History and Theology of the Ecumenical Movement in East Africa.* Kampala, Uganda: Fountain Publishers.

Chepkwony, Agnes. 1987. *The Role of Non-governmental Organizations in Development: A Study of the National Christian Council of Kenya, 1963–1978.* Uppsala, Sweden: University of Uppsala.

Economic Commission for Africa (UN). "African Alternative Framework to Structural Adjustment Programmes for Social-Economic Recovery and Transformation." From an undated document.

Gorbachev, Mikhail. December 7, 1988. Address to the 43rd Session of the United Nations General Assembly. New York.

Grinevald, Jacques. 1987. "Development of the Biosphere" in *L'homme Inacheve.* Cahiers de L'IUED. Geneva-Paris: Presses Universitaires de France.

Hebge, Fr. Meinrad. April 1990. Lecture at Hekima College. Nairobi, Kenya.

Karamaga, Andre. March 30, 1990. "African Aspirations and the Christian Response." Presented at the AACC General Committee meeting. Nairobi, Kenya.

Moisseyev, Nikita. 1987. *Man, Nature and the Future of Civilization.* Moscow: Novosti Press.

Mugambi, J. K. N. 1989. *The Biblical Basis for Evangelization: Reflection Based on African Experience.* Nairobi: Oxford University Press.

National Council of Churches of Kenya. 2013. *A Century of Ecumenism and Mission: The Story of National Council of Churches of Kenya 1913–2013.* Nairobi, Kenya.

Njock, Edward. May 2–6, 1990. "New Perspectives for Inter-African Co-operation in Science and Technology for Development." Presented at the Professors World Peace Academy. Nairobi, Kenya.

Prah, Dr. Kwesi. 1989. *The Bantustan Brain Gain.* Institute of Southern Africa Studies, National University of Lesotho.

Prah, Dr. Kwesi. April 1990. Lecture at All Africa Conference of Churches.

Raiser, Konrad. 1991. *Ecumenism in Transition: A Paradigm Shift in the Ecumenical Movement.* Geneva: World Council of Churches Publications.

Roberts, Allen R. October 1989. "The Illegal Depletion of Namibia's Resources." *Africa Recovery.*

"The State and the Crisis in Africa: In Search of a Second Liberation." May 12–18, 1990. Conference document, Mweya Lodge, Uganda.

Utuk, Efiong. 1997. *Visions of Authenticity: The Assemblies of the All Africa Conference of Churches 1963–1992.* Nairobi: All Africa Conference of Churches.

9
When Metaphors Collide: Reconciliation Roles for Nongovernmental Organizations in Africa

A metaphor that works is sufficiently unconventional and shocking that we instinctively say no as well as yes to it.

—SALLIE McFAGUE

Introduction

On no account is a "new world order" in place. But shifts and changes are in fact underway, informed by, among other factors, the demise of Marxist ideology and (at the time of the original writing of this reflection) the collapse of the Soviet empire. Like eastern Europe, Africa felt the full impact of the changes underway and was obliged to readjust relationships both within and beyond the continent to the new realities.

Against that backdrop, scrutiny of Africa's modernization project became a matter of considerable interest. In the Cold War period, it became evident that much of what had passed for development or modernization consisted merely of the crumbs that industrialized economies were prepared to share, representing not so much genuine change as the emergence in varying degrees of new dependencies. In a time of world economic recession, industrialized democracies found it easy to add conditionalities to diminishing bilateral and multilateral funds.

The consequences of such policies on Africa's fragile modern-sector economies became apparent and were to varying degrees negative. Across the continent, economic, social, and political indicators were down or in notable flux. What some observers referred to as the "second (political) liberation of Africa" reflected the engagements of a hard-pressed continent with persistent international forces.

While Africa's modernizing project was experiencing stresses and strains, the strength, content, and functions of its social, ethnic, and religious resources were being revisited. Until 1990, the East–West ideological matrix had served as a kind of buffer zone between Africa's own socioreligious resources and what were perceived to be modernizing resources available from both Western and Eastern spheres of the world. The collapse of the Soviet empire and the subsequent reassessment of ideology obliged Africa generally and the African church together with the NGO community in particular to revisit the continent's spiritual and cultural resources as alternative bases from which to address the challenges of coming decades.

Questions about the deployment or manifestations of such resources begged for fresh attention; they were of particular interest to both indigenous and foreign development and service-providing NGOs. In an attempt to identify the most helpful postures for such agencies, the first figure, Africa's Change Matrix, situates the continent's religious and cultural resources in the context of changes over the centuries, including more recent shifts.

For purposes at hand, the term *church* provides the perspective from which this paper is written. Historically, church was active in Africa before the term NGO was widely used. There is continuing debate as to whether church could or should be categorized as NGO.

Churches and Nongovernmental Organizations En Route: Participatory Restructuring

At independence time—during the 1960s and 1970s—the African body politic was greatly influenced by two formal-sector actors: the governments of the day and African church in all its diversity. To the extent that both actors were under the control and direction of Africans, they were for all practical purposes "on the same side." Both were in favor of

Africa's Change Matrix

Periods	Time Span
Slavery	1400s to 1800s
Colonialism	1800s to 1960s
East/West Ideology	1917 to 1990s
Neocolonialism	1960s to present

Projects	Medium
Political	Pan-Africanist Congresses Independent Statehood
Religious	Islam, Mosques Christianity, Churches
Economic/Industrial	Extractive (Commodity) Modern Sector Development

Current Project Expressions

Political	"Second Liberation" — Political Restructuring "Democratization" as Aid Conditionality
Religious	"50% Christian, 50% Muslim" (David Barrett, 1982) Conspicuous Fundamentalist Fringes Para-religious Service Organizations
Economic	"Open Markets" — Donor Conditionalities Flourishing of Informal Sector NGOs Welfare/"Development" Services

the development undertakings, both were committed to control by the African majority, and both were essentially committed to modernization ("Westernization") as the way into the future. If people at the grass roots of society were recognized at all, it was assumed that they were waiting with bated breath to be ushered into the precincts of the modern, postcolonial era by NGOs, governments, and churches who "knew best," in the direction of modernity.

While government and church shared public space, it was clear, nevertheless, that the state was the "first among equals." Church was seen to be carrying out projects for which government resources were not yet available, but that would eventually be taken over by the respective governments when circumstances permitted. There was the sense at the time that church was functioning as experimenter, innovator, and risk-taker. Government–church relationships were perceived as compatible, with each maximizing respective advantages, and both committed to the welfare of the community at large. Modernization theory was for all practical purposes alive and well.

During the late 1960s and into the 1970s, church was joined in its development efforts by a host of NGOs, in many guises and representing a dizzying array of interests and expertise. In the absence of a general catchall theory explaining their appearance, over time observers began to categorize this collectivity of activists according to function.

By the mid-1980s it was becoming clear that the NGO phenomenon in fact constituted a far-flung enterprise—a vast spectrum extending from within the northern industrialized nations to the far corners of the developing world, sometimes referred to, disparagingly, as the "third world." It was also becoming apparent that this broad category of actors would require some differentiation if there was to be any useful description or understanding of the various roles being undertaken.

There were donor NGOs, intermediary NGOs liaising between North Atlantic countries and African countries, "designer" recipient NGOs in host countries and communities, and the vast hinterland of African grass-roots groups, variously exercising traditional mandates, some of them adjusting to and being reshaped by the largesse of the greater NGO phenomenon. An inordinate amount of energy was invested in the sorting out of relationships between the respective functional NGO categories. Analyses of relationships between northern and southern NGOs generated a particularly vigorous debate, for overlaps and relationships were proving to be complex. One analyst posited that NGOs moved through several discernible phases.

Five-Generation Strategies of Development-oriented Nongovernmental Organizations

Strategy	Project
1. Relief and Welfare	Starving Children/ Refugees
2. Community Development	Community Self-help
3. Sustainable Systems	Development Policies/ Institutions
4. People's Movements	Self-managing Networks
5. Reciprocal Learnings	Spaceship Earth

Adapted from David Korten, 1990

Meanwhile, the discussion continued, reflecting a growing array of layered structures with the capacity to "network" in multiple directions. The appearance and proliferation of NGOs on the African scene could best described as an explosion. Political scientists were giving serious thought, belatedly, to this emerging collectivity of actors, tentatively describing its legitimate and acceptable function within the larger body politic.

Meanwhile, the original church and state players were falling on hard times. Across Africa, the state was perceived as incapable of meeting the basic needs of society. Church discovered, meanwhile, that it was no longer "on the same side" as the government of the day, acting instead, in many instances, as the "not-so-loyal opposition." Even more distressing for the church was the growing realization that its privileged position as the other major actor in society—alongside governments of the day—had been subsumed by or shared within the more generic category of "NGO." In the absence of clear guidance from either theologians or political scientists, the church was casting about for fresh definitions and designations for itself.

Governments in Africa, on the other hand, were under pressure from many quarters within and without, from the donor community and from the (post-ideological) mood of the times. Generally, those pressures were in the direction of more open forms of governance, perceived as calls for a "second liberation," the first having won independence from colonial powers. And whereas it had been assumed in the 1960s that people at the grass roots of society needed to be taught and led, it had become clear, meanwhile, that they were in fact being courted by governments, the church, and NGOs.

For it had become evident that much of the residual social cohesion on this continent was lodged at grass-roots level of society. Hence the question: to which degree could any one of the three major actors in modern Africa lay genuine claim to the loyalties of people at the grass roots? Generally, grass-roots peasants were perceived to be exceedingly circumspect in the husbanding of their loyalties vis-à-vis government, NGO, or church. As a modern-sector actor—more than government or NGO—church was widely present at the grass-roots level, but not exercising a controlling monopoly of grass-roots allegiances.

The ubiquitous presence of church could not everywhere be equated either with the stated values or essential (political) aspirations of the grass-roots majority. Churches "listened in" and even catalyzed such discussion, often as primary change agents. But generally societal issues were most seriously and most creatively addressed by people at the grass-roots level by means of neo-traditional, locally nuanced socioreligious dynamics.

Over time, governments acknowledged more readily that a debate was underway and that such debate would be crucial to more participatory futures. Growing self-aware ferment was no longer recognized as an extension of the "benign" development activity of the 1960s. Nothing less than a major participatory restructuring of the African body politic was being set in motion. Critical to this change process were the religious and metaphysical elements that had been variously articulated by African theologians under the general rubric of African Religion or as cultural factors according to social scientists.

Imagining a New African Order

Since 1900, Africa has been viewed by various of its ideologues as a unitary whole. It was a vision articulated by Africans in the diaspora and readily endorsed by African nationalist leaders on the continent. Beginning in 1900, a series of Pan-Africanist Congresses were convened as an exploration of the meaning and possibility of political independence for Africa. In this context the independence movement of the 1960s was realized, releasing a "wind of change" that swept across the whole of the continent and that, by the late 1980s, had left only a few pockets of the colonial structure intact.

Africa's political independence, constructed on the foundations of an essentially colonial state framework, quickly gave way to major disruptions. In many situations across the continent, the emergence of refugees provided tragic evidence of the stresses and strains inherent in the new order. But it was the widely publicized Biafra War of the late 1960s that shifted attention from the glamour of political independence to the dilemmas of postindependence civil war.

Apart from the events in Biafra, and later in the Sudan and other countries across Africa, churches and church-related agencies were preoccupied during the 1960s and 1970s with the southern Africa region; for decades the struggle against South Africa's apartheid governance system had provided a unifying focus for the Western church-related activist community. Changes in South Africa eventually surpassed all expectations and defied the gravest fears. Still, in the context of this survey, it must be noted that the achievement of majority rule in South Africa merely completed the original (1960s) Pan-Africanist vision for a politically independent continent. South Africa would assume a learning posture vis-à-vis the rest of the continent, obliged to revisit the nature of interethnic relationships and the religious and cultural matrix within which those relationships functioned. Given that Africa's first modern project—the independence project—was being realized, attention could then be focused on other paradigmatic shifts underway across the continent.

The 1990s opened doors to a new, but still undefined, vision of the future. Thanks to the collapse of eastern Europe, the whole of the ideological configuration within which Africa had functioned since the mid-1900s changed. No longer were "Western" socialist or capitalist models providing the ideological and economic options for African decision makers. In the absence of an articulated "new world order," African governments were left to struggle with the variously derived imperatives of multiparty democracy and its widely touted corollary "free markets." Meanwhile, there was a sense in some African quarters of being abandoned by the traditional donor community in favor of building, among other things, a "common European home."

If the economic and ideological adjustments underway in Africa were deemed demanding, so was the reawakening of the continent's ethno-cultural factor. This most vexing of Africa's "strengths" was being accorded a new legitimacy and a certain immediacy by the concomitant rise of ethnic-related conflicts in eastern Europe. Whereas both church and state in independent Africa had all along sought to keep the ethno-cultural dynamic under control (usually by denial or denigration), it had now become clear that the issue remained unresolved.

Africa's wars in the Sudan, Liberia, Angola, Mozambique, Ethiopia, Somalia, and Rwanda were all premised, in one way or other, on ethnic considerations. With the notable exceptions of Ethiopia and Uganda, where alternative approaches to the ethnic question were being tested, African heads of state insisted that a frontal encounter with ethno-cultural issues was at the very least highly controversial. On the other hand, there was among African theologians and philosophers a growing sense that the continent was reconstituting itself, that if a new order was to be realized it could only be achieved by taking careful account of the indigenous religious and cultural strengths of African peoples.

During the 1990s and into the year 2000, the concern for churches and NGOs focused on how things could come together again, on which foundations and within which configurations the continent of Africa was rearticulating itself. In theological and social science terms, it was a preoccupation with peace and reconciliation or, as Jesse Mugambi suggested, it was the project of reconstruction. For churches in Africa, these issues were particularly poignant, as many of them were typically divided or united just as the African body politic was divided or united. Still, observers insisted that churches generally numbered among the few alternative, "disinterested" mediating facilities with significant stature on this troubled continent.

In what way, then, did the African church or NGO and the related support community provide the leadership and process requisite to the imagining and articulating of a new continental vision? Some portion of the answer could be explored in a reflection on the metaphors or paradigms within which choices were consciously and unconsciously being made. For it was within the arena of contrasting metaphors and paradigms that some of the tensions between Africa and the modernizing/change project were located. Intriguing for purposes of this reflection were metaphors related to temporality and, by extension, the politics of time.

Linear vs. Spherical Paradigms

Every colonizing power has projected its own time values onto its subjects, arguing that its temporal affairs were organized as a reflection of the manner in which the whole of the universe was organized. The specific projects noted in the first figure above (Africa's Change Matrix), together with the whole of the colonial enterprise, represent particular understandings (there were a number of different colonial powers intervening in Africa, each with its own sense of time) of the phenomenon of time and its management. While the benefits derived from those interventions have been variously acknowledged, the related opportunity costs and religious and cultural costs have been noteworthy.

Until the modern era, concepts of time usually coincided with an intimate relationship between the rhythms of human sociability and the rhythms of the earth's living ecosystems. Preindustrial or nonindustrial civilizations were tuned in profound ways to the temporal cycles of nature, to the changing seasons, to the apparent changing constellations of stars in the heavens, to the snake shedding its skin, and to the migration of birds, among many other examples. Time, to a significant extent, corresponded to the cycles and rhythms of nature and life within the human community.

With the advent of technology, and the modern computer in particular, events were being processed at speeds that could no longer be consciously experienced by humans: a modern computer functions on the basis of a nanosecond, one billionth of a second. Not only does Western time move faster than the biorhythms of humans and nature, it moves in linear fashion from a static past into a future variously projected as controllable and manageable from the present or, alternatively, as a catchment area for either total despair or ultimate bliss. The following figure identifies some of the characteristics of Western time.

Western Time Values

Past	**Present**	**Future**
Written Record	Entry to Future	Well-being
Classic Categories	Management/ Planning	Perfection
Poverty	*Sufficiency*	*"Heaven"*
Nature	*Technology*	*Space Age*
Pristine	*Anxiety*	*Apocalypse*

In his comparisons between Western and African time schemata, John Mbiti posited that Africa functioned in the absence of a clear sense of the future. He sought to demonstrate that Africa was generally more inclined toward the past than toward the future, with past experience residing in the memory of living people who retained, interpreted, and variously acted upon their interpretation of accumulated ancestral wisdom. Mbiti critiqued this configuration as a paradigmatic handicap to be overcome. Was he was essentially attempting to accommodate the world of African temporal awareness within a linear, Western temporality?

Mbiti's thesis has been roundly criticized by fellow African academics who insist that Africans, like all peoples in the world, have the capacity to think into the future, to join the linear world of progress as championed and demonstrated by the Western, industrialized world or as outlined by the linear, eschatological understandings of Western Christian theology.

The linear/cyclical/spherical debate has been touched on by the now famous Canadian Jesuit scholar, Fr. Claude Sumner, for more than three decades an expert on the medieval wisdom literature of Ethiopia. He summarized his findings and impressions in rather obtuse but singularly understandable academic language:

> Does the "present" of the so-called advanced countries indicate the "future" of developing countries? Are not all of them living in the same "present"? Does not the question amount to asking that time be stopped for underdeveloped countries to catch up on advanced countries? To introduce novelty into history we must think of the future as new, as created together. This implies that the past, instead of being a mere continuation or expansion of the future, creates the future. The past would not act thus, were it not itself altered in some manner. But how can the past be altered unless it is present? In this present which endures, there is no distinction of a "before" and "after" side by side. In other words, as a "perpetual present" time does not unfold but, so to speak, returns upon itself; by this return the future is altering the past. Through this change the past is constantly renewed, this renewed past is none other than the sense of the perpetual present. There is hope only if this procession is changed into the intermittent acts of heroes, into the legend of nations.

The African worldview to which Sumner referred is most helpfully understood in the form of a sphere in which all life is interrelated. Dichotomies between living peoples and their ancestors, between animate and inanimate objects, are dissolved into a unitary whole. An all-encompassing "present" accommodates at once the modernity of the computer and the dynamics of the rural village.

Instead of the separation suggested by the linear metaphor of time, in which modernity is considered to be "out ahead," distanced from tradition, the spherical view would suggest a constant, proximate interaction among the several dynamics within the living "present." Indeed, "growth" (as contrasted with "movement" along a linear timeline) of the sphere of life would be contingent on interaction among the several components, between individuals and communities, between "past" and "present." A living and growing "present" would comprise creative contributions from all sectors of the community, including the unborn and the ancestors. The following figure expresses some of the active dynamics of Africa's spherical "present."

Linear vs. Spherical

Spirit/Matter Dichotomy	Biosphere/Noosphere (Jacques Grinevald, 1987)
Futurist/Eschatological	"Present"
Technical/Scientific/ Expert	Group Effort
Relational/Proximate	Community
Exclusive	Inclusive
Separate	Together

Conclusions: A Relational Ethic for the Future

Following the matrixes offered in this reflection, it is possible to locate church in the African setting. Its presence is evident in the major projects affecting this continent since the 1500s; together with Islam, church in various guises tolerated, blessed, or condemned the slave trade; church became ubiquitously present in large portions of the African continent as formal Christian institution. According to some statisticians, it was anticipated that by the year 2000 nearly half of all Africans would be adherents of the Christian faith. Additionally, Africa's Christian theologians have championed an analytic and reflection process that has rendered sub-Saharan Africa's religious and cultural matrix into an entity acknowledged as African Religion and thus an element of the modern religious project. Additionally, church and latterly the NGO have served as important actors in the economic or development project, each active on the basis of Western, linear assumptions. By the mid-1980s it became clear that the tensions between the social, economic, and political realities across Africa, on the one hand, and the African religious and cultural paradigms within which those projects functioned, on the other, were experiencing significant stresses and strains. The tension was merely exacerbated by the aforementioned end of the Cold War and the overwhelming influence of the globalized economy.

The metaphor of reconstruction suggests the possibility of Africa rearticulating itself, assuming, as does Sumner, that Africa with its spherical (or more accurately "spiral") temporal orientation offers the possibility of new dimensions of paradigmatic synthesis. Thus, if future relationships within Africa (and between Africa and the Western impulse) are to be life-giving and life-sustaining, they must be open to the possibility of metaphoric and paradigmatic syntheses within the existing African religious and cultural matrix.

Today's crises, whether economic or environmental, political or religious, can be understood in part as temporal crises. Those who would make peace between the conflicting pace or direction of change, between conflicting and contrasting perceptions of proper order, may need to cultivate an openness to alternative possibilities. Today's visionaries would insist that power is most legitimately exercised within participatory community. They would be tuned to nature, not merely as a resource to be exploited and tamed, but as a life force, as the temporal manifestation of nature's pace.

How does church, or NGO for that matter, live in the light of this vision? The German scholar Hans Küng suggests that an inclusive matrix for peace and reconciliation must comprise a course between the extremes, neither drifting into a random pluralism nor isolating oneself with claims to absoluteness: "We do not arrive at peace [wholeness] through syncretism (lowest common denominators) but through reform of ourselves; we arrive at renewal through harmony and self-criticism through toleration." His understandings can be summarized in the following figure.

An Ethic for the Future

- No human life together without a world ethic for the nations
- No peace among the nations without peace among the religions/cultures
- No peace among the religions/cultures without dialogue among the religions/cultures
- No peace ethic realized without reciprocal learning/acting

Summary

Ex Afrika semper eloquid novi ("out of Africa there is always something new") says the ancient Latin dictum. And indeed, during this century Africa has in many respects changed beyond recognition. It became the testing ground for at least three major projects: political independence, religious formation, and economic "development." All three projects were premised on initiatives from outside the continent, informed by ideologies and values largely alien to the continent. The dramatic ideological shifts at the beginning of this decade have demonstrated openly what has long been known: for centuries Africa has been shamelessly exploited, and has functioned for an extended period as a pawn between the ideological/economic "East" and "West."

While countries such as Somalia would seem to suggest collapse and failure in the aftermath of European intervention, what is striking instead is Africa's ability to survive. What is the nature of the strength undergirding Africa's ability to survive? This paper has suggested that, while the religious and cultural values of the continent have been under intense pressure, they have by and large been sustained. At its best, the African impulse is inclined to "include," to account for the dynamics of the whole community. In the context of such dynamics, how does the African church or the NGO in Africa function?

Functions of church and NGO in Africa have been diverse and changing. On the one hand, church in Africa, like church elsewhere and in other times, has on occasion been coopted by the state, by an ethnic group, by one or several warring factions, or to varying degrees, by Western cultural impositions. Obviously, NGOs are equally or even more diverse and therefore equally vulnerable to the manipulation of external forces.

If the dynamics of peace and reconstruction on this continent are to succeed in any measure, it seems clear that both church and NGO will need to be tuned to the continent's primary strengths. Those strengths, some dimensions of which have been cited here, have yet to be fully explored. If and when they are taken seriously, it can be assumed that positive (life-giving) change in Africa will be realized. It can also be assumed that, if church and NGO communities participate fully in Africa's change process on African terms, churches and NGOs will themselves be transformed, with new possibilities becoming apparent to all.

—Nairobi, Kenya, July 1994

Sources

Barrett, David B. 1982. *World Christian Encyclopedia: A Comparative Survey of Churches and Religions in the Modern World AD 1900–2000.* Nairobi: Oxford University Press.

Chipenda, Jose, Andre Karamaga, J. N. K. Mugambi, and C. K. Omari. 1990. *The Church of Africa: Towards a Theology of Reconstruction.* Nairobi: All Africa Conference of Churches.

Grinevald, Jacques. 1987. "Development of the Biosphere" in *L'homme Inacheve.* Cahiers de L'IUED. Geneva-Paris: Presses Universitaires de France.

Ikeda, Daisaku. "Toward a More Humane World in the Coming Century." *Security Dialogue.* Oslo, Norway.

Korten, David. 1990. *Getting to the 21st Century: Voluntary Action and Global Agenda.* Hartford, Connecticut: Kumarian Press Inc.

Küng, Hans. 1991. *Global Responsibility: In Search of a New World Ethic.* New York: Crossroads.

McFague, Sallie. 1982. *Metaphorical Theology: Models of God in Religious Language.* Philadelphia, PA: Fortress Press.

Prah, K. K. November 1991. "Vision for the Year 2000: Insights from the Pan-Africanist Experience." Paper prepared for the All Africa Conference of Churches Symposium, Mombasa, Kenya.

Rifkin, Jeremy. 1987. *Time Wars: The Primary Conflict in Human History.* New York: Simon and Schuster Inc.

Shorter, Aylward. 1991. *The African Synod: A Personal Response to the Outline Document.* Nairobi: St. Paul Publications.

Sumner, Claude. 1992. In the foreword to *Oginga Odinga: His Philosophy and Beliefs* by Odera Oruka. Nairobi: Initiatives Publishers.

10
Jubilee among the Gabra

IT WAS THE forty-ninth year, with preparations for the fiftieth, the Jubilee, underway. Wrongs were righted, sins forgiven, outstanding debts paid. Justice was being done. A myth from biblical times? No, it was a living tradition among the Gabra of northern Kenya. These herders of camels, goats, and cattle occupy one of the most arid portions of East Africa. Theirs is an endless monitoring of the vagaries of fickle rain, honed by many years of practice into a calendar of 365 days and into a cycle of years, typically in multiples of seven.

Bounded to the west by Lake Turkana and to the north by the Magado Escarpment, just inside Ethiopia's southern boundary, with Marsabit Mountain punctuating the southeast corner of the approximate quadrangle, is Gabra country. Included in its topographical diversity are the forbidding salt flats of the Chalbi Desert and, on the other extreme, the Huri Hills plateau, reserved by tradition for dry-season grazing.

Marsabit Mountain is a huge volcanic outcropping capped with magnificent forest—an island of green with its own mini-climate, surrounded by desert. Of the rains that come to northern Kenya, those that bless Marsabit Mountain are the most reliable. British colonial officers established a district administrative center at this five-thousand-foot elevation with its cool air. During the intervening years, this center evolved into a mini metropolis where the Gabra people met the outside world, where foreign tourists frequented a forest lake lodge, where government servants of independent Kenya mingled with neighboring ethnic groups—the Rendille, Samburu, and Borana, all of them rooted in the pastoral, semi-nomadic tradition.

Gabra life was hard not only because of scattered and uncertain rain. In 1878 cholera struck, decimating man and beast. A disease akin to polio further reduced the population in the following year. In 1880 the Gabra, together with their Borana neighbors, fought a final major skirmish with the relatively distant Maasai; the Gabra won the battle, but with heavy losses. At the turn of the century, Gabra livestock suffered an onslaught of rinderpest—a dreaded bovine disease that eventually ravaged the continent, having begun in Ethiopia and extending, finally, to Africa's southernmost cape. Soon after the rinderpest onslaught came a severe outbreak of malaria, a disease usually associated with heavy rains. Then came smallpox for the first time in 1891. There were further battles with neighboring groups in the early 1900s. Later there were bouts with chickenpox and whooping cough. By 1914 an additional six livestock diseases—including bovine pleuropneumonia—had taken their toll.

The widely publicized Sahelian drought of the mid-1970s also affected the Gabra. It was severe and devastating, but in many ways "normal." In 1913 there had been a similar drought, long before global media networks could spread the word, and long before the United Nations agencies had come into existence. For the Gabra people, life comprised a continuous series of challenges. In its own harsh manner, nature's ravages ensured that the population densities of humans and animals were maintained at more or less sustainable levels. Life continued, but selectively. It was the survival of the fittest. Modern Gabra are of spare, taut physique. Among them double chins and rotund girths are rare. Survival was demanding; it called for the ability to cover vast distances at the bidding of weather's whim. Theirs was an affirmation of the human body as a miracle of adaptation, of coping with adverse conditions.

But Gabra survival was facilitated not only by physiological or genetic dexterity. Like many indigenous African peoples, they had developed an elaborate understanding of the universe, a well-developed cosmology. Seven was a critical number. As in the Western calendar, their week featured seven days. But the Gabra thought of time and events as moving in cyclical patterns, while Westerners tended to think of time and events as moving in linear trajectories. Thus, among the Gabra, years were understood as clusters of seven. The seven years of the cycle were named after the days of the week: "Monday" was the name of year one in the cycle, "Tuesday" the name of year two, and so on. After seven years, another "week" of years began.

As in the Hebrew tradition (Leviticus 25), the Gabra celebrated a "Jubilee": after seven cycles of years had passed, it was time for a year of rest, of justice, of the restoration of right relationships. Their Jubilee year coincided with 1981; 1980 was deemed a year of preparation. Since most of their social and economic relationships were centered on livestock, it followed that preparation for the Jubilee involved the judicious exchange of livestock, concluding long-standing but incomplete agreements, giving legal status to an earlier handshake deal. Generally it was a time of putting things in order. For the Jubilee was best celebrated when all was forgiven, when relationships were restored.

Why, one would reasonably ask, had such systems evolved? Some of the answers would seem to be fairly straightforward. It could be speculated, for example, that a seven-year cluster was more readily dealt with in a predominantly oral society than a cluster of one hundred years—a century—would have been. In some nomadic communities, each seven-year cluster coincided with a distinct age group: puberty rites were held every seven years; a new age group was launched, a new social cycle begun.

Although not predictably consistent, weather cycles could be observed more easily in the context of seven-year clusters. A single cycle would feature rains and droughts. But rarely would the weather patterns of a given cycle resemble precisely those of an earlier one. Important for the Gabra was the perspective offered by a seven-year period. Droughts were resolved by rain, eventually, somewhere, within the accepted grazing territory.

One anthropologist described this observance of the seven-year cycle as a coping device, as a survival mechanism. It represented a careful exercise of collective memory. Events remembered by a collectivity provided the womb from which were born the myths that nourished and sustained a people. In times of uncertainty and distress, such myths became a kind of living survival kit. Among the Gabra there was also active adherence to cycles of both longer and shorter duration than seven years. Aspects of ritual, social, and even climatic events followed their several disparate rhythms. Whether longer or shorter, much of the Gabra world of meaning was most easily described and understood in terms of cycles. Theirs was a survival made possible by astute attention to cyclic patterns amid unpredictable climatic dynamics.

In this context, it is not difficult to understand the utility of cyclic temporal patterns. Somewhat less clear is the appearance of a justice theme in the midst of these cycles. Whence the idea of the fiftieth year? Was it only an element of a logical numerical sequence? Was this evidence of some Hebrew cultural fallout blowing across the lower reaches of the great desert? Or could one speculate that a year of justice, a year of peace appearing amid the cycles of years, was as natural as a leap year in the Western calendar?

Do nature's cycles bespeak renewal? Justice? Peace? Rest? Could one credit these systems to "natural revelation"? If so, how does one account for the rather elaborate theological understanding of God and universe among the Gabra? Or is even that thought simply an extended probe into nature's carefully guarded secrets? The questions could be extended indefinitely.

What transpired when the Gabra world met the Western world in the form of the missionary, the development worker, or a civil servant of the modern independent Republic of Kenya? Contrasts were profound. While the Gabra were guided by a seven-year cycle, the "Westerner," including the Kenyan civil servant, functioned in the context of one-year cycles. Budgets, salaries, contracts, parliamentary debates, and even perceptions regarding the rains were informed by one-year cycles, by the fiscal year.

Rains in Kenya's "down country" areas were more reliable than the rains of Gabraland. And of course the rains of North America's prairie belt and those of western Europe boasted an uncanny record of predictability. It was from those areas, the so-called rich "north," that development aid and development ideals emanated. Indeed, the modernizing process had to a large extent been honed and shaped in that context. A one-year cycle of four seasons in the "north" usually yielded a harvest, balance sheets, and profits/losses indicating surpluses/deficits from which the next year was planned, from which the next ventures were plotted, and from which the next packet of development aid was allocated. Aspects of this process, notably the annual report, were integral to the development process.

In Gabraland a three- to four-year drought was normal. Any modernizing presence from elsewhere would need to take that factor into account. And the project leader—typically on a two- to three-year assignment—could well conclude that massive relief aid was required. The Gabra, meanwhile, were informed by the perspective that came from the practiced monitoring of seven-year cycles. Of course they would accept relief aid in drought years. But relief of this kind bred its own negatives. As dependency on easy food handouts increased, the age-old skills of coping with sustained drought were compromised. For the Gabra, the twentieth century was underway—but in stilted form.

As noted above, 1981 was a Jubilee year for the Gabra. It was a form of justice or order chiseled into shape by a harsh, unrelenting environment. Whether the Gabra would in future celebrate the Jubilee year remains a moot question. The fact that the tradition was still alive bespoke their relative isolation. More positively, it reflected the wisdom of the *wazee* (elders), who understood that without the communal purge provided by the year of justice they would be less well prepared to cope with their harsh homeland.

The odds are against the Gabra way of life. The country's pastoral peoples are expected to participate fully in national life—it had become government policy. It was a policy that did not easily accommodate the nomadic lifestyle. Schools, as an example, were for people who lived in settled communities. Until now, the country's agricultural policies had been better defined than had the policies related to rangeland or pastoral land improvement. The tendency, therefore, was to apply agricultural policies across the board, touching range areas—like Gabraland—in which agriculture was not viable and where a settled existence of any kind was possible only with the most careful husbandry of available resources.

There was a kind of haste characterizing the modernizing process. And there was also some measure of competition among churches and among development agencies, vying to lay hands on one of the last of Kenya's untouched territories. The ensuing changes had little in common with the "timeless" cycle of years. Modern development insisted that drought was abnormal, an aberration. Drought now demanded a response from the aid agency. It took on the form of political pressure: "Do something, now!" If this government or that voluntary agency did not respond, then the other one would. Drought had been transformed from a normal climatic happening into something akin to disaster.

Where was justice? If the Jubilee were to come again for the Gabra, it would likely be in emaciated form. There was no doubt that a sense of justice also informed initiatives of the aid agency, the government settlement policy. It was often said, "The Gabra must not be left behind; they must enjoy the fruits of independence." But to what extent is justice informed or mitigated by a fragile environment? Did the largesse and the pace of the modernizing development dynamic bespeak any form of Jubilee?

A modest beginning for the aid or the modernizing effort, if only to enlarge its own perspective, would require, as a minimum, a seven-year budget. It would require personnel committed to seven-year contracts. Any definitive project reports could be expected to materialize only after an initial seven-year presence. Lesser perspectives and lesser aid cycles tend toward disruption and disorder.

—Nairobi, 1981

A version of the above article was published in the December 12, 1980 issue of *Missionary Messenger* (Eastern Mennonite Board of Missions). Another version, entitled "Jubilee 1981 among the Gabbra," was published in the *African Ecclesial Review*, Vol. 23, No. 6, December 1981.

Addendum

My interest in the Gabra Jubilee was triggered by a missionary friend who was working at the time in Gabraland. During a routine morning devotional reading with his Gabra workers, the focus was on Leviticus 25, an elaborate description of the "Jubilee," the fifty-year biblical justice cycle. As workers sauntered off to their respective tasks after the devotional exercise, my missionary friend overheard them remonstrating with each other: "How did our story get into that book?" The question stimulated further inquiry, both by the missionary and by myself, and resulted in this essay.

More than thirty years later, there was encounter with several ethnographic studies of the Gabra, the Borana, and related groups clustered within the Kushite religious and cultural tradition of northern Kenya, southern Ethiopia, and the greater Horn of Africa. A careful reading of those studies soon made it clear that my 1981 reflection on the Gabra Jubilee constituted but a faint facsimile of an exceedingly complex religious and cultural tradition. It seems that the Kushite empire—to which the Gabra are heir—had flourished along the Nile Valley and into the Horn of Africa region more than three millennia earlier. In succeeding centuries, an elaborate Kushite cosmology was expressed within intricate religious and cultural norms. Parallels and cognates between the Kushitic and the biblical Hebrew traditions are alluded to in the modern ethnographic studies. Regrettably, my foray into the land of the Kushitic peoples as a staff member of the National Council of Churches of Kenya was lacking in adequate orientation, resulting in a deficient reflection on Jubilee 1981.

Sources

Bassi, Marco. 2005. Translated by Cynthia Salvadori. *Decisions in the Shade: Political and Judicial Processes among the Oromo Borana.* Trenton, New Jersey: Red Sea Press.

Fariji, Salim. 2012. *The Roots of Nubian Christianity Uncovered: The Triumph of the Last Pharaoh.* Trenton, New Jersey: Africa World Press. Includes reference to Kushitic culture.

Leus, Ton and Cynthia Salvadori. 2006. *Aadaa Boraanaa: A Dictionary of Borana Culture.* Addis Ababa, Ethiopia: Shama Books.

Tablino, Paul. 1999. *The Gabra: Camel Nomads of Northern Kenya.* Nairobi, Kenya: Paulines Publications Africa.

Vantini, Giovanni. 2009. *Rediscovering Christian Nubia.* Verona, Italy: Collegio delle Missioni Africane. Includes reference to Kushitic culture.

Wood, John C. 1999. *When Men Are Women: Manhood among Gabra Nomads of East Africa.* Madison: University of Wisconsin Press.

11
Jubilee for Africa's Debt Burden: The All Africa Conference of Churches in Reflection

Introduction

Virtually every day, the media comments on the debt burden that is strangling the aspirations of people on the African continent. Debt management has become a huge, complex consideration. With few exceptions, debt is accepted as a negative element in the African economic body politic. Because the World Bank and the International Monetary Fund are the prime sources for large loans at very low rates of interest, and because these institutions are strongly influenced and managed by Western powers, many Africans are convinced that the politics of debt have much to do with oppression and domination.

Calls for the alleviation of the debt burden have come from many quarters, including the ecumenical community and, latterly, the world of business. For, while it is understood that little economic progress can be achieved without borrowing money from sources external to a particular national economy, there is also the understanding that there must be some proportionality between the debt incurred and the ability of the respective economies, whether personal, national, or continental, to "service" such debt.

There is general agreement that Africa's debt burden has rendered the economies of the continent dysfunctional. In the case of Mozambique, for example, the government expends twice as much on servicing its debt as it does on the provision of basic services such as primary health care and education. Africa's debt burden cannot properly be "serviced" or sustained on the basis of the existing economic structures. In other words, the present situation has become untenable. New beginnings must be made. Bold strategies must be articulated. However, because of the complexity of Africa's debt burden, there is also the need for careful analysis, both for the effective deployment of a variety of alleviation strategies and for the purpose of forensic specificity. For the debt configurations in Africa's more than fifty national economies and in the regional entities (e.g., the East Africa Cooperation/Community, Intergovernmental Agency for Development, and Southern African Development Community) vary enormously.

Among the many protests on this subject has been the pioneer voice of the African Christian ecumenical community. With its theological base and its access to powerful biblical images and metaphors (e.g., the Jubilee), the ecumenical community is well placed to make a contribution to the current debate and to the calls for radical change. This essay recounts aspects of the ecumenical posture assumed among African churches in the past while reflecting as well on current sentiments as stated in forums such as the Seventh General Assembly of the All Africa Conference of Churches, held in October 1997 in Addis Ababa, Ethiopia. It calls for careful examination of the variety of debt-relief instruments, including a rather more expansive interpretation of the call for a debt Jubilee.

All Africa Conference of Churches Initiatives on Africa's Debt Burden

Tutu Statement on Debt

By far the most high-profile comment within the All Africa Conference of Churches (AACC) context on the debt burden in Africa was made by Archbishop Desmond Tutu in his capacity as the chair of the AACC during its Seventh General Assembly in October 1997. In his report to the assembly, Tutu expressed his own frustration with Africa's debt burden and proposed specific action that was subsequently and variously endorsed by plenary and subgroup discussions during the assembly. Herewith the relevant excerpt from his report:

I called long ago for the cancellation of the crippling debt we have had to bear for so long. The IMF and World Bank are using their crippling structural adjustment programs (SAPS). These are immoral, for they care nothing about the suffering of people. Jesus objected to such conduct. He said people were more important than even religious rules. He broke these to serve people. The Sabbath was made for us and not we for the Sabbath. Anything that imposes unnecessary suffering on those for whom Christ died, is wrong and immoral. SAPs do this and they must be condemned as wrong and immoral.

There are others who have joined their voices in this campaign. There is something called Jubilee 2000. We ask our friends to stand by us in this new moral crusade to have the debt cancelled following the biblical principle of Jubilee. Basically it says: "Everything belongs to God; all debts and mortgages must be cancelled in the Jubilee Year to give the debtors a chance to make a new beginning."

I suggested that there should be a six-month moratorium on debt repayments just to ensure that this cancellation would benefit the people, not some new elite.

The conditions should be:

a. True democratization—when it is clear that the people participate in decision making;
b. Respect for human rights;
c. Demilitarization;
d. Redirecting money thus saved for the benefit of the so-called ordinary people.

If these conditions are met, then debts should be cancelled.

In earlier pronouncements, Tutu had focused primarily on the issue of human rights as a conditionality for the cancellation of debts. In this subsequent challenge, he alluded to a "basket" of conditionalities on which basis consideration should be given to the possibility of such cancellation. In several of the assembly documents and mandates there was acknowledgment and endorsement of Tutu's call, though the complexity and specificity of the required action was not elaborated upon.

In the context of AACC deliberations on the African debt conundrum, Tutu's challenge no doubt constituted the most specific, focused challenge to date. A quick review of past ecumenical deliberations and initiatives are instructive, for they indicate the range of debate and the priority concerns related to the effect of debts and international monetary instruments.

Missionaries and Dependence

In his sweeping review of ecumenical institutions and initiatives in Africa, Efiong Utuk, a Nigerian theologian, noted the importance of the post–World War II period for purposes of ecumenical formation. Emerging African church structures birthed by the missionary endeavor were heavily subsidized by overseas "mother churches," while recognizing that much of local or rural church infrastructure was locally funded. Counterpart government infrastructure was heavily underwritten by the Bretton Woods institutions, namely, the World Bank and the International Monetary Fund. Utuk elaborated: "When the history of the Christian missionary enterprise in Africa during the twentieth century comes to be reviewed, it will be tempting to draw the conclusion that missionary funds and personnel from Europe and North America were indispensable. . . . This situation will be seen as a paradox, because much of the 'aid' received will not have helped to root the Gospel in the African cultural soil." In the 1970s this point was extensively discussed in the context of the so-called moratorium debate that called for the cessation or drastic reduction of overseas funding and personnel, thus providing a breathing space during which the self-identity of African churches could be developed. The quest for authenticity in African ecumenical life, according to Utuk, had been relentless.

Summit—All Africa Conference of Churches Commission on International Affairs

In 1986 the AACC's Commission on International Affairs convened a "summit" meeting for church leaders in Cairo, Egypt. Typical of ecumenical discussion in those days, there was much focus on South Africa's apartheid regime and the need to bring that evil system to an end. Apartheid was seen as an affront to human dignity and a gross violation of human rights. Resource persons to the summit spoke eloquently of the biblical basis for human dignity. Indeed, subsequent ecumenical discussions in Africa have rarely exceeded the heights of those insights and the related "laying claim" to God's provisions for the fullness of life. Throughout these discussions, the detrimental effects on human dignity in Africa inflicted by the debt burden were cited with great effect.

Human Rights—Debt Crisis

Later, in 1990, the AACC's Commission on International Affairs convened a major consultation in Lesotho to consider "The Debt Crisis as It Affects Human Rights." In Lesotho, the deliberation became specific. It dealt with questions related to the rule of law, the rights of the child, and the church as an actor in political affairs and a healer within the body politic. In its recommendations, the Lesotho convocation considered the ethics of lending and borrowing, citing the following criteria: (a) loans for development must accrue to the benefit of the people as a whole; (b) loans should be apolitical; (c) loans should not be tied to the purchase of capital goods or the deployment of personnel from the lending government/institution; (d) loans should not be used for military purchases; (e) negotiations on loans should be democratic, involving representatives of the general public; and (f) the administration of loans should be publicly monitored.

More recently, other recommendations urged the churches to become active in raising awareness within Africa and among their overseas partners on the intricacies and acceptable ethics related to loans, debts, and economic issues generally. Very relevant to this present deliberation, the Lesotho convocation recommended that the AACC together with the World Council of Churches call for a "Year of Jubilee," advocating a restructuring of the whole of the international monetary system as a basic requirement.

Economic Literacy

In 1997 the Women's Desk of the All Africa Conference of Churches published its *Economic Literacy Manual*, which was officially launched at the Seventh AACC General Assembly, thus fulfilling with one remarkable effort a number of recommendations that had been accumulating in successive ecumenical gatherings in Africa. The manual featured eleven modules covering a range of issues, including a broad examination of the configuration of African economics, structural adjustment programs, and the debt crisis, moving near the end of the manual toward creative, human-centered economic visions for Africa. While the manual was intended primarily for the use of economic literacy trainers, an accompanying video entitled "To Be a Woman" had been launched already in 1994, designed for educating and raising the awareness of a wide range of women and men within and outside the church. This combination of resources comprised a tour de force in the ecumenical effort toward basic economic literacy and remedial action.

The Specter of African Debt

The manifestations of debt in Africa are manifold, from classic public articulations to the more obscure and poignant. Herewith selected samples.

Item: Disempowered Governments

Many people in Africa have experienced the effects of debt in terms of the severe structural adjustment programs (SAPs) that have been prescribed in one country after another on the continent. Typically, the SAPs invoked several or all of the following elements: (1) an emphasis on export production, (2) higher interest rates, (3) removal of trade and export controls, (4) privatization of public resources, (5) currency devaluation, and (6) reduction of government spending (effectively curtailing expenditure on social services). "Governments [that are] . . . no longer able to respond to the basic needs of their people embark on ruthless repression to silence the people. In many places government workers are unpaid for many months, the universities are closed and workers laid off from jobs. Africans . . . [want] a system that [puts] food on their tables, medicine in the hospitals, and allows education to function and economies to grow" (Ngoy Mulunda-Nyanga).

Item: Repaying Debts for Genocide Tools

In 1994, people around the world watched aghast while tens of thousands of people were slaughtered in Rwanda with machetes, grenades, and small arms. The former Government of Rwanda had imported those lethal weapons en masse for the precise purpose of facilitating the genocide. This importation of tools for slaughter constituted the single largest importation during the previous twenty-year period in Rwanda. Ironically and tragically, the successor Government of Rwanda was saddled with the debts incurred by the importation of those lethal weapons. Tragedy follows tragedy: the survivors of colossal genocide and their children will be penalized by the repayment of this debt. Where in the long chain of misgovernance, immoral use of borrowed money, actual genocide, and now in the payment of the related debt might a Jubilee be launched and celebrated?

Item: Debt Repayment to Political Nonentities

Anglican bishop Dinis Sengulane of Mozambique noted that African states, including his own, were being required to pay for debts incurred with political entities that had long since ceased to exist. Independent Mozambique was paying for debts incurred with the former Soviet Union and the former German Democratic Republic, neither of which exists any longer. Perhaps more important, such loans were typically availed and such debts incurred for reasons of ideological solidarity rather than economic advancement. They were promoted and made available at a time when Africa was shamelessly tossed about as a pawn between Eastern and Western ideological power blocs. When "the wall came down," allowing the Western powers to claim victory, countries such as Mozambique were left holding an empty solidarity bag. From an African, or more particularly from a Mozambican, point of view, clearly no form of the Jubilee could be equated with the demise of the Berlin Wall.

Item: Debt and Conflict

While it was difficult to make the precise link between debt and conflict in Africa, there was a widespread sense that economic deprivation or economic constraints gave rise to armed conflict. In the absence of stable and growing economic sectors, opposition leaders and leaders of marginalized minorities in Africa were quick to "take to the bush," waging rebellion against existing authorities. Liberia was the conspicuous case: Charles Taylor took to the bush against the backdrop of his own massive financial irregularities. For purposes of accumulating power, African leaders preyed on the discontented, the unemployed, and the marginalized as a means of accumulating power. Indeed, in Africa stable economic systems had given way variously to political regimes that gained, held on to, or changed power by means of mobilizing the marginalized languishing outside the modern-sector economic order. Many people on this continent would resonate with the passage in I Samuel 22:2: "People who were oppressed or in debt or dissatisfied went to him [David, the rebel leader against King Saul], about four thousand men in all and he became their leader."

Item: Per Capita Debt—Tanzania

On Sunday March 15, 1998, President Benjamin Mkapa of Tanzania made a scholarly thirty-minute presentation on the nation's external debt. The facts, as he recounted them, were stark. Tanzania's external debt stood at US$7.9 billion. If this national debt had been distributed equally among the population, every Tanzanian citizen would have been indebted to the sum of $250. Or, in more graphic terms, if the country had deployed its entire export earnings without importing a single aspirin or a liter of petrol, it would have required ten years to repay the outstanding national debt.

Who was to blame for getting Tanzania into this impossible situation? According to the newspaper article reporting on the speech, many badly conceived and poorly administered development projects were to blame. Former President Nyerere always insisted that such projects benefited donors more than recipients. But what was to be done? Resignedly, the article concluded: "More needs to be done to reduce Tanzania's indebtedness, not necessarily by repaying cash, but by using more dynamic and imaginative and feasible remedies" (*East African*, March 23–29, 1998).

Quite apart from the heartrending effects of debt in Africa, it was also understood that Africa's debt configuration had become exceedingly complex. Much of the literature on the subject was presented in generic terms, citing (in incomprehensibly huge figures) the total continental debt load and the debt-servicing ratio, again on the basis of generic continental figures. While those general statistics may have been helpful to expert debt managers, they obscured, in fact, the great diversity that existed. Some African nations were poorer than others; some had refused to become enmeshed in accepting major international loans (e.g., Eritrea), while others (e.g., Kenya) had accumulated internal or domestic debts that inflicted greater sacrifices from ordinary citizens than did the loans accepted from global institutions such as the World Bank. African debt could not easily be identified as a single unitary debt. It was better understood as a "basket" of debts: some of them were official (World Bank, IMF), some multilateral (European Community, Lomé Convention), some bilateral (between two consenting countries), some commercial, and some had been incurred internally by governments of the day (e.g., Kenya).

Moreover, debt statistics were lodged largely in the hands of the industrialized world where they had been generated in the first place, publicized and managed with powerful (some would say neocolonial) effect. A former senior bank official who must remain anonymous cited the extreme reluctance of African governments to release and publicize statistics related to debt. Imbalances between debtor and creditor nations were constituted by more than mere figures. For years Africa was heavily reliant on the external world for functional information on the full dimensions of its debt.

In 1990, Amos Wako, Kenya's attorney general, cited debt statistics gleaned from public sources: In 1985 Africa had a debt burden of US$100 billion. At the time, Sudan and Ghana had a debt service ratio of 155 percent and 40 percent, respectively. By 1990 Africa's debt was projected to reach $230 billion; the same presenter predicted that by 1995 the debt would have reached $605 billion. Debt servicing was projected to reach 167 percent of the gross national product, and by the turn of the century it was anticipated that the cost of servicing Africa's debt would be 293 percent of the continental gross national product. If statistics of this kind are to be meaningful, they must be rendered manageable and approachable if any form of Jubilee is to be realized.

Revisiting the Jubilee Injunction

In its most popular form, the term "Jubilee" is usually associated with fifty-year anniversary celebrations—a jubilee wedding anniversary refers to a fiftieth wedding anniversary. The present convocation is preoccupied with one aspect of the biblical Jubilee, namely, the cancellation of debts. However, a careful reading of the relevant biblical text indicates that there were at least four components of the prescribed fiftieth-year Hebrew celebrations (an elaboration of the understanding of the Sabbath): (1) leaving the ground fallow, (2) the remission of debts, (3) the liberation of slaves, and (4) the return of respective family property to relevant individuals.

According to the most vigorous scholarship, "the entire body of jubilee prescriptions, including the element of land redistribution, was never practiced on a regular basis, yet [the Jubilee as metaphor] nonetheless remained alive in the collective mind and culture of Jews." There is evidence that food shortages were experienced on a six-year cycle, lending some evidence to the likelihood that the prescribed practice of fallow farming had indeed been practiced. Thus, if the validity of the Jubilee was based on the actual precedent of Jewish practice or if today it was invoked merely as a legalistic device for the accomplishment of justice, its appeal and significance would be missed. On this point, John Howard Yoder (*The Politics of Jesus*, 1994) quoted Donald Blosser (*Jesus and the Jubilee*, 1979):

> The Jubilee is not simply a theological concept providing insight into the nature of God, it is a guide for living which is to be observed in normal daily practice among believers. . . . These Jubilee acts are not simply to be expected in the future, they are

> to be given concrete expression among the people of God in the present . . . what had been expected in the future can now be experienced in the present because we are now living in the new age . . . characterized by Jubilee activity among the believers.

The essential premise of Yoder's thesis in his widely recognized study was that the "Year of the Lord," Isaiah's rendering of the Leviticus Jubilee, was permanently inaugurated (invoked) with Jesus' reading and pronouncement in the Nazareth synagogue (Luke 4:16–18). Thus are believers in the Judeo-Christian tradition invited to give witness to the ethical demands of the Jubilee in a world that has become increasingly interdependent and increasingly complex. "When one member suffers, all suffer" is no longer a pious adage; it has become as compelling and current as the daily CNN broadcast.

As with many fundamental ethical principles, the practice of a cyclic invocation of justice was not confined exclusively to the Judeo-Christian story. Echoes of this ethic are found among practitioners of African Religion. From the Gabra people of northern Kenya comes the account of a fifty-year justice cycle. While there was some debate about the precise prescriptions being followed, evidence seemed to suggest that certain of the Jubilee requirements were indeed practiced, the most recent version of such a cycle having been celebrated in the early 1980s.

Toward an African Debt Jubilee

Selecting Debt-Relief Tools

Just as there are many kinds of debts, so there exists a bewildering "basket" of tools designed to mitigate debt. In the case of official debt, there are the tools designed by the consortia of creditors. The relatively informal group known as the Paris Club developed elaborate tools that facilitated the turning over, consolidating, or rescheduling (among other options) of existing debt, usually for purposes of rendering a debtor nation eligible to receive another tranche of aid which could then be applied toward interest payment on previously incurred debts! Another instrument designed jointly by the IMF, the World Bank, and the Paris Club was known as the Highly Indebted Poor Countries Initiative. Uganda, as a favored student of official debt managers, was the first country in Africa to benefit from the deployment of this instrument; debt to the tune of US$385 million was scheduled to be cancelled.

In addition to the official instruments of so-called debt relief, there were on offer market-controlled debt-relief instruments. These included debt-conversion funds that involved the use of discounted debt to buy shares on local stock exchanges, or asset swaps in which creditors would sell their privately held debt for approximately 75 percent of the face value, then resell the local currencies for dollars. There were market instruments known as debt buybacks and mezzanine debt instruments, among others, involving exceedingly complex management regimes. By any measure, debt management, including debt relief by means of existing instruments, placed on offer extraordinarily complex options.

Selecting Jubilee Instruments

Inasmuch as we deliberate as a Christian community, let us as a first order of commitment embrace the biblical Jubilee as a foundational ethic by which the faith community lives. By definition, such a commitment would take the form of a continuous relational process among all members of the committed ecumenical community. In this case, Jubilee 2000 could serve as an important symbol of the commitment, but would not by itself constitute the essence of the Jubilee ethic. For Jubilee is an ethic for life, not merely an event to be celebrated symbolically every fifty years.

Taking into account some of the peculiar debt patterns in Africa, giving consideration to the variety of debt and the variety of debt alleviation instruments, there were obviously some genuine problems with cancellation as a solution for existing debts. The most straightforward problem had to do with specificity. Which debt was to be cancelled? If there was to be cancellation for an official debt incurred thirty years ago, what was the educational or remedial value for those involved in administering the governments in Africa today? Did not the cancellation option become a matter of "easy come, easy go," thus making a mockery of what should otherwise be considered serious economic and political process? Which economic instruments would best be deployed to move into the vacuum left by the politics of debt and debt repayment? Does the debt cancellation process promise any insights or participatory education on the manner in which good loans must be acquired, serviced, and monitored by well-informed, democratically appointed watchdog agencies? In short, the successful and celebrated cancellation of debt, however selected, might have offered a necessary but certainly not a sufficient exercise for the reconstruction of Africa.

Public Information on Debt

For many reasons, expertise on the debt phenomenon was dominated by northern industrialized countries. Debtor countries were delighted to have their debts forgotten by creditor nations or creditor agencies. In some African countries, no payments on debts were made until the creditor nation or agency came around to collect! (Kenya's Central Bank only recently instituted a debt-monitoring department. Previously, the bank waited for the creditor to tinkle the deadline or due-date bells!) It may well be that debts in Africa were incurred too easily and shrouded in too much secrecy or too much "expertise." Should not loans entered into by a state be publicly debated and publicly implemented? Do African parliaments have sufficient voice or expertise in this regard? Indeed, why should the acquisition of official loans not be dependent upon referenda, seeking approval from the respective publics, both in the creditor and the debtor nations? Obviously, mechanisms governing those kinds of issues require high levels of expertise. And they require high levels of collaboration between informed publics in both creditor and debtor nations.

Ecumenical Mobilization of Debt Relief

If it is accepted that Jubilee is an ongoing process and if it is generally accepted that money is necessary to the economic advancement of peoples, then it becomes abundantly clear that concerned communities in the north and south, in debtor nations and creditor nations, will need to develop and mobilize much more sophisticated tools of analysis, access, and mutually beneficial action. Let it be agreed that a symbolic cancellation of specifically identified African debt may be both necessary and helpful as a global symbolic event in the year 2000. But let it also be agreed that such an event would not be sufficient to resolve Africa's debt burden. An embrace of the Jubilee would call for commitments to new relationships between the creditor north and the debtor south, between the ecumenical north and the ecumenical south. It would call for new forms of governance in Africa in which monies acquired and monies expended would benefit all people in a public, participatory manner. The Jubilee-informed life together is vastly more demanding than is a single Jubilee event.

—(written for/with) Ngoy Mulunda-Nyanga
Secretary to the All Africa Conference of Churches
(International Affairs Desk)
Nairobi, Kenya
March 1998

Sources

Blosser, Donald. 1979. *Jesus and the Jubilee: The Year of the Jubilee and Its Significance in the Gospel of Luke.* (PhD dissertation.) University of St. Andrews.

Brown, Gordon. February 21, 1998. "Debt and Development: Time to Act, Again." *The Economist.*

"Hard Choices for Nyachae." March 13, 1998. *The Weekly Review.*

Karaimu, Benedict. March 12, 1998. "Solution to Debt Problems." *The Star.* Nairobi, Kenya.

Mutumba-Lule, A. March 9–15, 1998. "After IMF Review, Uganda Still on Course for Debt Relief." *East African.* Nairobi, Kenya.

Rweyemamu, Robert. March 23–29, 1998. "Tanzania's Huge Debts: Who? Why? How?" *East African,* Nairobi, Kenya.

Utuk, Efiong. 1997. *Visions of Authenticity: The Assemblies of the All Africa Conference of Churches 1963–1992.* Nairobi, Kenya: All Africa Conference of Churches.

Wako, Amos. September 8–13, 1986. "African Charter on Human and Peoples' Rights." Cairo, Egypt: Commission on International Affairs of the All Africa Conference of Churches. (Report.)

Wako, Amos. September 26–30, 1990. "Debt Crisis and Human Rights." Maseru, Lesotho: Commission on International Affairs of the All Africa Conference of Churches.

Yoder, John Howard. 1994 (second edition). *The Politics of Jesus.* Grand Rapids, Michigan: Wm. B. Eerdmans Publishing Co.

12
The Horn of Africa Project: Modeling Alternative Conflict Resolution

Purpose

This essay reflects on an experience in conflict resolution. As the title indicates, the focus of the action was the Horn of Africa. The purpose of the venture was rather grandiosely projected as "Peace for the Horn of Africa." In more sedate language, the project was intended to test the ability of the voluntary agency community to undertake longer-term peace initiatives as opposed to the more conventional focus on the logistics and urgencies of relief aid. For purposes of this experiment in conflict resolution, the immediate setting was provided by the family of Mennonite institutions and by the dynamic of the Mennonite international service tradition. This essay follows the initiative from its inception through the formative period and into a description of the major activities. Within the Mennonite community, the experience established precedents. Beyond the community, a range of relationships with voluntary coalitions and independent actors was formed. Writ large was the project's eclectic pattern, with the possibility of replicability being left entirely open.

In 1984–85, African famine was broadcast to the world. Around the globe, images of hunger and starvation filled television screens. In equally unprecedented fashion, responses to the tragedy were mobilized. The world remembers Live Aid, the globally televised benefit concert, and Band Aid, one of the more illustrious relief efforts mobilized in response to the Ethiopian drought. There were many other responses to the tragedy, coalescing within the Western world into a vastly expanded awareness of the African continent. Would a more timely response have inflicted a lesser assault on African sensibilities? Debate took various directions.

For centuries Ethiopia had been recognized by Africans on the continent and peoples in the diaspora of African descent as a lone outpost of independent black African rule (Liberia also had a long history of independence, but was viewed usually as an ex-slave settler country, whose establishment had been initiated from North America) and thus as a unifying symbol for the whole of the continent. Although occupied for a short time by Italians, Ethiopia was never colonized by metropole powers, as was the remainder of the African continent. During his thirty-year reign, Emperor Haile Selassie—the last of Ethiopia's emperors—played exceptional roles in world forums, projecting the image of a world-class statesperson and an African nationalist. With his overthrow in 1974, Ethiopia's mystique faded quickly to reveal deeply rooted cleavages, informed on the one hand by the imperial tradition of the emperors and resisted on the other by increasingly self-aware dissident groups.

During the formative period of the Horn of Africa Project (HAP), the political situation within Ethiopia was characterized essentially by stalemate. The Government of Ethiopia insisted—as had the emperor—on territorial integrity as a sine qua non in any negotiations, while groups such as the Eritrean People's Liberation Front insisted on their right to self-determination. Conflict in the north of Ethiopia generated refugees who fled to neighboring Sudan. Sudan, meanwhile, had become a conduit for both civilian and military aid to antagonists in disputed areas. The Ethiopian government was providing bases in the southwest of the country from which the Sudanese People's Liberation Army was launching military forays against the Khartoum government. Likewise, Sudanese refugees fled for asylum into southern Ethiopia. This configuration was reinforced by strong support from the Soviet Union for the Ethiopian government, while the United States provided support for the border states of Somalia, Kenya, and Sudan. Thus, in addition to the interlocking complexities of national and regional politics, the bipolar East–West dynamic served to position the region in a global context. Perestroika was still in its infancy.

Although the conflict issues within Ethiopia had meanwhile remained essentially unresolved, significant shifts were nevertheless in evidence. In March 1988, the Eritrean People's Liberation Front dealt a decisive blow to the Ethiopian military in the Eritrean town of Afabet. According to the front's claims, three divisions from the Ethiopian forces, totaling between 18,000 and 20,000 men, along with their equipment, were annihilated. Several thousand government troops were captured, while the Eritreans seized some fifty tanks and sixty rocket launchers. During the same month, the Tigray People's Liberation Front announced the capture of several towns in the province of Tigray, killing or wounding thousands of Ethiopian soldiers and capturing unprecedented quantities of war materiel. With additional subsequent military action, the front gained virtually complete control of the province. The military stalemate between the dissidents and the Ethiopian government was rendered essentially complete.

In neighboring Sudan, a similar military stalemate between the Khartoum government and the Sudan People's Liberation Army was in effect. Here vigorous interparty debate within the Khartoum government and protracted but promising negotiations between Khartoum and the Sudan People's Liberation Army portended for a while the possibility of a negotiated settlement. The whole of that tortuous process was overtaken by a military coup on June 30, 1989. Initially, the political colors of the coup makers had not been fully declared, but there were indications that the fundamental grievances of southerners were not being addressed in any creative fashion. Indeed, there were signs of a reversion to confrontational postures. And while Somalia had achieved a peace of sorts with Ethiopia, severe strains within the country—conditions approaching civil war—promised to keep internal tranquility at bay into a troubled future.

All of these dynamics coincided with big power shifts in the region, and in particular with the Soviet Union's growing articulation of perestroika. That policy seemed to favor movement toward negotiated settlement of the conflicts and, if events in Namibia provided precedent, some eventual diplomatic role for the United Nations. In the longer term, Soviet policy was expected to become notably less strident as a big power actor in its relationships with countries of the region. Under President Bush, United

States foreign policy had pronounced itself ready to respond to any initiatives that might be initiated by the Soviets, an ambiguity not entirely negative in its portent, but not promising either.

A comment on the nongovernmental organization (NGO) scene is in order. In the period after 1984, when proposals for HAP had been discussed initially, the focus of the NGO community had shifted dramatically. In Somalia NGOs were relatively few in number and had assumed very low public profiles. In Ethiopia, where NGOs had been accorded extremely high visibility during the famine relief period, the government imposed stringent regulations regarding their presence and function, bringing them closer to the country's declared development goals. And in Sudan, much of the NGO energy had been expended on cross-border relief efforts—again relatively high profile—in attempts to meet the needs of the war-ravaged south of the country. Relevant to the longer-term prospects for peace in the Horn of Africa was the birth and activity of NGO coalitions in Europe and the United States. Similar to the purposes of HAP, theirs were commitments, generally, to so-called second-track diplomacy, with all the attendant concerns. From mid-1988 to mid-1989 coordination among the coalitions had been strengthened.

A Mennonite presence in Ethiopia long predated the famine. Having functioned in both "development mode" and the traditional mission, church-planting mode, that presence continued in modified form. The Mennonite Central Committee's Africa Department mobilized very substantial quantities of relief aid during the drought period amid assurances all around that distribution of such assistance had been reasonably equitable and remarkably well coordinated. But within the NGO community generally, and within the Mennonite Central Committee particularly, some disquieting questions were begging for consideration: Had drought been the sole cause of the famine? Did continuing armed conflict between the government in Addis Ababa and the dissident movements within the country bode ill for longer-term food security and political stability? Could such longer-term questions be addressed in any way by the NGO community?

Together with staff members of the Institute of Peace and Conflict

Studies, Mennonite Central Committee urged that greater attention and effort be directed to the larger objective of peace for Ethiopia. There was of course awareness that no single undertaking could bring the desired peace. But it was considered, nonetheless, that preliminary initiatives could be undertaken and that a beginning needed to be made. A graduate student was employed to assemble an initial survey report on Ethiopia, identifying relevant historical factors, outlining the then current sociopolitical conditions, and offering suggestions for an NGO action agenda.

The ensuing report offered a variety of action proposals to be considered by Mennonite Central Committee. According to the introduction, the report was intended to (1) present a synopsis of the conflict in Ethiopia, (2) discuss the need for reconciliation, (3) discuss possible options for North American Mennonites in reconciliation and conflict resolution, and (4) provide a resource list of persons with expertise relevant to the situation in the Horn of Africa. Together, all of these factors and dynamics constituted the arena of action and concern for HAP.

Administrative Structure: Eclectic and Flexible

HAP was hosted by the Institute of Peace and Conflict Studies, an institute established by and ensconced within Conrad Grebel College. The college in turn was sponsored by the Mennonite Conference of Eastern Canada and affiliated for academic purposes with the University of Waterloo. In addition to hosting HAP, the Institute of Peace and Conflict Studies provided the physical and institutional space for Project Ploughshares and the related Service Education Program. The former was devoted to the study of the political and economic consequences of militarism, while the latter was a combined effort by Canadian Mennonite colleges and Mennonite Central Committee to articulate an understanding of Christian service—encouraging students to consider service vocations at home and abroad.

HAP itself was a minimalist operation. Physically it occupied a two-meter-by-five-meter space within the Project Ploughshares office complex, and it functioned with only one full-time staff person. A second person, seconded from Mennonite Central Committee, was part time. An advisory committee—comprised of the director of the Institute of Peace and Conflict Studies, the coordinator of Project Ploughshares, and two people from the local Mennonite Church community—served as a sounding board for the activities of HAP. The project rendered its accountability to Conrad Grebel College by sharing significant documentation and by the presence of the institute director on various administrative committees of the college.

HAP's fundraising experience reflected the diverse character of the project and its several relationships. Initial core funding was provided by Mennonite Central Committee, but it was intended to cover only the first two years of the life of the project. Thus the search for funds from other sources soon became integral to HAP's ongoing agenda. In May 1987, HAP submitted a major funding proposal to Partnership Africa Canada, making application, essentially, for access to Canadian government funds. Partnership Africa Canada had been established under the legal auspices of the Canadian Council for International Cooperation (an NGO umbrella organization) as a way of managing development funds that had become available through Africa 2000, a government program launched by the Minister for External Affairs. As a coalition of Canadian nongovernmental organizations, Partnership Africa Canada was intended to have access to half of Africa 2000 funds, operating autonomously with its own general assembly, board of directors, and program committee.

The initial application to Partnership Africa Canada was rejected. It was rejected on the grounds that HAP did not qualify as a bona fide NGO, that HAP appeared to be a university-based research project, that it apparently lacked close links with other NGO efforts of a similar nature, and that its proposed budget was too high. A revised application responding specifically to the partnership's initial queries elicited a second response. This time HAP was informed that its application was approved, but "constraints external to the PAC process do not allow PAC to fund the project. At the last PAC Board meeting CIDA representatives informed the members of a CIDA policy of which PAC was not aware. This policy stated that projects dealing with militarism/peace issues will not be accepted for funding by CIDA."

In response to the second rejection, HAP sought the assistance of Canadian Council for International Cooperation staff, appealed the rejection, and expressed its astonishment regarding the Canadian International Development Agency's (unpublicized) powers to overrule Partnership Africa Canada decisions. HAP's disappointment was particularly acute in view of the partnership's prior encouragement and guidance in the preparation of HAP's revised application. Meanwhile, a strange ambivalence prevailed: The Partnership Africa Canada Board's approval of HAP's was "on the books" at the same time that the Canadian International Development Agency's refusal was in effect.

Having failed in its pursuit of substantial government funds, HAP was obliged to seek alternative donors. For those purposes, a distinction was made between core funding and event funding. Initial core funding from MCC was in place. But given HAP's intent to support consultations among diverse people from the Horn of Africa, additional event funds would need to be found. In anticipation of its November 1988 consultation, HAP directed an appeal to more than fifty Canadian NGOs. Contributions from ten Canadian organizations were eventually received, covering most of the projected costs of the November event.

Accountability for both core and event funding was undertaken in quite deliberate fashion. Because of the nature of the consultations, donors were fully advised on details of the meeting, but were not expected to attend the consultations. However, for purposes of accountability they were subsequently sent copies of the proceedings and invited to convenient locations for detailed briefing on the November event. Within the HAP advisory committee, this pattern of detailed briefing with the several donors was itself considered integral to the networking character of the project process.

Liaison and accountability relationships with Mennonite Central Committee had taken the form of periodic face-to-face debriefings. In general, Mennonite Central Committee policy called for the support of short-term catalytic action. In the case of HAP, the organization's core funding was extended beyond the launching period but was not intended to continue indefinitely. It considered that HAP was in any case a relatively short-term venture. On the other hand, if the issues which engaged HAP proved sufficiently compelling and if HAP's performance proved sufficiently convincing, Mennonite Central Committee assumed that both core funds and event funds for the longer term would become available from a variety of donor organizations.

In retrospect, the merits of this approach became clearer. HAP was not exclusively academic in its character, nor was it wholly an NGO venture; as a project it incorporated aspects of both and maintained links with both. For the donor community this proved problematic. Clearer project designations would possibly have attracted more ready funding. Like other projects of ambivalent category, HAP was easily attracted by the security that lump-sum grant funding offered. On the other hand, it was recognized that a lean hand-to-mouth existence served to discipline both the direction and the content of the project. Necessity had to some degree become a virtue.

Project Process: Consultative and Open-ended

From its inception, HAP was intent on the goal of contributing to reconciliation or peace in the Horn of Africa. The means and activities through which such a goal could be realized were open to experimentation. In the Conrad Grebel College calendar of 1989–90, HAP was described as a study project, examining North American perceptions of conflict in the Horn of Africa. And, indeed, one of the very first HAP activities was focused on a survey of five major print media bodies and their reporting on conflict in the Horn of Africa. The findings of that research survey provided the initial database upon which people from the Horn of Africa were invited to reflect. Present at a consultation for that purpose were academics, students, administrators, and publishers who resided in various parts of North America but who came originally from some part of the area designated as the Horn of Africa. (For purposes of the Horn of Africa Project, the Horn of Africa comprised Ethiopia, Sudan, Somalia, and Djibouti. A United Nations–initiated agency known as the Intergovernmental Agency for Drought and Development included, additionally, the countries of Kenya and Uganda. This six-country grouping acted as the only officially constituted African entity that conformed in general terms to what was accepted within HAP as the Horn of Africa region.) The "edited proceedings" of the November 21–23, 1986, meeting appeared in the form of a published document entitled *Consultation on the Horn of Africa* (dated January 1988). Additional documentation produced by that original consultation, and supplemented by subsequent consultative vetting and editing, was entitled *War and Famine: Indigenous Perspectives on Conflict in the Horn of Africa*. It was dated March 1988 and designated as a public education document.

A second consultation was convened in April 22–24, 1988. Its purpose was to explore avenues toward peaceful resolution of conflict and to identify some of the obstacles encountered en route. Among the issues considered during the consultation were the nature and validity of the contributions to be expected from voluntary associations operating in Africa, opportunities and problems inherent in external initiatives toward conflict resolution, and the relevance of traditional (African) approaches to conflict resolution. As in the case of the previous consultation, transcripts of the proceedings were submitted to participants for editing. The proceedings were subsequently published in April 1989 under the title *A Review of Conflict Resolution Agenda in the Horn of Africa*.

In November 25–26, 1988, HAP organized a third consultation—"Conflict Resolution in the Horn of Africa: Envisioning Alternative Futures." In addition to repeat invitations to participants who had attended previous consultations, special invitations were sent to persons living in Africa. The intent was to enliven the discussion with comment and insight informed by the realism of conditions as they prevailed within the Horn of Africa. Happily, an academic from the University of Addis Ababa, Ethiopia, consented to present a paper and to participate in the discussions. Although not officially delegated by the Ethiopian government, it was understood that he came with the full knowledge of the government and that his paper reflected then current policy formulations. From Kenya came a person who had participated in a local (Nairobi) peace group committed to the exploration of peaceful resolution of conflict in the region and to continued networking with groups of like mind both within and outside of Africa.

In December of 1988 there was opportunity for a HAP staff person to travel to Europe to become acquainted with the newly formed Working Group on the Horn of Africa. Bringing together representatives from nearly a dozen western European NGOs from as many countries, the declared purpose of the working group focused on lobbying influential politicians on matters related to the Horn of Africa. Functioning under the broad umbrella of the working group, but sponsored directly by the Life and Peace Institute in Uppsala, Sweden, was a "sister" Horn of Africa Project that monitored events in the region and published a periodic information bulletin. Without specifying follow-up details, it was agreed during this visit with the various people concerned that every opportunity for exchange of information and networking should be seized.

During a period of particularly intense reflection and planning for the future of HAP, it was decided that a visit to Africa would be in order. Thus in February 1989 a trip to Africa and Europe, involving two HAP staff, was planned. Included was Kenya, where time was devoted to interaction with the fledgling Nairobi Peace Group; Ethiopia, where hosting was expertly done by an academic friend who arranged for exposure to decision makers within the Ethiopian government; Sudan, where there were exploratory conversations with the newly constituted Institute for the Study of the Horn of Africa; and London, where—at the initiative of HAP—a one-day networking meeting was attended by representatives from the European Working Group on the Horn, the Washington-based Coalition for Peace in the Horn, the Canadian Council for International Cooperation, and the Sweden-based Horn of Africa Project, in addition to interested individuals with experience in or connections to the Horn of Africa region. Special effort had been made to invite two participants from Africa to join the one-day meeting, one from the Nairobi Peace Group and one from Sudan representing the churches and the newly formed Institute for the Study of the Horn of Africa. No "action plan" was drawn up at the meeting, but the links established on this occasion were variously pursued.

In June 1989 representatives from HAP and the Horn of Africa project in Sweden met in Washington, DC, for a one-day planning session. With the full endorsement of the respective advisory committees, these two institution-based projects considered the possibility of convening a joint consultation on the tentatively identified theme "Search for Peace in the Horn of Africa: NGOs in Supportive Process."

Product: Publications, Networking, and Serendipity

The most obvious product of HAP activity took the form of the documentation already noted. More intangible but also more moving was the comment from a participant in one of the consultations: "Under normal circumstances we would be shooting each other. Here we are eating, talking, and laughing together." HAP provided a sustained forum around which representatives of the most diverse opinions gathered for discussion, debate, and trust-building exercises. The mysteries of networking were in evidence. Because of connections fostered through HAP consultations and related activities, events took place and connections were made that otherwise would not have been made. The following were among the specific contributions effected by HAP:

- As a direct consequence of HAP's networking links with East Africa, one of the faithful consultation participants, Dr. Hizkias Assefa, was serving as resource person to several conflict-resolution seminars in East Africa (August 1989). Already in early 1988, Assefa's book *Mediation of Civil Wars: Approaches and Strategies—The Sudan Conflict* (Westview, 1986) was widely distributed in East Africa by HAP, providing access to the memory of that 1972 mediation event and also providing an introduction of the author to networking partners in East Africa.
- The visit of HAP staff to Ethiopia provided opportunity to "express a concern" to well-placed officials of the Ethiopian government.
- There was opportunity to meet the general secretary of the Eritrean Peoples' Liberation Front; an opportunity again to express concerns and to be instructed in the ways that HAP could be most helpful.

- HAP had the opportunity to host visitors from the Horn of Africa region, including representatives from the Ethiopian Orthodox Church, a professor—long outspoken on conflict issues—from the University of Khartoum, and a delegation from the Sudan Council of Churches.
- In a variety of conferences and academic institutions, there was opportunity for HAP staff to highlight both the conflict issues from the Horn of Africa region and to reflect and report on initiatives taken by HAP to address those conflicts.
- Repeated coverage on HAP activity in local and regional media introduced the public to the intricacies of conflict issues in the Horn of Africa. HAP provided in-depth information and interaction with issues in the Horn of Africa that the Mennonite Central Committee in the context of its normal program would not have had the facility to pursue.
- For Conrad Grebel College and the University of Waterloo's Peace and Conflict Studies Program, HAP provided a window onto active conflict situations. Documentation produced by HAP circulated in the Horn of Africa and within the exile and expatriate Horn of Africa community in North America, thus providing access to opinions and discussions from this deeply divided community.
- HAP initiated and facilitated a one-day "get-acquainted' meeting in London, UK, bringing together for the first time the European Working Group on the Horn, the Washington-based Coalition for Peace in the Horn, the Canadian Council for International Cooperation, representatives from a number of mission/service agencies, representatives from partner agencies in Africa, and a variety of interested individuals.
- Together with Life and Peace Institute's Horn of Africa Project in Uppsala, Sweden, HAP took initiative to convene a jointly sponsored consultation in Europe. This effort was seen both as a continuation of the consultation series conducted by HAP and as a way of collaborating more intently with a counterpart project.

HAP as Conflict Resolution Model: A Peace Tradition and Beyond

As a model, HAP could be viewed in two ways: (1) as heir to Mennonite and Quaker peace traditions, as well as an example of increasing diversity and creativity within the larger NGO community; and (2) as a specialty project, eclectic in its institutional and relational arrangements. There was little evidence from HAP files of focused reflection either by the staff or by the host institutions regarding the ideological or theoretical bases for initiatives taken. Rather, there was the sense that the project was infused—consciously and unconsciously—by the accumulated corpus of Mennonite peace theory and praxis.

The Mennonite Church was widely acknowledged as one of the historic peace churches, both by the religious community and by the respective North American governments. Within Mennonite theological circles much had been written on the Mennonite peace position, and from the annals of Mennonite Central Committee activity, beginning in 1920, there had been repeated examples of Mennonite peace initiatives. Praxis and theory had been woven together within the Mennonite community into an awareness of the peace option. Armed conflict was not countenanced as a means of settling either communal or national disputes. Indeed, much of the early Mennonite peace effort had addressed issues related to conscientious objection to war. Only in more recent decades had the "peace testimony"—as frequently referred to—coalesced into specific peace or conflict-resolution skills and initiatives.

Within the Mennonite Central Committee's institutional framework, trained staff were offering mediation skills under the rubric of Mennonite Conciliation Service. This service had meanwhile addressed a wide range of issues both within and outside the Mennonite community: from traditional "fence-row" disputes to marital problems; from legal disputes to disputes in Nicaragua between the Miskito Indians and the national government. The latter experience approximated the nature of the issues addressed by HAP; issues of international relevance, appealing to specific conciliation skills.

If Mennonites had nurtured their own peace tradition, they had long been profoundly aware of and influenced by the conciliation work of the Quakers. Like Mennonites, Quakers were usually included in the cluster recognized as the historic peace churches. British Quakers in particular had long demonstrated strong initiative in what is now identified as "second-track diplomacy." Their efforts had been associated with the negotiations between East and West Germany during the building of the Berlin Wall, the mediation of the India–Pakistan wars, the negotiations leading to the establishment of Zimbabwe as a modern nation, and many other conflict or transition situations. Quakers initiated the establishment of the School of Peace Studies at Bradford University, located in the British midlands.

A literature search on second-track or alternative diplomacy leads almost invariably to the Quaker experience in international conciliation. Within the peace church community and within the larger community of nongovernmental organizations, there is no doubt that the Quakers have played pioneering and exemplary roles. But their ideological claims and their success claims were consistently modest. Any such initiative, they say, starts not with a grand design, but with a "concern," and proceeds on the assumption that "there is that of God" in all people, to which a reasoned appeal for peace can be addressed. Thanks to their extraordinary vision and singled-minded tenacity, for years they occupied the field of conflict resolution virtually by themselves. But there were reasons to believe that changes were underway.

Beyond the worlds of Quaker and Mennonite initiatives, the NGO community had meanwhile proliferated on both formal and informal levels, vastly enlarging the arena for potential debate and action on conflict issues. In 1907, there were by one count approximately two hundred international NGOs. Today the figure has been pegged, by one estimate, at eighteen thousand. With the advent of each new disaster (such as war or famine), additional NGOs are birthed, and they move, according to accepted NGO theory, through several recognizable phases: (1) relief work, (2) development activity, and (3) networking. This sequence is recognized as a shift from single-issue NGO activity toward open-ended interaction with a wide range of issues, including, latterly, questions of equitable access to resources and related tensions or conflicts. Such NGO configurations, working more or less from the top down, have been complemented by the appearance of myriad grass-roots groups emerging in countries around the world from the bottom up.

Together these dynamics set the stage for greatly enlarged NGO participation in the affairs of the world. The much-touted "global village" may well be leading toward common awareness. But the proliferating NGO phenomenon would seem to indicate the emergence of many diverse voices.

HAP functioned quite self-consciously in the networking mode, situated deliberately within a world of conflicting constituencies. During its formative period, there was the idea that conflicts in the Horn of Africa could best be addressed by an informed Mennonite constituency or, on another level, by an informed Canadian public. HAP, it was deemed, would therefore serve to educate the several constituencies accordingly. In the event, the focuses of HAP included a strong documentation and education component. But as the project proceeded, it was drawn additionally toward a variety of other points of concentration.

As indicated earlier in the narrative, people from the Horn of Africa region, in particular those attending the periodic consultations, became the primary focus of the project. A second focus centered on networking with a variety of specialist coalitions whose concerns also centered on the Horn of Africa. At a tertiary level there was focus on donor and host communities, with HAP providing orientation and briefings on project activity. With the dynamics among the actors in the Horn of Africa region changing weekly, sometimes daily, a fourth-level focus centered on monitoring exploratory negotiations underway and fine-tuning HAP plans for subsequent initiatives. In its directional shifts and changing focuses, HAP followed the pattern suggested by the Quakers: starting with a specific concern and proceeding—often intuitively—with that concern in ways that offered potential to advance the possibilities for peace.

The HAP's institutional arrangements reflected a certain logic. There had been easy access to communication facilities, conference facilities, and resource libraries, and there was the possibility of engagement within a climate of common concerns. In addition, there had been a sense that the institutional base provided legitimating links with the Canadian Mennonite constituency—HAP functioned, after all, as part of the Mennonite family. It could be debated whether the institutional arrangement was a necessary or a sufficient condition for the success of HAP. Certainly the institutional links proved extremely useful. But the absolutely indispensable ingredient that in the final analysis carried the project along was the quality of flexibility. At every point where the project touched institution, structure, dynamic, or precedent, the persons or institutions involved proved themselves totally flexible and accommodating. Nobody insisted on "the right way of doing things"; everything was an experiment, everything served as precedent.

Future parameters of HAP-like initiatives will most likely be determined by a number of factors: discussion within the networking coalition community regarding the most useful support roles to be played by projects of this kind needs to continue; careful planning around continued exchange of views within the coalition community would serve as critical variables to the future of such projects; project effectiveness would be enhanced by critical midcourse changes or timely termination.

Finally, there was the imperative of examining the original goal of the project, "peace for the Horn of Africa." Given the complexities of the issues to be considered in the region, the goal as originally stated could be recognized as naive at best and cavalier at worst. The journey from that original formulation to subsequent understandings was rendered complex and diffuse by encounters with a variety of realities. Substantial expectations for informed constituencies and publics may in fact have been achieved, but were difficult to quantify and even more difficult to mobilize. More readily realized were the active networking linkages with working groups or coalitions on the Horn of Africa. While it was generally accepted that all of the conflicts in the region had in one way or another intersected, in the real world of negotiations only one issue at a time could be addressed.

Just prior to this writing, peace talks between the Eritrean People's Liberation Front and the Government of Ethiopia in Addis Ababa were becoming a possibility. All approaches were delicate, all advances were incremental, and no one had a clear concept regarding a grand design for the region that would eventually provide the framework for political stability. As the possibility for talks became greater, the immediate locus of support shifted, subtly, from NGO working groups and coalitions to a tightly knit "shadow cabinet" of exiled Ethiopians who were in positions to provide specific week-to-week guidance for the process that would hopefully lead to substantive talks. In response, HAP, together with other projects and support groups, shifted focus more clearly on secondary and long-term support strategies. Change of nuance was constant, allowing for no easy project stability.

Conclusion

As this narrative indicates, HAP developed its own modest expertise and trajectory as a project. But it also fine-tuned the project process to include close networking relationships with other support groups; it acted as a reference point for liaison and contact among both primary and secondary actors; it became attuned to the weekly, almost daily, changes in the fortunes of the Horn of Africa region. The line between reflection and action became blurred. Some portions of the drama normally categorized as "field experience" were effectively bent to intersect with HAP; in other words, "field experience" visited HAP's institutional base. On the other hand, HAP staff made numerous visits to a variety of fields related to the Horn of Africa. Can such diverse activity be seen in any sense as a model to be emulated? Similar attempts around conflict issues in other settings, by other institutions, would almost certainly take their own distinct trajectories. Broad patterns would be generally recognizable, while details would be expected to vary enormously.

As a category of second-track diplomatic activity, HAP's efforts functioned amid a variety of unclear designations, none of which fully captured the range of nuances at work. Political scientists who observe and analyze from a distance offer generous recognition of the NGO contribution toward a reordering of the African political configurations. They write tentatively of a "second liberation" for Africa, facilitated and informed by an engaged, organized citizenry, both inside and outside the African continent. HAP played its role in the midst of that dynamic, a dynamic still awaiting definitive christening.

—Harold F. Miller
Ronald J. R. Mathies
Menno F. Wiebe
August 1989

Produced at the Horn of Africa Project, Institute of Peace and Conflict Studies, Conrad Grebel College, Waterloo, Ontario, Canada. A version of this paper appeared as a chapter in the book *Aid as Peacemaker: Canadian Development Assistance and Third World Conflict* by Robert Miller, ed. (1992, Carlton University Press, pp. 179–198). Reproduced with permission of the publisher and the co-authors.

Sources

Bailey, Sydney D. 1985. "Non-Official Mediation in Disputes: Reflections on Quaker Experience." *International Affairs.* p. 208.

Boulding, Elise. Fall 1987/Spring 1998. "The Rise of INGOs: New Leadership for a Planet in Transition." *Breakthrough.* p. 14.

Durning, Man B. January 1989. "Action at the Grassroots: Fighting Poverty and Environmental Decline." *World Watch Paper 88.* p. 10.

Hershberger, Guy F. *War, Peace, and Nonresistance.* Scottdale, PA: Herald Press.

Korten, David. Autumn 1987. "Third Generation Strategies." *World Development.* Vol. 15. pp. 147–149.

"The State and the Crisis in Africa: In Search of a Second Liberation." 1987. *Development Dialogue.* p. 5. Uppsala, Sweden: Dag Hammarskjold Foundation.

Yarrow, C. H. Mike. 1978. *Quaker Experience in International Conciliation.* New Haven, Connecticut: Yale University Press.

13
Nongovernmental Organizations at Large: A Taxonomy

Introduction

This brief overview of the NGO world is focused on five points: (1) a broad comparative configuration of NGOs, (2) origins and trajectory of the donor NGO community, (3) the host NGO community configuration, (4) unfinished NGO business, and (5) the future of NGOs.

First, a brief note on terminology. The acronym NGO stands for nongovernmental organization, an unfortunate negative designation that provides very little enlightenment for the uninitiated. A broad spectrum of development literature on Africa refers almost uniformly to development initiatives apart from those taken by governments as NGO initiatives.

In African countries, where organized religion acts frequently as the other major formal entity within the body politic, churches have assigned themselves advocacy roles, while governments regard churches to be subservient nongovernmental entities. Given such assumed dominance, one can readily speak of all activity not initiated by governments as nongovernmental. In the United States, where the role of capital and the marketplace is strong, nongovernmental activity is referred to as private voluntary activity, and the actors as private voluntary organizations. For practical purposes, these designations are interchangeable. But they all constantly beg for clarity.

The Macro Configuration

Most people in the world are aware of the idea and the function of organized government at the state level. (There are some interesting exceptions, of course: in a *New Yorker* article on Mozambique, a roving reporter happened upon people in that war-torn country who had never heard the term *Mozambique* or the name of the country's president! And of course they had never heard of the United States or Canada!) But the nation state, as recognized in the modern world, is of relatively recent origin. Today there are approximately 193 recognized nation states in the world, nearly all of them members of the United Nations. However, we must remind ourselves that the United Nations organization was established relatively recently, in 1948, and that many of its member nations are even younger.

Both the United Nations and its predecessor, the League of Nations, have at various times and under varying circumstances exercised supervisory jurisdiction over so-called trust territories. For example, South West Africa (today's Namibia) was a trustee territory under the League of Nations, and after 1948 under the United Nations, with South Africa administering the trusteeship mandate. Nation states undertake remarkable initiatives and undergo remarkable changes—China, Poland, the USSR, Hungary, Argentina, and Panama provide examples from the past. Generally, there is much less cognizance of the eighteen thousand—by one count—international nongovernmental organizations (INGOs) that are believed to be functioning in the world. That figure becomes even more impressive when compared with the estimated two hundred INGOs in the world in 1907.

While the world has witnessed a significant increase in the number of nation states and in the range of their individual and collective undertakings, it has also witnessed a dramatic increase in the number and activities of INGOs. Importantly, vast portions of INGO activity take place outside the immediate control of any nation state apparatus. Thus are INGOs only partially true to their "international" designations, for they operate within, outside of, between, and often in spite of nation states. Later in this brief overview there will be consideration of the respective differences between donor and host INGO communities.

However, the really big surprise comes at yet another level. Throughout the non-Western world, there exist multitudes of organized people groups for which the general designation "NGO" is highly inadequate. Herewith arbitrary time-bound examples of the diversity and numbers of such groups:

- In Bangladesh, 1,200 independent development organizations have been formed since 1971 and have become engaged in all manner of health and income-generation activities.
- In Brazil, 100,000 Christian Base Communities with 3 million members have been established with 1,300 neighborhood associations in São Paulo alone.
- In Burkina Faso, 2,500 NAAM peasant associations (informed by traditional age-group organizational and leadership patterns) are focused on self-help activities, inspiring similar movements in the neighboring countries of Senegal, Mauritania, Mali, Niger, and Togo.
- In India, an estimated 12,000 independent development organizations are functioning, with additional grass-roots groups numbering in the tens of thousands.
- In Indonesia, there are 600 independent development groups focusing on environmental issues alone.
- In Kenya, in addition to large numbers of projects carried out at the parish level by a variety of churches, there were by one count 16,232 women's groups with 737,000 members in 1984, with the estimated number of groups rising to 25,000 in 1988.
- In Mexico, there are at least 250 independent development organizations.
- In Peru, 300 independent development organizations engage in a variety of activities, including the operation of 1,500 community kitchens.
- In the Philippines 3,000 to 5,000 Christian Base Communities provide focus for change activity.
- In Sri Lanka, the Buddhist-inspired Sarvodaya Shramadana village movement touches 8,000 villages, mobilizing 3 million people in a variety of activities.

To be relevant and useful to analytic reflection, lists of such organizations and related activities would need to be extended and updated almost indefinitely. Durning has noted that the world's people at the grass-roots levels "are better organized in 1989 than at any time since European colonialism disrupted traditional societies centuries ago."

A broad configuration of the major change actors—including INGOs and NGOs—in our world can be summarized thus: (1) At the macro level, nation states clearly dominate the scene: there are more than 193 of them. They in turn control and, to varying degrees, manage global organizations such as the United Nations. (2) At an intermediate level, there are large numbers (perhaps eighteen thousand) of international nongovernmental actors, in addition to many nongovernment actors that function formally, informally, regionally, nationally, or locally—here the categories and numbers are in flux. (3) Finally, at the micro level around the world there are estimated to be tens of thousands of groups providing on the one hand the primary glue to the prevailing social mosaic, and on the other hand offering the impetus for change that emanates uniquely from large numbers of organized small groups. At this level something akin to absolute diversity reigns.

Whence the Donor Nongovernmental Organization Community?

Just as there is some confusion regarding the nomenclature related to the NGO community, there has been continuing discussion regarding their functional categories. In recent years the multilateral organizations of the world, such as the World Bank, the International Monetary Fund, and the United Nations, have increasingly sought collaboration with NGOs as "development partners," viewed as persons or agencies with the ability to deliver ideas and services to grass-roots communities. In that regard, NGOs were viewed as small or village versions of the "adult" multilateral development undertakings. Hence the view that NGOs were development writ small, while authoritative initiatives of the development enterprise were more properly generated in New York, Washington, or London.

Alternatively, the NGO community can be understood to have generated, over time, its own authentic trajectory. True, some NGOs followed a course remarkably parallel to the "official" development dynamic. But there is also the sense that a certain uniqueness of insight and emphasis has characterized the NGO enterprise. In fact, both tensions and complementarities have prevailed, a spectrum of conformity as well as deviancy. The following is an adaptation of descriptive/functional NGO categories as formulated by David Korten.

Relief: NGOs in the Western world have generally been born in clusters. Their collective births were typically occasioned by some calamity or disaster such as war or major drought. Thus at the end of World War II a large number of American agencies were born to deal with the devastation that had been inflicted on Europe. Forty-three such agencies agreed in 1946 to form an umbrella organization known as the American Council of Voluntary Agencies for Foreign Service. This agency expended vast energies in mobilizing food for the hungry and services to refugees, leading—among much else—to present-day official American food aid programs, as provided by Public Law 480, and to the formation of the United Nations High Commission for Refugees.

Subsequent calamities birthed clusters of NGOs that became active in Korea, Biafra, Vietnam, Cambodia, Ethiopia, and Central America—the continuities have been remarkable. Always there has been much room for new agencies and for a replication during each disaster of the relief and welfare actors. With its dramatic images and generally low levels of analysis, the modern media exercises a capacity to hype both the crises and the relief and welfare response to disasters. In spite of repeated proposals toward collective preparedness in anticipation of more reasoned and programmed responses to successive emergency situations, experience has demonstrated that each disaster functions as something of a precedent, replaying both the worst and the best of voluntary response. In the relief mode, NGOs tend to take high-profile postures, exercising exceptional, sometimes exclusive, initiatives and functioning as the ultimate delivery system, shifting goods and services from those who have to those who require the services.

Development: In the post–World War II era, the United Nations declared the 1960s and the 1970s the First and Second Development

Decades. Dislocation effected by World War II was already receding in the public's awareness and was followed by the birth around the world of new nations, emerging from long-standing imperial rule. Such new nations eagerly sought and assumed membership in the United Nations and claimed the right of equitable access to the wealth of the world. This massive shift from subservience to sovereignty set in motion what might be called, for lack of a better term, the "development imperative."

If the First Development Decade shepherded new nations into existence, the Second Development Decade articulated the development agenda. Beginning in 1972 with a UN conference on issues related to the environment, there followed a most incredible train of global UN conferences on subjects as diverse as food, population, water, health, deserts, technology, and energy—eighteen within one decade, recognized subsequently as development agenda or categories.

Against this backdrop of fresh agenda, agencies born in the immediate post–World War II period found themselves with new leases on their institutional and operational lives. Typically, they shifted programmatic emphases from relief to development, championing now the aspirations of the newly independent nations around the world. It was the discovery of the development agenda that brought into focus a series of counterpart or partnership questions. Words such as participation or reciprocity came into vogue. Relief efforts had been largely one-way streets, with Western NGOs building up quickly around emergencies and disasters, but just as quickly fading away or shifting to the next emergency scene. Longer-term development initiatives obviously required infrastructure in both the donor and host communities, as well as a greater degree of participation by all concerned, especially by host or receiving communities. Much of what is now recognized as NGO structure was formed within this context.

Networking and linkages: Networking in general refers to the sharing of information in nonconventional, alternative ways. As a process it emerged from the belief that scientific or professional means of dispensing information tended to render information expensive and exclusive. Networking was deemed a form of resistance to the "development establishment." Typically, the ubiquitous newsletter served as a primary communications vehicle, focusing on single, specialty themes or as a mini-catalogue on multiple themes.

Some NGOs specialized in networking or low-profile information sharing. They shifted with perceived needs, with possibilities, and with changing political or opinion climates. Such flexibility, however, was not to be confused with passivity. In fact, networking NGOs featured well-defined opinions and values reflected in the information shared.

Networking ideology, if it can be referred to as such, recognized information as power. True to its latent subversive nature, networking tended to dissipate power by sharing information and demonstrating multiple ways of applying any given technology. It sought, ideally, to demystify seemingly complex knowledge or technical systems, rendering them accessible to the poor, the disadvantaged, and the marginalized. Whereas the greatest portion of the early development enterprise was more or less a one-way delivery system—from the developed to the less developed countries and communities—the networking dynamic pointed its delivery and receiving systems in all directions. There was the implication that everyone, in every community, had something to share and, by the same token, everyone had the capacity to receive new or alternative information, ideas, and values.

The above configuration provides a general overview of the source of successive generations of Western NGOs and the general trajectory followed by them. It also implicitly suggests—particularly under the development and networking categories—that both initiatives and responses from host or receiving communities functioned as significant contributions to the larger NGO initiative, demonstrating an ability to play normative roles within the development enterprise with increasing vigor and self-awareness.

Nongovernmental Organization Host Communities

In Africa, the broad outlines of the NGO phenomenon can be divided into several distinct sectors.

INGOs in host countries: Armies of INGOs are present in Africa, emanating largely from the industrialized countries, acting as donors on behalf of their civil society constituencies or donor governments. For purposes of counterpart or partnership relationships in host countries, such INGOs may relate either to a local NGO, to a consortium of NGOs, or to the host government. Alternatively, some INGOs function in host countries as implementers of projects that they have themselves funded, relating for these purposes directly to the host village, community, organization, or government department within which the project was being implemented.

Local NGOs in host countries: In many host countries, there exist groups of local NGOs that act as receptors, responding to initiatives taken by INGOs. Some such local NGOs were originally created by INGOs, precisely to act as local alter egos, functioning as local subsidiaries of a multinational or transnational INGO conglomerate. On the other hand, some local subsidiary NGOs declared independence, setting their own operational criteria and diversifying their funding sources as well as their range of activities. Still other local NGOs were stimulated in their formation by the lure of available resources from the INGO community. A local NGO or NGO network—KENGO (Kenya Energy NGOs) is an example—might foster a wide network of relationships with the Kenyan government and with other Kenyan NGOs, while the greatest portion of its budget originates with external donors.

Host country grass-roots organizations: In host countries, many of the aforementioned grass-roots groups are uncomfortable with the NGO designation. Rather, they perceive themselves variously as women's groups, peasant associations, work groups, or savings groups, fulfilling a variety of self-determined purposes. Some were formed for purposes of survival—"many hands make light work." Some were formed precisely to establish some distance between their own initiatives and the oppressive hand of an insecure government. Others undertook similar actions, but for opposite reasons—their organizing was undertaken precisely to access services available from the government of the day or from other formal sector institutions such as banks. Still others were variously discovered, assisted, or exploited by both national and international NGO communities. But, in general, these groups were not to be thought of as devolved extensions of either the government or the NGO community. Whether as primary producers in the rural areas or as subsistence communities in the urban areas, they were first of all deemed accountable to themselves, providing the glue for much of African society.

Unfinished Nongovernmental Organization Agenda

Relationships: Over the years there has prevailed vigorous debate between two broad categories of NGOs: the so-called northern and southern (for the latter, read "African") NGOs. Southern NGOs have been making the case for a division of labor, suggesting and, in some cases, effectively demanding that northern NGOs provide funds and expertise only as requested and determined by African NGOs. Here the issue had to do with the setting and the management of criteria governing NGO activity in Africa. In some measure the debate continues, and is unresolved for the most part. One of the factors had to do with the way in which the donor NGO community related to its supporting constituency or to its supporting donor government.

When northern NGO communities engaged their constituencies for purposes of relief activity, relationships all around were fairly straightforward. Urgency required or was believed to require haste and unilateral action. Relational finessing fell by the wayside. When northern NGOs shifted to development activities, all manner of criteria and conditions came into play. Some of these were easily translated and understood by host NGO communities. However, the donor communities usually controlled the funds, the criteria for dispersing funds, and the names (jargon) for the fads and fashions in the development enterprise.

The attempt to render this complex mix of development language and structure understandable to host communities led easily to the sense of domination and control by donors. Host communities wanted access to resources without strings attached, while donor NGO communities—if they were to stay alive as organizations—were expected to meet stringent criteria set out by donor governments while retaining current and understandable relationships with their supporting constituencies. Such tensions were exacerbated when bilateral or multilateral resources became available to and through the NGO community.

Throughout the whole of the NGO enterprise, there has been the question of its identity and its link with either host or donor governments. For a variety of purposes, donor governments were quite happy to collaborate with the NGO community as surrogates. In other words, donor governments perceived that they increased their international flexibility by channeling resources through NGO channels. The same was not necessarily true for host governments. Host governments were happiest when relationships with INGOs were contractual and integral to negotiated government-to-government contracts. In the midst of these dynamics, the multiplicity of NGOs in host countries became increasingly confusing and threatening. While there was a recognized need for at least some of the services offered by NGOs, within the African body politic the rationale for and the structured presence of the NGO community was in flux. Some of the confusion was dealt with, however inadequately, by means of multi-tiered coordinating structures within the African NGO community.

Coordination: In Africa, precise counterpart NGO coordinating structures—comparable, for example, to what is known in Canada as the Canadian Council for International Cooperation or in the United States as InterAction—have not been developed. Instead, there existed an unofficial continental coordinating body known as the Forum of African Voluntary Development Organizations, while various regional coordinating forums were taking shape as well. In Anglophone Africa, governments have established National Councils of Social Services for purposes of registering a wide range of local and national NGOs. For the most part, such councils proved only marginally effective. The registration and coordination of INGOs in African host countries varied substantially—even within a single country, a certain unevenness prevailed. In general, there were some tensions between top-down coordinating efforts and bottom-up grass-roots dynamics. For example, West African peasant associations and other grass-roots groups were not particularly eager to join or to be directed in their formation by the likes of the Forum of African Voluntary Development Organizations. They perceived themselves to be authentically rooted within the indigenous social fabric, while coordinating organizations such as the forum were seen to be artificially structured from the top down.

Some local African NGOs perceived their mandates to be broader than was suggested by national boundaries. Thus were they established themselves as NGOs with regional mandates, rendering them not entirely beholden to the regulations of any single government. Examples of co-ordinating structures elsewhere in the world proved interesting; with a base in Geneva, an organization known as Integrated Rural Development provided a reference point for a range of peasant associations from West Africa. The organization claimed to act as a networking facility between various African groups and similar groups around the world. As for the large number of INGOs working in Africa, they were subject to diverse, sometimes fragmented, host-country coordinating guidelines. Indeed, the whole of the NGO coordination scene experienced great flux, reflecting the general ambiguity surrounding the roles played by the NGO community in Africa.

Training: Within African NGO communities, there was considerable emphasis on training (later known as "capacity building"). Much of the focus was on learning how to manage NGOs as rational bureaucracies. From the International Council of Voluntary Agencies in Geneva, a newsletter entitled *NGO Management* was published as the "Newsletter of the NGO Management Network." One article in the newsletter opined that, in their search for improved performance, African NGOs may have been borrowing excessively from organizations whose mandates were quite distinct from NGO mandates, focusing too readily on the business models of efficiency and effectiveness rather than on the ambiguities of creativity and flexible relevance.

Some of the pressure for focused training originated with donor governments that supported INGOs. Many INGOs depended for more than half of their budgets on donor government monies, a fact that rendered them beholden to government guidelines with regard to their management policies. In subtle ways and otherwise, these pressures were passed along to counterpart African NGOs, resulting in an African NGO structure that was more recognizable to the person on the street in an industrialized country than to a peasant from an African village. Training as a posture and as a process provided a window onto one of many ambiguities within the African NGO world.

Into the Future

While African governments were struggling to identify an appropriate modus vivendi with the NGO phenomenon, and while NGOs experimented with ever-changing relational models, political scientists—off to one side—offered observations. They pointed out that development patterns over the decades were changing markedly. During the period 1955 to 1965, development efforts in Africa were characterized by the concept of "trickle down," functioning at the time in the dominant central-government mode. From 1965 to 1975, the development enterprise was characterized by decentralized administration, strategies promoted by the international development community and informed by the concept of "integrated development." "Small is beautiful" functioned as a lead concept between 1975 and 1985, drawing attention especially to the plethora (and possibly to the success) of grass-roots groups and generally pointing toward more participatory modes of development. From 1985 onward, political scientists were claiming to see an enlarged role for intermediary NGOs, providing that necessary but thankless function that Korten referred to as "networking"—forging relationships in all directions.

Finally, some political scientists observed that the NGO enterprise at its best possessed the overall potential of "re-legitimating" the African state apparatus. That sentiment did not reflect in any accurate fashion either the conscious intent of the NGO community or the latent expectation of the African state with regard to NGOs. African NGOs, in many respects, were continuing a search for their own legitimacy, while African governments found it difficult to identify authentic space for NGOs. The African NGO quest was complicated, additionally, by the diverse taxonomy of its far-flung community, by the expectations raised and the pressures implicit in relationships with northern INGOs, by the self-assured bottom-up voice from the grass roots, and by the high degree of dependency that already characterized the "meso" levels of the African NGO community.

If Canadian NGOs hoped for authentic relationships with the African NGO community, they would do well to examine, constantly, the function and the definition of the NGO alternative. If Canadian NGOs act merely as extensions of government policy, and if the assistance they offer is simply warmed-over government assistance, it can hardly be expected that African NGOs will then by some administrative magic render such assistance into genuine alternative development patterns. If partnership between Canadian and African NGOs is to have any meaning at all, it does at the very least imply that the hard, contradictory issues can never be fully laid to rest by either side of the partnership equation. Relational and smooth-operating bureaucracies may be a necessary condition for the maintenance of NGO partnerships, but never a sufficient one.

—June 16, 1989

Prepared at Conrad Grebel College, Waterloo, Ontario, for presentation to the Ontario Africa Working Group Seminar: "African–Canadian NGO Perspectives of Partnerships."

14
Between Northern and Southern Nongovernmental Organizations: In Search of Relational Models

Placing the Nongovernmental Organization Enterprise

On the international development scene, nongovernmental organizations play important roles. This reflection is focused on aspects of the relationships among the several categories of NGOs.

NGOs for the most part enjoy the warmth of acceptance and approval within the modern development establishment. Neither their virtues nor their vices have been exhaustively scrutinized. They live, therefore, with the legitimacy offered by open-ended categories and broad, but not carefully tested, assumptions. Among those assumptions are the following:

- In a world dominated by superpowers, NGOs bespeak the strength and diversity of small-scale efforts.
- In a world tending toward generic development, NGOs reflect creativity as diverse and complex as the human community itself.
- In a world that assumes the rightness of top-down, center-to-periphery dynamics, NGOs champion the creativity of the margins.
- In a world that assumes the need for capital inputs in any change process, NGOs are concerned with mobilizing the wisdom of people.
- In a world order based on privileged access, NGOs open information to all.

- In a world of fragile nation states, NGOs seek to build relationships across national and state boundaries.
- In a world where access to food is informed by the calculus of market politics, NGOs sabotage the media in favor of the hungry.
- In a world of rising unemployment, the NGO community offers employment opportunities both within formal and informal sectors.
- In a world of stifling institution, the NGO community claims to offer more "humane" organizational options.

These assumptions persist in part because they remain relatively unchallenged by formal scrutiny, but also because the NGO phenomenon has been so diverse until now that it yields only reluctantly to rigid analysis. The diversities are real, but then so are the broad commonalities. In fact, NGOs emerge from reasonably clear dynamics, the outlines of which have been tentatively identified. It is hypothesized that NGOs wax and wane in cyclical fashion. They explode into new energetic outbursts during major paradigm shifts or natural/human-made disasters; they follow a predictable maturation trajectory, with the first generation focusing on relief and welfare, the second generation on small-scale, self-reliant local development, and the third generation on the development of sustainable systems.

But is there in this scheme of growth and development too easy an assumption that normalcy patterns for NGOs do exist? Are there more subtle and more fundamental shifts underway? Is a return to or an achievement of any kind of normalcy precluded by the cumulative factors at work in Africa and in the world at large? Can it be assumed reasonably that the efforts of a multidirectional, multilevel NGO community will coalesce into coherent, manageable wholes, or is that community simply aiding and abetting a tendency toward negative synergy? In Africa there would seem to be considerable "need" or opportunity for NGO activity, but there are also more questions from host governments on the desirability of NGO proliferation. Those questions come from nation states increasingly hard-pressed to sustain their own political survival and economic growth.

It is not clear whether NGOs operating in Africa see themselves as alternatives to mainstream development, as supplementary service appendages to a struggling public sector, or as parallel structures to the whole of the formal modern dynamic. Neither the international NGO community nor host governments have clear understandings regarding the role of indigenous or neo-indigenous NGO configurations. Do the growth and strength of this category of NGOs render modern African states more or less governable? Does international NGO support of such groups render them subversive? Or is it by this time clear that at least some portion of the future must be built upon understandings inherent in indigenous grassroots groups?

One of the persistent trends within the development enterprise in Africa has been that of opting for a kind of generic development—change patterns and priorities that correspond to internationally accepted nomenclature and category. Is the search for appropriate institutionalization a move in the direction of greater self-determination for the peoples of Africa? Is it a process intended to strengthen the modern or public sector? Or is the whole of the present direction inherently a drift toward greater dependencies? Does the institutionalization of NGOs and community initiatives render them more easily coopted by dominant forces in the world? Are the less formal NGO options too easily lost in directionless anonymity?

In this reflection there is a basic acknowledgment that the NGO phenomenon is exceedingly diverse. But given the sensitivities of host governments and host communities, it is further assumed that diversity without the guidance of certain parameters constitutes part of the development problematic, and only with deliberate and self-conscious "placing" or characterization of NGO function can such diversity play positive roles in the overall change and development effort. Development operating in a free-for-all environment is easily bent in the direction of dominant international power brokers.

Development Context and NGO Action

NGOs are born in particular contexts. There are no "immaculate NGO conceptions"! How NGOs function in the world has much to do with their circumstance of birth, which in turn has much to do with the subsequent functions undertaken. Here is a cursory review of both context and function.

NGOs tend to be birthed in clusters. These cluster births coincide with stress periods or with major paradigm shifts. While the effects of the great African drought (1984–85) provided an immediate context for this reflection, other larger paradigms provided context as well. For example, the shift from the colonial period to the era of independence (1960s) was for many developing countries formative (or reformational) in fundamental ways.

That shift gave rise to the so-called development decades (the 1960s and 1970s), so designated by the United Nations as a period for special attention to the needs of new emerging nation states in the third world. The United Nations' contribution to a realization of development was further focused by eighteen global conferences (between 1972 and 1982) on development categories that have since then taken on generic character. Agenda items from the UN conferences included environment, water, population, health, desertification, food, and energy. Together, these processes influenced development aspirations on a global scale.

Meanwhile, it was debated whether development, as broadly understood, promised solutions to Africa's problems or whether the development process itself, as generally formulated, was indeed part of the problem. The debt crisis, for example, seemed to suggest that the negative characteristics and effects of the development model had coalesced into dynamics that became untenable and unsustainable. Ours has become an interdependent world. But there is no ready consensus on whether such interdependence is positive or negative. Academics have offered a range of formulations in an attempt to sharpen understanding of this disparate world. They write of the following:

- The *modernist neoclassical school*, which emphasizes the dual nature of many developing countries and advocates some form of industrialization to fill the gaps and lead the way toward sustained development.
- The *orthodox Marxist school*, which emphasizes the need for developing countries to transit from colonialism through capitalism to socialism.
- The *dependency school*, which connotes metropole centers and their outlying counterparts; development and underdevelopment are seen as two sides of the same coin.
- The *soft state theory*, which identifies the less-than-effective African state on the one hand and the "primordial public realm" on the other as the source of development's failures. "Soft states" ruling over primal public realms are said to be guided by an "economy of affection," leaving governments with only coercive, top-down development options. In response, the general populace and the peasants in particular exercise the option of withdrawal, rendering the state apparatus "soft." Many situations in Africa are therefore readymade for exogenous penetration by NGOs or, alternatively, for more significant roles played by indigenous or village-related NGOs on the inside.

Inasmuch as the NGO community is non-establishment, it is on the one hand very flexible and on the other hand vulnerable to cooptation by the dynamics suggested above. The central issue turns on the diverse nature of the NGO role. Are there optimal distances to be maintained between NGOs and the public weal, and between NGOs and the development dynamic? And are those proximities or distances critical to the self-definition of NGOs? Is such distance particularly critical in the case of indigenous NGOs, which in the best of times are only marginally recognized by the respective governments?

Nongovernmental Structure and Behavior

Until now the NGO community has functioned in the context of negative definitions. In African countries, governments rank easily as the prime movers for most sectors of national life. Governments function as the chief employers, governments control the high points of the economy, and governments manage much of the educational and health infrastructure. In such contexts, activity initiated by nongovernment entities becomes conspicuous as exceptions to the norm and gives rise to the phenomenon now readily referred to as nongovernmental initiative.

By contrast, in a strongly capitalist setting such as the United States different terms are used to describe a similar phenomenon. There is reference to the "not-for-profit" or to "private voluntary organizations," reflecting the dominance of the "for-profit" category and the current bias within the capitalist world toward private (corporate) as opposed to government initiative. Both in the West and in Africa, NGO or private initiative has been dependent for its identity on the nondominant or non-establishment sectors of the public realm, all of which leaves the NGO community with identities not of its own making.

During the early postindependence days in Africa, there was an assumption that much of the activity of NGOs (especially in the fields of health and education) would eventually be handed over to government control and thus become part of establishment or government-provided services. NGOs were seen to be performing interim supplementary roles during periods when governments were still growing into or upgrading their capacities. Just where NGOs were expected to go after having surrendered their experimental or interim contributions was not clear.

Meanwhile, it became obvious that African governments did not have infinite capacity for enlarging the civil service establishment; they were unable to meet all development expectations, nor were they willing or able to absorb without careful consideration any number of nongovernment actors into the body politic. The problem became particularly vexing when the grass-roots, indigenous NGO sought validation at the national level or when it became clear that a national NGO was staking out permanent territory within the public weal, either as supplement or alternative to established government structures.

Among the more controversial issues within the international NGO community were the terms of employment and how such terms were translated into the transnational NGO context. Some sectors of the NGO community functioned as rational international bureaucracies, patterned after entities such as the United Nations. Others assumed that factors relating to employment or remuneration within the NGO sector should be pegged to high levels of motivation and relatively modest salary levels.

When either of these assumptions was translated to the African setting, invitable distortions became apparent. Not uncommon were senior NGO salary scales that easily superseded those on offer to civil servants in the respective host governments or those offered to professors by the typical African university, resulting in an attrition of the brightest and best into the NGO circuit and away from what some observers would consider coherent development planning and implementation offered by national government structures. On the other hand, appeals to high motivational levels become obscured in situations of limited job opportunities. Any job was considered better than no job. From an international perspective the typical NGO job on offer was positioned at the low, informal end of the spectrum. From the perspective of an African school leaver or even a university graduate, a job with an NGO provided entry into a multi-tiered, relatively open world of formal sector activity.

In the real NGO world there was in fact great differentiation, not lending itself easily to all-encompassing characterization. Indeed, the variety of NGO structures corresponded to diverse relational patterns. What follows is an attempt at creating an NGO typology and its attendant characteristics, both in terms of function and in terms of the relationships emanating from such function. It should be clear that the ideal types are not mutually exclusive—there are obvious overlaps—nor is the list exhaustive. These are intended only as recognition of the range of dynamics that come into play within the NGO community and to suggest that they have much to do with relational options.

The Classic Western Nongovernmental Organization

The origins of the dominant Western NGOs must be sought in the immediate post–World War II period, especially relevant to the USA. There, a cluster of more than thirty NGOs burst onto the scene for the purpose of meeting the needs of war-torn Europe. This cluster quickly coalesced into an umbrella organization known as the American Council of Voluntary Agencies for Foreign Service.

The council embraced two major agenda items: food and refugees. Upon the cessation of wartime hostilities, food surpluses had quickly accumulated in the United States, thanks to massive mobilization of farmers during the peak of the war effort. Surplus food had remained relatively stationary until members of the council lobbied for ways of making it available to hungry Europe. Thus was initiated the famous Public Law 480 legislation, which in various subsequent guises rendered American food surpluses available to people in postwar Europe and much later to Africa and many other parts of the world (during times of famine and during times of normal harvests, it might be added).

Similar efforts were made with regard to Europe's displaced people. It was the refugee committee of the American Council of Voluntary Agencies for Foreign Service that lobbied successfully for the formulation and eventual adoption of the 1951 UN Refugee Convention, which defined the legal status of a refugee, including their privileges and rights. Subsequent lobbying by the committee helped to situate the United Nations High Commissioner for Refugees as the implementing agency for the Refugee Convention and related provisions.

This cluster of American NGOs made the massive shift in the early 1960s from their traditional preoccupation with food and refugee concerns in postwar Europe to development activities in Africa, very much as prescribed by the aforementioned UN development conferences. There were of course notable exceptions that saw individual agencies extending solidarity to nationalist initiatives in Africa, viewing such solidarity as a precondition for self-determined development activity.

Church-related American Council of Voluntary Agencies for Foreign

Service member agencies participated in the structuring of counterpart coordinating bodies throughout Africa, now recognized as conciliar or ecclesial infrastructure in the form of national Christian councils or national secretariats for the Roman Catholic Church. Subsequently there was support in a similar vein for regional or continental infrastructure, such as regional offices for the Catholic Church collectivity and the continental All Africa Conference of Churches for the Protestant counterparts. Secular NGO members of the council forged relational links with host governments or entered into a variety of collaborative alliances with bilateral or multilateral agencies. The ensuing structures in fact facilitated long-term relationships between post-independent African NGOs and a range of Western postwar NGOs. Indeed, those institutions and those relationships in many ways constituted a generational norm.

Meanwhile, those structures and relationships variously flourished, diversified, or collapsed. Within the African conciliar community, it became common practice to rely on donor "roundtables" as a means of assuring sustained funding. It was argued that this pattern represented a breakthrough toward participatory negotiations between northern and southern NGOs or, conversely, represented a breakdown of the earlier reliance on formal sector bureaucracy and communication systems. Alternatively, the observation was made that the conciliar community with its traditional donors had fossilized into symbiotic dependency relationships that no longer creatively informed either northern or southern constituencies.

Dependency theory spoke to some of the characteristics of this NGO cluster, but not to all of them. True, there was upward accountability and on the part of African counterparts there was what seemed like undue reliance on overseas funding. On the other hand, the multiplication of donors had provided donees with funding options, a degree of freedom to shop around, and nominal freedom to set or change the criteria for receiving overseas aid. This generation of NGOs was influenced still by the rhythm of disasters, but much less so than were younger NGOs. At its best, this generation of NGOs was invested in relationships that enlarged mutual understandings. The magic of project or technique had given way, at least marginally, to the knowledge that both developing and developed communities increasingly shared common interdependent global agendas.

The Multinational Nongovernmental Organization

There seemed to be an uncanny similarity between the structure of the international corporate organization and this "type" within the NGO community. The corporate multinational structure was typically headquartered in one or several northern cities. Branch or daughter companies were located around the world, all of them sporting the same slogans, logos, and computerized spreadsheet accounts.

Almost by definition, multinational NGOs were characterized by an accountability flow that moved from the peripheries toward the metropoles. Program focus was centralized; there was an efficient delivery of services, carried out in businesslike ways, serviced by rationally organized bureaucracies. Staff were recruited both in metropole countries and internationally on the basis of professional qualifications. Within hard-pressed host economies, there was the effect of siphoning well-trained local talent away from an already fragile indigenous modern sector. Multinational NGOs were accused of offering salaries at levels that could not be sustained by the host economies, thus contributing to the establishment of a parasitic class of professionals. A counter view emphasized that local talent was being equipped or capacity built for greater creativity in the employ of well-financed, well-equipped multinational NGOs.

Meanwhile, it became clear that the multinational NGO, like its corporate multinational counterpart, was integral to a politically right-of-center international order. This category of NGO functioned as a delivery system, making needed or desired goods and services available, but delivering them in nearly antiseptic fashion from the metropole to recipient communities. Their role reflected the dual nature of the world economy and in particular the dual nature of African economies. Efforts by African individuals or organized collectivities to penetrate or to render this type more participatory were only marginally successful. This type of NGO was accused, rightly and wrongly, of creating and coopting African elite into an international circuit, away from the priorities and power of locally generated agenda.

The Holistic Nongovernmental Organization

A holistic view of the world suggests the integrity of the whole while providing for the integrity of the parts. Following strictly the design of a hologram, there was the suggestion that each of the parts constituted a small universe, each containing elements of the whole. Thus, only if the parts had the integrity of completeness could the whole have meaning. Such, one was told, were the insights and requirements of modern physics.

The real world was not so generous or egalitarian; in that world, there was mention of centers and peripheries. And it was generally taken for granted that centers dominated over peripheries. That assumption was mitigated somewhat by a growing awareness that centers easily became sterile, while peripheries sported residual or growing evidence of creativity.

Within the NGO community, this type suggested some interesting demands and concessions, among them the integrity of the peripheries, insisting that peripheries possess their own dynamics. Indeed, the holistic NGO dynamic seeks to enhance the validity of the peripheries, ensuring that creativity in those sectors not be lost to or coopted by dominant centers.

Almost by definition, the holistic NGO functions as a networking facility. The goal of networking, obviously, would be to ensure that peripheries interact, be heard, and speak to and influence the prevailing tendency of centers to dominate. Ideally, the discussion here is of a whole comprising respective and respected parts.

A number of remarkable networking NGOs based in Africa or touching Africa in various ways are in fact operational. As a kind of ideal type, one could cite Integrated Rural Development, based in Geneva, Switzerland, with a field office in Harare, Zimbabwe. Better than many others with similar claims, Integrated Rural Development articulated a rationale for the networking posture. Theirs was not so much to "know all" as it was to "facilitate knowing." Typically, Integrated Rural Development arranged for a given NGO to learn from or contribute to another NGO's knowledge pool. While accumulating information in the process, the stated reason for their existence was to facilitate information availability, to make information accessible.

At its best, the holistic networking NGO functions in a post-dependency mode. Its inherent process collaborates with, but does not become beholden to, existing modern-sector institutions. "Process" is writ large; "institution" is writ small. Accountability is lodged within the authenticity with which information is communicated. Authentic information is almost by definition generated in the real world of praxis and shared optimally by and among practitioners.

The Gifting or African Nongovernmental Organization Type

"Gifting" in Africa has to do with contributions toward the sustenance of life processes. A ready and somewhat ironic example relates to the importance of contributing toward the cost of a funeral within a given community. Funerals in Africa are not superfluous or optional happenings. They are perceived to be part of the life process. To bring a gift to the occasion is to endorse the life of the community.

But there is more: there is the sense that the African gifting process in supporting life or death has to do with keeping community alive. Celebrations, rituals, and storytelling informed by the past keep options for the future open. For neo-traditional but self-aware communities in transition, this deployment of story translates into what is easily recognized by development practitioners as process. It is a process readily sustained by traditional forms of gifting: sharing food, sharing work, sharing celebration, and of course sharing a common history.

To highlight the indigenous African practice of gifting as a model for NGO behavior is of course problematic. Africa's modern-sector expectations for NGO activity are already very high; there is the expectation of formal structure, of salaries, of program. But there is nevertheless something to be said for the "unstructured" character of the African sharing culture. It is a practice bespeaking an awareness of the whole of the life process; an awareness of the right to life. Even more radically, it suggests that life in community is not so much a matter of expertise as it is a matter of common knowledge. In this context, relationships are seen more readily as the essence of community rather than as some abstract product of an expert process. In many respects, this model conforms to what was described as the holistic model. If there is a difference, it lies in the emphasis on life in community as a central focus rather than on the networker function of the holistic model.

There is an additional consideration regarding the function of the sharing culture. It is accepted that myriad groups function at grass-roots levels. They can be identified as work groups, savings groups, or religious groups, among many other categories. African governments have recognized the existence of such groups by registering them at various administrative levels, but in general these groups (frequently characterized by ethnic loyalties) are not easily accepted as part of what is now known as the NGO category, patterned as it is on the international NGO community. Indeed, it is not unusual for African governments to discriminate against the diversity (confusion?) of grass-roots organizations in favor of more "articulate" NGO communities with formal structures and international links, the latter ensuring access to formal sector resources. And it is equally difficult for modern-sector NGOs to be informed in their operating modes by the "soft" patterns of community traditions.

The Transformation Type

As an operative term, "transformation" functioned as a relative newcomer to the development lexicon, but was used by an innovative NGO minority, of both religious and secular hues. It was deployed most effectively by sectors of the Catholic Church community, giving attention to the writings of South American Paulo Freire, an advocate of radical literacy, and to the writings of Ivan Illich, the development iconoclast. Both would have been comfortable with E. F. Schumacher's small-is-beautiful development ethic. And, like others of similar suasion, they were informed by a powerful sense of vocational calling and celebration.

There must be no illusion about the ready transferability of transformation as modeled by the Catholic activist community. Much of its motivation can be traced to the disciplines inherent in long-established religious orders, infused by vows of poverty, chastity, and obedience, functioning within secure, supportive communities. Moreover, some portion of the activist Catholic agenda was lodged within the traditional cleavage between laity and clergy. During the 1970s and 1980s, this activist agenda as pursued in East Africa ignited stresses and strains within the hierarchical character of the Catholic Church. Similarly, inasmuch as such church-related activist agenda affected established political and social structures, it was perceived in some quarters as subversive.

In the continuing search for legitimate NGO function, on the one hand, and suitable government polity space, on the other, the notion of NGOs as subversives has not been particularly welcome. Although this type does insist on keeping all options open, it is not advocating mindless anarchy. There is the assumption that the established order, if it is to serve a nation or a community effectively, must always be subject to renewal and fresh direction. If the transformation process is indeed participatory, then there is reasonable hope that its new levels of understanding and action will enhance the common good.

Writ large in this model is process. It does not accept that development has to do only with infrastructure and the acquisition of modern-sector skills, however important these may be. Nor does it accept that development choices are value-free. On the contrary, values are deliberately considered and embraced, preferably in the context of due process. Relationships are carefully scrutinized. Technique, project, and institution become subservient to continued deliberative process. This NGO type anticipates the point that NGOs in their non-establishment mode work the margins and creatively deploy the space between the more established sectors of society. Renewal, not subversion, is the intent.

Summations

The basic directional thrust of the NGO phenomenon has been from the so-called developed toward the so-called developing world. Seen against the broadest backdrop, NGOs from the industrialized countries have been integral to the historic expansion of North Atlantic countries, variously taking the form of exploration, empire, religious proselytism, humanitarian services, and what has since the decades of the 1960s and 1970s been recognized as the development enterprise.

Until now no single, widely accepted theory adequately accounts for the reality of the NGO community. Those who write about NGOs seek to place their function largely in the context of generally accepted development theories. The task is made no easier by an expanding pluralism within industrialized countries, on the one hand, and the felt need in African countries, on the other, to control or to account in political and policy terms for the presence and action of the NGO community.

NGOs are actors within the existing order of international relationships. However, some NGOs are more established than others. Differences between the functions of the various NGOs can be attributed to various factors: the timing of their "births," the timing of their subsequent patterns of intervention, the degree of specialization reflected in their programs, or the nature of alliances formed with the non-NGO community. Some NGOs insist on maximum access to unencumbered operational space; governments, they say, are clumsy and confuse the issues. Others actively seek out legitimacy for their existence vis-à-vis both donor and recipient countries, with the UN or with other multilateral actors. There is little unanimity on the appropriate proximity or distance to be maintained between the formal public (government-related) realm and the world of NGOs.

A closer look at the NGO typology spectrum only reinforces the impression of rich diversity. NGOs committed to transformation as a modus vivendi would seem to be opting for a fluid role in society, always playing the margins, never yielding either to cooptation by the establishment or to the stagnation of specialization. They are happy to play the perpetual role of the devil's advocate, speaking and working on behalf of the world's peripheries. At the other end of the spectrum are NGOs more formally linked to imperial and postimperial history. Because of fortuitous or unfortunate timing, they have become part of the established order, though perpetual questions regarding operational territory remain: which is obviously government turf, which is established NGO turf, and where and how, if at all, do the two intersect?

African governments are encountering NGOs from two directions—from without and from within the body politic. Those from the outside are weighted with imperial history or with the cyclical thrusts of ideological or political paradigm shifts, or of disasters, whether natural or human-made. Those from within vary in character: they may function as the mirror-image counterpart to an international NGO, having been created for that purpose; they may be genuinely grounded in local dynamics, but for purposes of acceptable category they take on the recognizable face of a modern NGO; or there may be, finally, the indigenous grass-roots NGO, seeking degrees of legitimacy from the government in power or deliberately withdrawing into non-formal collaborative circuits. Responses from African governments to these several NGO strategy modes vary, but there are discernable trends.

In general, the tendency among governments is toward control. Indigenous NGOs are perceived to require control because of their potentially divisive character based, as they frequently are, on ethnic dynamics. External NGOs elicit other responses. The strong host government may choose cooptation, assigning the external NGO to relationships with local counterpart NGOs, created for the purpose. They may be assigned thematic space beyond which they are not to stray, or their services may be accepted only in collaboration with external bilateral or multilateral development programs. In the absence of comprehensive understanding of the NGO phenomenon, the strong host government response to NGOs is usually a judicious mix of political expediency, bureaucratic rationality, and control.

Meanwhile, governments in Africa are unable to maintain development momentum commensurate with existing aspirations. Whether because of government "softness" or because of willing concessions, the space occupied by NGOs is substantial. African NGOs—across the spectrum—are beginning to lead their own lives. They play the range of relational options with international NGOs; during periods of heightened activity (such as drought or other natural disasters), they can play their roles, as it were, in a "donee's market." They can at such times set the criteria by which relationships with international NGOs are constituted. But not always and not on a stable basis.

In the quest for stability and for a permanent niche in the existing order, African NGOs are taking the route of institutionalization. To put it more precisely, the modern generation of African NGOs works its way toward additional layers of institutions. The most readily available space is regional—between nation states—but somehow parallel to certain regional formal-sector entities.

The current preoccupation with institutionalization has everything to do with relational options, because relationships between NGOs and with governments are premised on particular choices. Those choices hinge upon the particular role that an NGO chooses to play, whether that role is closer to the transformation end of the spectrum or to establishment structure and process; whether accountability is primarily upward toward the donor community or downward toward an engaged devolved constituency; or whether a given NGO plays a counterpart role or the role of aggressive initiator, with only residual dependence on external donor communities.

For the present and for the immediate future, north–south NGO relationships seem to be functioning with some degree of equilibrium. Northern NGOs survive variously by supporting African NGOs. Meanwhile, African NGOs have learned to fundraise, to implement projects, and to live within the space available either nationally or regionally. There is symbiosis, though not a steady-state symbiosis. The NGO phenomenon is still unfolding and establishing new categories.

For the longer term, there are questions about the effects of the NGO factor. Does the NGO community point toward a new pluralist world? Or does it represent the multiplication of dependencies? Does the inherent pluralism of the NGO world militate against the governing ability of the African nation state or will NGOs be viewed, alternatively, as the purveyors of fresh options?

Seen from almost any perspective, NGOs are a part of the changing order. Their effectiveness over the long term will be determined in the interface between stifling institutionalization on the one hand and creative relationships with living constituencies on the other.

Originally written for a conference in Khartoum, Sudan, January 10–15, 1988. Updated May 2005.

Sources

Brodhead, Tim. 1988. *Bridges of Hope; Canadian Voluntary Agencies and the Third World.* Ottawa, Canada: North-South Institute.

Chepkwony, Agnes. 1987. *The Role of Non-governmental Organizations in Development: A Study of the National Christian Council of Kenya (NCCK) 1963–1978.* Doctoral thesis. Uppsala, Sweden: University of Uppsala.

Crowley, Jerry. 1985. *Go To the People: An Experiment in African Education.* Eldoret, Kenya: Gaba Publications.

Curti, Merle. 1963. *American Philanthropy Abroad.* New Brunswick, New Jersey: Rutgers University Press.

FORUM. A newsletter of Development Innovations and Networks. Geneva, Switzerland.

Goulet, Denis. Autumn 1985. "The Global Development Debate: The Case for Alternative Strategies." *Development and Peace.* Vol. 6.

Hyden, Goran. January 1984. "Ethnicity and State Coherence in Africa." *Ethnic Studies Report.* Vol. II. No. 1.

Korten, David. Autumn 1987. "Third Generation NGO Strategies: A Key to People-Centered Development." *World Development.* Vol. 15. Supplement.

Mponsusu, Bukasa Tulukia. October 1986. "The African Tradition of Sharing." *The Ecumenical Review.* Vol. 38.

Van der Poort, Kees. October 1986. "Resource Sharing and Project Funding with Special Reference to Zimbabwe." *The Ecumenical Review.* Vol. 38.

15
Ethics for the Future

Review of *Catholic Theological Ethics Past, Present and Future: The Trento Conference* by James F. Keenan (Orbis Books, 2011)

DURING THE MONTH of July 2010, six hundred theological ethicists from seventy-five countries met in Trento, Italy, to examine a formidable array of ethics considerations from the past, present, and future. These included encounters with interreligious dialogue, the interface between history and theological ethics, marginalized voices, moral reasoning, political ethics, health issues, identity and familial issues, global social challenges, and the future of theological ethics.

Four years earlier, a similar convocation at the University of Padua brought together four hundred theological ethicists from sixty-three countries. It was determined at Padua that a subsequent meeting of ethicists should take place in the city of Trento (anglicized to Trent). Why Trento? Trento evoked memories of powerful precedent. From December 13, 1545, to December 4, 1563, Catholic ethicists had deliberated in what became known as the Council of Trent on issues arising from the emerging Protestant Reformation. Historians now refer to that deliberative marathon as the beginnings of a counter-reformation, instigated by a church intransigent, in its definitive repudiation of the Protestant reformers. According to reflections in this book, "Trent was faced with a decadent church."

If the sixteenth-century Council of Trent marked the demise of ethical and theological consensus within the European Christian body, the Trento convocation of 2010 signaled the urgency of considerations regarding global ethics, drawing now on insights from a plethora of faith traditions and a cornucopia of secular and political claims on the realm of ethics.

During the 475-year period spanning the two deliberations at Trento, the world became an intensely interrelated, interactive village. From every perspective, globalization beckons and, indeed, has already rendered any consideration of ethics internal and integral to the welfare of the global human community. There was the sense in the 2010 convocation that "globalization has created a value system of its own." Hence, theological ethicists were invited to bridge the gulf "between who we are and who we can be," beginning with the premise that there was an "ethical deficit of location" that needed to be remedied.

Ethics as a field of study and concern is located, in the modern era, in diffused form within a virtual tower of Babel. However, it was clear to both organizers and participants in Trento 2010 that the future of humanity's ethics lies not in a cancellation or homogenization of differences. Rather, the future of ethics must be informed by universal core values, expressed in myriad fashion. From its Christian premises, Trento was committed to a fresh exploration of its own biblical and historic precedent, and committed as well to considerations of ethics as espoused by other faith traditions and within a range of secular formulations.

Within church and its exercise of theological prowess, the quest for an acceptable ethics had moved over the centuries toward increasingly ethereal formulations. Generally, Christian theologians have located ethics within an envelope of transcendence, inseparable from the ethics of love for the other and grounded in the hope of eternal covenant. In Trento 2010, deliberations were focused on rendering accessible these and other spectra on the scope and complexity of modern ethics. It was staged as a Christian theological initiative, but deliberately open to reflections from diverse religious, cultural, and technological perspectives. Precedent loomed large, having been deployed by the Catholic magisterium over the centuries both as positive and systematically constrictive ethics formulas.

Organizers of this convocation deliberately engaged both foundational and auxiliary issues of the day. Was the very structure of the Catholic Church inimical to the task of discernment on ethics? Was its authority exercised as the key of Peter, or was it derived from "the people," however defined and wherever located? Failings within the church regarding racial inclusion or sexual abuse weighed heavily. In what measure did lament, as penitent posture, offer the way forward?

According to one presenter, the Christian occident had learned to live with losses: loss of identity, face, and even of a sense of the sacral nature of the human body. Nation states, "the containers of society," long viewed as reliable conversational partners with the church as sub-containers of society, deferred increasingly to corporate power at macro levels, and to the wiles of social media at micro levels. A Muslim participant regretted that, despite its legacy of moral and ethics engagement, Islam was yet to move beyond preoccupations with its own posture vis-à-vis the modern world toward a collective realization of global ethics. In a globalizing world "the architecture of thinking, acting, and living with state-cum-social spaces and identities is collapsing." The global culture of modernity is evolving into a "third space" where former fixities and unities are dissolved and where new negotiations of power and ethics can occur between people of difference. If it is to survive and contribute to the creation of a new world, the future of church will be located and engaged within this evolving dynamic.

If in the past ethics was guarded by disparate faith communities or lodged in the legal systems of secular states or exercised within the confines of discrete ethnic communities around the world, an ethics for the future must be adequate to the sustainability of life on the planet. According to a 2010 presenter on sustainability: "Humanity is going through an original ethical experience . . . contradictory and differentiated." We are invited "to rediscover ourselves as a human family deeply involved in global solidarity and concerned with our origin and our destiny, a solidarity that looks beyond the present moment" and beyond the present truncated categories of ethics. Human beings, it is widely recognized, can and do, to a significant extent, shape their own environment: "The planet is almost completely hominized." According to Benedict XVI, it is incumbent, then, on the human family "to hand the earth on to future generations in such a condition that they too can worthily inhabit it and continue to cultivate it."

But whence an ethics adequate to such a lofty calling? To this end John Paul II called for an "ecological conversion." One presenter stated that "the house of life that is bestowed on us is also the precious space in which the word has erected its tent" (John 1:14). According to Bujo, the word spoken (palaver) in community must create and celebrate the awareness of the human being as integral to the cosmos, as a summation of the totality. It is the path to be taken toward an ethics for the future. Everything about the realization of this project invites the church and every other segment of the human community to be engaged.

Trento 2010, well captured in this extensive summary volume, constituted a bold examination of an ethics of the past, a broad multifaceted survey of the current spectrum of ethics discourse, and a daring expectation of an ethics leading toward a common future.

—Nairobi, Kenya, October 2012

16
Closure for an African Century

Introduction

By any measure, the century coming to an end has been extraordinary. Over the past hundred years, the fortunes of the world and the fortunes of Africa have changed dramatically. This brief survey is intended as a review of reference points significant to an understanding and appreciation of the circumstances prevailing on the continent. In the concluding remarks, consideration is given to elements of Africa's religious and cultural heritage, the revisitation of which may prove critical to the reconstruction of the continent in the twenty-first century and the third millennium.

It is helpful to recall the advent of Christian faith in Africa. In Acts 8:26–29 there is an account of the "Ethiopian eunuch," a proselyte of the Jewish faith, returning to his home after a pilgrimage to Jerusalem. He was reading but apparently not fully comprehending the meaning of the book of Isaiah when he encountered Philip, the deacon. According to the account, the "Ethiopian" welcomed explanations regarding the Isaiah passage as well as baptism offered by Philip.

This unnamed Ethiopian (Nubian) man has been identified as an official of the royal court of Meroe, located some 250 kilometers north of present-day Khartoum, the capital city of the Sudan. As a treasurer of the Kandake (queen), he had been on a business trip to Jerusalem, where he also performed the rites of a religious pilgrimage. In the opinion of some writers, this man became the first Christian of the African continent.

According to philologists and historians, the Greek word *Aethiopia* (land of the blacks) was applied to all territories lying south of Egypt, including modern Sudan. The title *Kandake* (anglicized as Candace) was associated with the queens of the Meroitic kingdom. No doubt the eunuch had become acquainted with Judaism on his travels to Egypt, where there was a large Jewish community on Elephantine Island, located near the town of Aswan. Hence his acquaintance with the book of Isaiah. According to a legend found in the writings of Origen (AD 250), the converted eunuch became the first evangelist of Ethiopia (Nubia). The subsequent mass conversion of Nubia began in AD 543, focused on the kingdoms of Nobatia, Makuria, and Alodia. These Christian kingdoms prevailed in shifting forms for nearly a thousand years, even as the region slowly succumbed to Islam, thanks in no small part to the excessively "statist" or courtly nature of the Nubian Church.

While the Christian kingdoms of northern Sudan have long ceased to exist, today's Egyptian Orthodox (Coptic) Christian community can readily be traced to the very origins of Christianity itself. It is generally accepted that St. Mark became the first bishop of Alexandria in AD 62, a date that can reasonably be referred to as the founding date of the Christian Church in Egypt. The early beginnings of Ethiopian Orthodox Christianity can be traced to the ordination of Frumentius by Athanasius, Patriarch of Alexandria, as Bishop of Aksum in the AD 340. Abuna Salama Frumentius was a student of philosophy, having come from the Middle East to Ethiopia in the company of soldiers who brought him to the king's court at Aksum, where he was engaged as a teacher for the princes Ezana and Zazana. In exercising his zealous Christian faith, he had taken the initiative to ask the Patriarch of Alexandria for the services of a bishop. In the event, he impressed Athanasius with his ardent Christian faith and became the first ordained bishop in Ethiopia.

Centuries later, Portuguese explorers in West Africa established contact with the Bakonga people who, according to legend, were expecting the return of their ancestors. According to their lore, these ancestors, presumably because of their long absence, had become white. The Portuguese, in turn, had been inspired in their explorations to seek out the legendary "Prester John," a powerful Christian king, located in "Africa" or some other locale farther afield. This legend had originally surfaced during the Crusades, bespeaking an eminent Christian ruler serving as both priest and king. Eventually, it became apparent to the Portuguese that the home of Prester (priest) John (Gian, a title given to Ethiopian kings) was in fact Ethiopia. Meanwhile, thanks to landfall in 1491 of the Portuguese in West Africa, King Afonso developed a Christian community, which survived into the nineteenth century. The Portuguese made similar contacts in what is now Zimbabwe and Mozambique.

Islam entered Africa soon after its founding in AD 622, ironically in the immediate context of the Ethiopian Church. Several of the persecuted followers of Prophet Mohammed found protection under the Christian king of Ethiopia. To this day, both Ethiopian Islam and the Ethiopian Orthodox Church acknowledge a special relationship because of this early encounter, a fact that has only marginally mitigated the subsequent stormy relationships between the two faith communities. In later centuries, Islam spread and became firmly established on both the west and east coasts of Africa. Indeed, Islam had been established in Africa for nearly a thousand years by the time Christianity made its second major entry into Africa under the auspices of the modern nineteenth-century missionary movement initiated from Western countries.

After centuries of plunder and slave trade in Africa by European, Arab, and Turkish swashbucklers, the major European powers agreed to formalize their heretofore informal forays into Africa. On November 15, 1884, an international conference was convened in Berlin, Germany. Represented was every nation of Europe (save Switzerland) and the United States of America, fourteen countries in all. No African state was represented. The closest approximation to an African voice was representation from the International Association of the Congo, a philanthropic organization founded by King Leopold II of Belgium, ostensibly to end slavery, but in fact intended as the vehicle for the fulfillment of his imperial dreams. Africa was recognized as a great imperial treasure, awaiting appropriation at the hand of the expansionist European powers of the day. In its formal agenda, the conference dealt first with the regulation of navigation on the Rivers Congo and Niger, and second it purported to define the conditions under which future territorial annexations in Africa might be recognized.

In fact, however, this imperial convocation served as a forum in which the delicate balance of power among European nations was played out and as a projection of their growing mercantile interests around the world. Under Otto Bismarck, chief minister of imperial Germany, the country had rapidly established itself after the Franco-Prussian War of 1870–1871 as a major European power. Taking cues from other European powers that had already staked out claims in Africa, Bismarck announced protectorates in South West Africa (modern Namibia), Cameroon, and Togo. During the conference, Germany was negotiating the final details regarding the acquisition of the Tanganyika (modern Tanzania) colony.

The conference agreed to freedom of navigation on West Africa's major rivers; it agreed that any European power annexing an African territory would notify all signatories to the conference and establish political stability in the said territory. The German claim to Cameroon was recognized; French rights along the Congo River were recognized; the limits of the Portuguese (present in Africa since the 1500s) territories were clarified; and Leopold II's sovereignty over the Congo Independent State (virtually his private property) was legalized by treaty. Whereas the plunder of Africa prior to this time had been, for all practical purposes, an imperial free-for-all, the Berlin Conference "punctuated the fact of Africa's partition" by and among European powers. The borders of Africa's modern nation states owe their genesis, in large measure, to the deliberations of the Berlin Conference. Thanks to a collective decision made early on by African heads of independent states in the context of the Organization of African Unity, those borders have remained relatively intact to this day.

If the Berlin Conference formalized colonial hegemony over Africa, the Pan-Africanist movement was the beginning of its undoing. Pan-Africanism can be understood as a reaction during the latter part of the 1800s to the prevailing colonial reality in Africa and its supporting imperialist and racist ideologies, and as the culmination of a long history of preoccupation on the part of Africans in the diaspora with "Africanism," i.e., "an active claim for the blacks of Africa for real equality of human value with other peoples."

Organizationally, Pan-Africanism took the form of a series of five congresses convened between 1900 and 1945, initiative for which had been taken by Harry Sylvester-Williams, a barrister from Trinidad. Equally prominent in this undertaking was the world-famous academic William Edward Burghardt Du Bois, whose opening sentence in a summary paper of the first congress has since become an oft-cited classic: "The problem of the twentieth century is the problem of the color line, the question of how far differences of race . . . will hereafter be made the basis of denying to over half the world the right of sharing to their utmost ability the opportunities and privileges of modern civilization."

Thirty-two black people attended the first congress of the series, four of whom were born in Africa. Subsequent congresses were held in the context of a World War I peace conference, calling for the protection and advancement of "the natives of Africa and the peoples of African descent." Later during this period, Marcus Mosiah Garvey, Jr., a sometime rival of Du Bois, was championing a "back-to-Africa" movement under the slogan: "Africa for the Africans, those at home and those abroad." Meanwhile, any positive effects of the congresses were competing with the "successful" march of colonialism toward continental hegemony.

However, by the advent of the fifth Pan-Africanist Congress convened in Manchester, United Kingdom, the tide was beginning to turn. Attended by ninety delegates, together with other participants, it broke new ground by shifting the locus of the conversation from the black (Caribbean and the United States) diaspora to the African continent. Symbolizing this shift was the presence at the congress of people such as Kwame Nkrumah, later to become the first president of Ghana; Jomo Kenyatta, later to become the first president of Kenya; and I. T. A. Wallace-Johnson, a nationalist leader from Sierra Leone. Other personalities critical to the success of this congress included C. L. R. James from Trinidad and George Padmore of Guyana, later to become the "right-hand man" (ideologue) to President Kwame Nkrumah of Ghana. Manchester was clear in its final call: "We are determined to be free. If the Western world is still determined to rule mankind by force, then Africans, as a last resort, may have to appeal to force in the effort to achieve freedom."

The Pan-Africanist Congresses opened the gates to new, far-flung initiatives. In 1947, the first African Studies Program in the United States was launched at Northwestern University. In Africa, meanwhile, momentum toward political independence developed apace, advancing more rapidly than some expected, and not as quickly as others had hoped. Ghana became the first sub-Saharan African independent state in 1957, leading the way to an initial tidal wave that eventually swept across the continent. However, it was soon realized that the southern tip of Africa would yield more slowly to the quest for independence. The Portuguese had no intention of surrendering their African territories (Mozambique, Angola, Guinea Bissau, Cape Verde)[1] after a five-hundred-year presence. Rhodesia (Zimbabwe) dug in its heels when the white-minority government in 1965 announced a "Unilateral Declaration of Independence." South West Africa (Namibia) was being administered by South Africa as a League of Nations (later a United Nations) trust territory, while South Africa itself had had white minority rule in various guises since the late 1600s, and the harsh apartheid regime under the white/Afrikaner-dominated Nationalist Party since 1948.

Enter the Organization of African Unity in 1963, Africa's premier continental political independence forum. Constituted by the heads of African independent states, the organization's mandate had been to work for the total independence of Africa, including that reluctant southern tip. One of the vehicles to this end was the Organization of African Unity's Liberation Committee, based in Dar es Salaam, Tanzania, in support of the variety of political movements from the southern part of Africa engaged in the liberation of African countries still under European or minority white rule. President Nyerere of Tanzania served as chair both of the Liberation Committee and the so-called Frontline (independent) States, a sub-regional alliance of independent states and liberation movements. As can easily be imagined, Dar es Salaam in those days was immersed in a virtual Pentecost of political opinion and a diversity of leading African personalities variously managing their political organizations as well as their armed military movements in the respective wars of liberation scattered across southern Africa.

1 Portugal's African territories were not held as colonies; they were administered as integral parts of greater Portugal. Their African subjects in these territories were encouraged to become *assimilados* and thus gain some status approaching citizenship according to strictly prescribed criteria set by the Portuguese.

As a result of those strong initiatives, the second wave of independence was finally realized, sweeping the Portuguese territories to independence in the mid-1970s, Zimbabwe in 1980, Namibia in 1990, and, finally, South Africa in April 1994. Some portion of the dynamic triggering this dramatic independence "landslide" (majority rule in South Africa came relatively quickly and nonviolently) was facilitated, ironically, by the collapse of the Berlin Wall. The rupture of the global East–West ideological divide unleashed a domino-style wave of changes across the globe, depositing Africa into a new post–Cold War world order, not entirely of its own making and not in every way to its advantage. Still, it could be argued that the final realization of the Pan-Africanist goals had been hastened by catching a piggyback ride on the momentum of this global restructuring.

Thus, after a century of struggle, political independence in Africa was finally accomplished. But was it a Pyrrhic victory? Already by the end of the 1980s, there was a growing consensus that the nation state model was not functioning well for Africa. A veteran Africanist described it as "the black man's burden." Some analysts were clear about the reasons for this debacle. According to them, "it was the failure of our rulers to reestablish vital inner links with the poor and dispossessed of this (continent)" or "it was the failure of postcolonial communities to find and insist upon means of living together by strategies less primitive and destructive than rival kinship networks, whether the 'ethnic' clientelism or its camouflage in no less clientelist 'multiparty systems.'"

It has been pointed out repeatedly by political observers that postindependence civil wars in Africa had everything to do with the search for viable and inclusive governance systems. Typically, rebels were pressing their claims for inclusion with the larger body politic. It has also been pointed out that those wars had begun long before majority rule was achieved in South Africa, that supreme jewel in the African independence crown. Indeed, Mozambique suffered a ten-year civil war after achieving independence in its effort to identify an acceptable governance model.

By far the cruelest manifestation of this syndrome was observed in Rwanda. In that country, during the month of April 1994, between half a million and a million people were killed when the ruling Hutu majority government determined to destroy in systematic fashion the rival minority Tutsi community. This gruesome, calculated slaughter took place precisely when Nelson Mandela was being installed as the first black majority president in South Africa. Africa was witnessing, at once, the most hopeful and the most distressing events imaginable. The advent of South Africa as an independent nonracial country, now to be ruled for the first time by a black majority government, was viewed by many anti-apartheid workers as a sign of hope, a way of moving toward a new African future. Archbishop Desmond Tutu had frequently tossed a challenge to leaders of the continent: "If Africans in South Africa can overcome the monstrous evil of apartheid, surely the lesser problems in the rest of Africa can easily be resolved."

In retrospect, the demise of apartheid seemed to signal the fulfillment of the hundred-year-old Pan-Africanist vision for a politically independent African continent, even if it was now segmented into more than fifty nation states and not a United States of Africa as frequently proposed by Kwame Nkrumah during the heady pre-independence days. Like Ghana, South Africa had joined the club of African independent states. In subsequent years, nearly all of Africa's independent countries became variously preoccupied with the postindependence imperative toward Western-style "development" and "modernization," strongly informed by the criteria established in a series of United Nations conferences.

Between 1972 and 1982, twelve major global conferences sponsored by the United Nations were staged to discuss an astonishing range of issues, among them environment, women, water, food, population, and health. Each of these conferences set out criteria by which newly independent countries in Africa (and around the world) could determine their development status and their development needs. It followed that the newly formed independent governments of the day were expected to work for the attainment of the identified development goals. Those goals have proven hopelessly unrealistic, in part because of their excessive Western orientation and the concomitant donor fatigue, and also because the governments of the new nation states in Africa were not adequately prepared to undertake the arduous task at hand. Few of Africa's nation states were economically prepared for anything but the most basic subsistence economies.

In the view of Basil Davidson, the postindependence period in Africa demonstrated, rather unequivocally, the unviable and unsuitable nature of the nation state to Africa's needs. Indeed, he, among a number of observers, argued that the nation state in Africa was "dying." Given this dire prognosis, what, according to him, constituted a sign of hope? Together with other political scientists, he claimed to see hope in the range of regional entities such as the Southern African Development Community, the Economic Community of West African States, the Intergovernmental Agency for Development, and the East African Cooperation/Community.

Initially, such regional entities were created as responses to economic imperatives, since individual countries on their own remained economically unviable. Larger market catchment areas, it was believed, would ensure greater economic viability. Given the subsequent turmoil experienced by individual or contiguous nation states, a number of these regional entities have additionally developed peacemaking or peacekeeping facilities. The notable example here was the Economic Community of West African States, whose forces intervened in the Liberian civil war, nursing negotiations along until a reasonably satisfactory peace agreement was achieved. The Intergovernmental Agency for Development has provided the designated forum for official negotiations between the southern Sudanese rebels and the Government of Sudan. The Southern African Development Community also developed a certain peace mandate for itself, but faltered when confronted with the complex multi-nation conflict in the Democratic Republic of the Congo. Additional time and much more experience with the emerging regional configurations in Africa will be needed before their utility and sustainability can be declared secure.

Africa's political project during the whole of the century just coming to an end was informed by the imperative implied in the Pan-Africanist independence vision. That vision had been developed as a strong reaction to the European colonial project in Africa, officially launched by the 1884–85 Berlin Conference. At the risk of trivializing an extremely weighty process, it could be said that the whole of this century was preoccupied with a decisive African (including the African diaspora) response to the European imperial presence on the African continent. That response, predictably, was dictated largely in terms of European categories: Africa adopted the Western nation-state model; it developed strong links with European economies; its education systems were modeled on colonial metropole structures; and, as will be noted subsequently in this reflection, Africa also responded massively to the Western version of Christianity.

In remarkable ways, Africa's rebellion (in many cases taking the form of extended wars of liberation) against the European colonial presence constituted more nearly an adaptation to, rather than a refutation of, alien regimes. Thus, the net effect has been that Africa joined the world largely on European terms, rather than its own terms. Indeed, the period between 1900 and 2000 could be referred to as Africa's European century.

The establishment of Africa's ancient churches and the truncated Christianizing forays by the Portuguese in the 1500s have already been noted. Western Christian missions made their way into Africa in the shadow of the colonial enterprise, at times seeking its protection, at times disputing and resisting its claims, but rarely existing for long beyond its influence.

Modern Western Christianity's advent in Africa is in fact of very recent origin. David Livingstone, that pioneer of the modern mission movement, launched his missionary journeys in the 1840s and continued till his death in 1873. One must recall that Livingstone's work was dependent upon, and in some measure facilitated by, the trading networks of Muslim Arabs whose mercantile tentacles stretched right across the continent and down to modern Botswana. Islam had already been present along the east and west coasts of Africa for a thousand years.[2]

Within the current decade, many mainline churches in Africa have been celebrating their first centenaries, including Mennonites in the Democratic Republic of the Congo. The Mennonite presence in East Africa dates from the mid-1930s. During this relatively brief period of the modern Christian mission advance, nearly half of all people in Africa became professing

2 By the year 2000, Africa will be 48 percent Christian and 41 percent Muslim, with a corresponding statistical decline in adherents of indigenous religions.

Christians. Within less than a century, the Christian presence in Africa shifted from negligible numbers to become the numerical center of world Christianity. In the history of Christianity's spread around the world, such rapid growth is unprecedented.

These astonishing facts become even more compelling when the pronouncements of the Edinburgh Mission Conference of 1910 (a precursor meeting leading to the formation of the World Council of Churches) are taken into account. Having been convened as a recognition of a just-concluded hundred-year-period of Christian missionary activity in other parts of the world, conference participants opined that the Christian Gospel was unlikely to be readily accepted in Africa because of its strongly held "traditional religious or tribal beliefs."

The political nationalist fervor of the 1960s that led to the formation of independent nation states was accompanied by an ecclesial counterpart. Across the continent, mainline mission churches were transiting from missionary to African leadership, reflecting the spirit of the times. Exceptions to this general trend were found in the Catholic Church, which pursued its own training regime for the priesthood. Missionary councils or fellowships that had been developed as early as the 1940s for purposes of coordinating education and health services were, by the 1960s, being transformed into national councils of churches. At the continental level, a Protestant ecumenical body known as the All Africa Conference of Churches was established in 1963, just two months prior to the founding if its political counterpart, the Organization of African Unity.

Just as the heads of state in the Organization of African Unity enjoyed a fragile unity in their opposition to the South African apartheid government and the other remaining colonial states in southern Africa, so the AACC, in collaboration with its national and global counterparts, lent its aid to the project of liberation by maintaining a degree of common purpose. In his address to the 1974 All Africa Conference of Churches General Assembly, held in Lusaka, Zambia, General Secretary Burgess Carr presented a spirited defense of the deployment of armed resistance in the final push for the total liberation of the African continent: "We must give our unequivocal support to the liberation movements because they have helped the church to rediscover a new and radical appreciation for the cross. In accepting the violence of the cross, God, in Jesus Christ, sanctified violence into a redemptive instrument for bringing into being a fuller human life." As might have been expected, this rather daring exegesis of Christ's death raised theological eyebrows within the All Africa Conference of Churches constituency and beyond. Rarely, if ever, has this theological formulation touching on violence been cited in subsequent All Africa Conference of Churches literature. At the time, it will be remembered, liberation wars were in full swing throughout southern Africa, with ultimate victory against the colonial legacy virtually certain. Under these circumstances, what seemed to some like theological license was accepted, if somewhat reluctantly.

Bolstering this general commitment to liberation were a number of subsidiary initiatives. In a high-profile undertaking, the World Council of Churches organized the Program to Combat Racism, which, during the height of the armed struggle in southern Africa, made monetary grants to the humanitarian programs developed and administered by the liberation movements. In tune with the times, theologians of the region promoted "black theology" or "liberation theology," drawing inspiration from African American theologian James Cone. At a critical juncture, prominent ecumenical leaders selected Desmond Tutu as the appropriate clergyman to focus on the anti-apartheid struggle. After demurring initially, he accepted the challenge. As the world knows, he was to play a most remarkable role during the final throes of South Africa's liberation process. For Africa's Protestant ecumenical community, these were high-profile, bold initiatives for what was deemed a supremely important cause. Victory was never in doubt, though for some people it came earlier than expected.

In April 1994, Nelson Mandela was installed as the first black African president of South Africa. Africa and the world watched with bated breath and exhaled in solidarity. After several hundred years of domination by a white minority, and from 1948 to 1994 ruled by the explicitly racist Nationalist Party, South Africa was now joining the community of free nations, putting in place democratic regimes of governance intended to include everyone in what was called a "rainbow nation." Altogether, this remarkable train of events constituted a magical moment in the history of Africa.[3]

Liberation Realized

With this moment, the Pan-Africanist vision was fulfilled—nearly a hundred years of struggle and organization was vindicated. The dreams of the Organization of African Unity, the Frontline States, and the liberation movements had been accomplished. So also was the vision of the ecumenical community. Although the early leaders of the All Africa Conference of Churches had remonstrated against an excessive preoccupation in the churches with "nationalism," it had become abundantly clear that liberation was indivisible, whether it was being discussed within the context of the state or the church. Nearly half of the staff of the South Africa Council of Churches joined the new government of South Africa (presumably, now to implement the vision for which they had struggled so long and hard). Even the retired Archbishop Tutu accepted a government appointment as chairman of the national Truth and Reconciliation Commission, which launched a remarkable quest for the healing of a wounded South Africa. Meanwhile, donor support for the South Africa Council of Churches virtually evaporated.

Canons to Live By

Liberation accomplished remains stillborn if not informed and guided by overarching long-term visions. Although inspired originally by the Pan-Africanist vision, Africa's liberation was pushed along in its momentum by a diverse collection of creeds and ideologies. As noted, the African National Congress had been influenced by Gandhian nonviolence. Later the ideologies of Marxism and capitalism vied for the soul of Africa. Indeed, during the Cold War period the African continent became a virtual pawn amid

3 Mandela came to power as a result of the political (violent armed resistance) work of the African National Congress (ANC), the premier anti-apartheid party (origins date to 1912). One of the prominent ANC leaders was the Rev. Albert Luthuli; influenced by Tolstoy, the Russian pacifist, he was a strong advocate of nonviolence, a principle reflected in early ANC documents. Luthuli received the Nobel Peace Prize in 1961. De Klerk and Mandela were jointly awarded the Nobel Peace Prize in 1994.

East–West rivalry, with a generation of African leaders obliged to define themselves within that tension-filled context.

Just as the United Nations and many other agencies, including the churches, became enthusiastic about development, people such as Walter Rodney reminded the world how Europe had underdeveloped Africa. In formulating the next steps after independence, church leaders and political leaders vacillated.

Theology of Reconstruction

In the All Africa Conference of Churches, this lacuna had been anticipated in an extensive theological reflection process under the general rubric of a "Theology of Reconstruction." In ecumenical forums, this inquiry focused among other things on this question: If Africa is to embark on reconstruction, upon which foundations will it rebuild? And, given the burgeoning interest in peace work, the parallel questions: What is the nature of the wholeness by which peace work is guided? How can peace be realized when visions of the whole are not articulated? Indeed, African theologians repeatedly noted the prevailing alienation widely experienced by people living within several seemingly incompatible worlds.

Africa's Religious and Cultural Heritage

One element critical to the discussion on reconstruction was embodied in what is now increasingly referred to as "African Religion." Even though African Religion is in some sense "primordial" or ahistorical, there has been neither longstanding inquiry nor clear understanding of its nature. Indeed, the first serious inquiry into this subject (as recently as the 1940s) is usually associated with the Belgian Catholic missionary Fr. Placide Tempels. On the basis of many years of missionary work in the Congo, he wrote a treatise entitled *Bantu Philosophy* expressing the view that "the peoples of the Bantu language group (which includes most of west, central and southern Africa) shared a common philosophy centered on a concept of vital force. Everything in the universe possesses this force, including inanimate objects, but it is most powerful and important in human beings

. . . active in the departed ancestors as well as the living." Whether or not they agreed with Tempels's basic premises, subsequent writers on African theology or philosophy rarely ignored his inquiry and original formulation.

In a similar vein, John Taylor, a British missionary working in Uganda, characterized the African religious heritage as a "primal vision . . . a world of presences, of face-to-face meeting not only with the living, but just as vividly with the dead and the whole totality of nature. It is the universe of I and Thou." Taylor's formulation was long considered one of the most empathetic of reflections by European missionaries with regard to the African religious worldview. Then, in 1969, a Kenyan theologian, John Mbiti, published what has subsequently become a classic: *African Religions and Philosophy*. It was one of the earliest widely disseminated books by an African theologian, providing a detailed overview of the continent's religious heritage. Since its original publication, it has enjoyed many subsequent editions and regular textual revisions to reflect the growing body of relevant research.

More recently, Laurenti Magesa has outlined in comprehensive fashion the basic tenets of African Religion, drawing on a wide range of research. In his book *African Religion: Moral Traditions for Abundant Life*, in which he explains in careful detail the moral and ethical nature of African Religion, Magesa is concerned that there be a clear recognition of its living reality.[4] Moreover, he is concerned that there be a recognized conversation or discourse between African Religion and Christianity—between African Religion and the modern world. African Religion "must not be buried underground, but must be helped to emerge from centuries of ridicule so that it can interact with other religious orientations for its own benefit and theirs as well."

4 African Religion posits certain core affirmations reflected variously throughout this book, all of which impinge upon or inform the morals and ethics requisite to abundant living. Among these are the following tenets: the belief in the creator God as the primal source of all life; human beings as the crown of God's creation and endowed with special responsibilities of fecundity, community, and sharing; the individual and the community of persons together constitute a microcosm of the universe; all human beings are children of God; no one can claim ownership over that which is placed in the public trust by the creator God; the universe has been lent by God to humanity by the ancestors and living leaders for the promotion of life, good relations, and peace; personal identity is found in group identity, e.g., "life is when you are together—alone you are an animal." Harmony is the agent of freedom.

Dialogue Between African Religion and Christianity

Dialogue is being actively stimulated by African theologians such as Kwame Bediako. Quoting Mbiti, he noted the ready cognates between primal (African) religion and Christianity: "The man of Africa will not have very far to go before he walks on familiar ground. For the wholeness of African life found an echo and an answer in the wholeness of the Gospel of Christ." Further noting the interaction between Christianity and African Religion, he cited Andrew Walls: "The notion that religions are not mutually exclusive entities which succeed one another in the process of conversion, but that the whole social life of a community must be taken together was perhaps more readily learned in Africa than elsewhere." Finally, citing Bediako directly: "It is in Africa that the opportunity for a serious theological encounter and cross-fertilization between Christian and primal traditions (African Religion), which was lost in Europe, can be regained; and Africa may well be the place for redeeming wrongs done not to her alone in the name of mission."

Conclusion

Whatever the nature of Africa's future, it is now clear that its dual religious heritage in the form of African Religion, received through religious and cultural practice, and Christianity, received via encounters with the Western missionary initiatives, will be in the service of the continent's reconstruction. The powerful liberation and modernization dynamics that characterized and formed the twentieth century in Africa have reached an important juncture. While these have been necessary to the dramatic achievements to date, they are probably not sufficient as a vision appropriate to the next century.

As Bediako suggests, such sufficiency or adequacy will more likely be located, among other places, in the serious cross-fertilization between Christianity as adapted from the West and the power of the African religious heritage. In this regard, there is a considerable literature and some consensus that Africa's future will not be secured by wholesale adoption of Western economic, technical, and social models, though it is clear that it has been enormously influenced by them. In a globalized world, Africa cannot be an island to itself. But its future, if it is to be at all promising, will surely include well-articulated perspectives, based in some measure on Africa's religious and cultural heritage.

For those from outside Africa who accompany this quest, the challenges are particularly daunting. In the shift toward more adequate understandings and redefined relational frameworks, it may be necessary to pronounce a conscious "closure" to the past, to this century, and to its cozy but inequitable relational niches. Authentic accompaniment calls for clear understanding of Africa's "holocaust" past, recognition of its fragile present, and commitment to the realization of life abundant for all in the future.

An oral version of this paper was presented to the annual Mennonite Retreat in Limuru, Kenya, in December 1998.

Sources

All Africa Conference of Churches. *The Struggle Continues.* 1975. The official report on the third General Assembly of the All Africa Conference of Churches. Nairobi: All Africa Conference of Churches.

Barrett, David. 1982. *World Christian Encyclopedia: A Comparative Survey of Churches and Religions in the Modern World AD 1900–2000.* Nairobi–Oxford–New York: Oxford University Press.

Baur, John. 1994. *2000 Years of Christianity in Africa: An African History 62–1992.* Nairobi: Paulines Publications–Africa.

Bediako, Kwame. 1995. *Christianity in Africa: The Renewal of a Non-Western Religion.* Maryknoll, NY: Orbis Books.

Davidson, Basil. 1993. *The Black Man's Burden: Africa and the Curse of the Nation State.* Nairobi: East African Educational Publishers.

Davidson, Basil. 1994. *The Search for Africa: A History in the Making.* London: James Currey.

Hastings, Adrian. 1994. *The Church in Africa: 1450–1950.* Oxford: Clarendon Press.

Howe, Stephen. 1998. *Afrocentrism: Mythical Pasts and Imagined Homes.* London: Verso.

July, Robert W. 1992. *A History of the African People.* Nairobi: East African Educational Publishers.

Magesa, Laurenti. 1997. *African Religion: The Moral Traditions of Abundant Life.* Maryknoll, NY: Orbis Books.

Mbiti, John. 1969. *African Religions and Philosophy.* London: Heinemann.

Mugambi, J. N. K. 1995. *From Liberation to Reconstruction: African Christian Theology after the Cold War.* Nairobi: East African Educational Publishers.

Reader, John. 1999. *Africa: A Biography of the Continent.* Vintage.

Taylor, John. 1963. *The Primal Vision: Christian Presence Amid African Religion.* (Republished in 1987.) London: SCM Press.

Vantini, Giovanni. 1981. *Christianity in the Sudan.* Bologna: Collegio delle Missioni Africane.

About the Author

Harold Miller was born in Canton, Ohio, in 1935. He was nurtured to Christian faith within an Amish and Conservative Mennonite church community near Hartville, Ohio. From 1955 to 1958 he served in Germany as "PAX boy" in a program sponsored by the Mennonite Central Committee (MCC), building houses for European Mennonite refugees. He graduated from Eastern Mennonite College in Harrisonburg, Virginia, with a BA in History, and later earned an MA in International Affairs at Pittsburgh University.

After teaching history and civics at Eastern Mennonite High School in Harrisonburg, Virginia, from 1963 to 1965, he was seconded by Eastern Mennonite Board of Missions (EMM) to the Christian Council of Tanzania in Dar es Salaam, Tanzania, to the position of Secretary for Relief and Service from 1965 to 1971. For most of the period between 1972 and 1974 he was seconded by EMM in collaboration with MCC to the Sudan Council of Churches with its base in Khartoum, Sudan, as logistics officer. From 1974 to 1981 he was seconded to the National Council of Churches of Kenya based in Nairobi, Kenya, to the position of Secretary for Rural Development. From 1981 to 1987 he served as MCC's East Africa representative, providing administrative oversight for variously placed North American volunteers and workers, and for program initiatives that included a brief entitled "Food and Peace." From 1987 to 1989 he was appointed by MCC as co-administrator of the Horn of Africa Project, an initiative ensconced within Conrad Grebel College in Kitchener-Waterloo, Ontario. From 1989 to 1999 he was seconded by MCC to the All Africa Conference of Churches based in Nairobi, Kenya, to the position of consultant in its Department of International Affairs. From 1999 to 2005 he served as MCC's co-representative (together with his wife, Annetta) to Sudan, based in Nairobi, Kenya. Since 2005 he and Annetta have lived as retirees in Nairobi, Kenya.

www.ingramcontent.com/pod-product-compliance
Lightning Source LLC
Chambersburg PA
CBHW021923040426
42448CB00008B/890
* 9 7 8 9 9 6 6 7 3 6 0 2 4 *